A Book of
Modern
American Poetry

PERSPECTIVES IN LITERATURE

A Book of Short Stories—1
A Book of Poetry—1
A Book of Nonfiction—1
A Book of Drama—1

A Book of Short Stories—2
A Book of Poetry—2
A Book of Nonfiction—2
A Book of Drama—2

Modern American Prose
A Book of Modern American Poetry
A Book of Drama—3

Modern British Prose
A Book of Modern British Poetry
A Book of Drama—4

PERSPECTIVES IN LITERATURE

A Book of Modern American Poetry

JANE McDERMOTT
THOMAS V. LOWERY

HARCOURT BRACE JOVANOVICH, INC.
New York Chicago San Francisco Atlanta Dallas

Cover Photos: The front cover is by Lee Lockwood, from Black Star. The back cover is by Jerry Cooke, from Photo Researchers, Inc.

ISBN 0-15-336900-0

Contents

Additional Poems
for Comparison, Contrast, and Study

INTRODUCTION

Modern American poetry can be said to have begun when American poets stopped imitating English literary works and started writing about American experiences in a distinctively American style. In the nineteenth century, two American poets—Walt Whitman and Emily Dickinson—made major contributions toward changing the course of American poetry from imitative to individual. Whitman extolled democracy and individualism, and praised the virtue and strength of the common man. His poems were written in free verse, a form that reflected the informality and vitality of the American spirit. Like Whitman, Emily Dickinson drew her imagery from the ordinary things around her. In contrast to the vague imagery of the English poets of the time, Emily Dickinson's images were clear and concrete.

It was not until the twentieth century that a major change in the direction in American poetry became clear. The change was indicated by the publication of poems about American life—particularly small-town life—as it was actually lived and not as people liked to romanticize it. American speech rhythms and colloquial expressions were grafted onto traditional English meters. Edwin Arlington Robinson was an originator of this type of poetry in the United States, and Edgar Lee Masters, Robert Frost, and Stephen Vincent Benét were others who worked in this tradition.

Many poets, however, were not satisfied with a mere adjustment of traditional verse meters to accommodate American speech patterns. Following Whitman, they believed that free verse was necessary to achieve a truly American poetry. Some of these poets, notably Carl Sandburg, continued to write about America. Others, particularly a group of poets known as the Imagists, concentrated on writing poetry that contained clear, specific images. These images, drawn from the spectrum of human experience, were set in lines of irregular meters, rhythms patterned after ordinary speech. These poets helped make American poetry international in scope and influence.

The Imagists were originally led by a young poet named Ezra Pound, who was to have an enormous influence on the development of modern American poetry. Not only did Pound personally influence several important American poets, but he was also responsible for the introduction of many experimental poets to the American literary public—through *Poetry: A Magazine of Verse*, of which he was one of the editors. Moreover, from his doctrine of Imagism to his command "make it new," Pound set goals for poetry that a great many American poets tried to reach.

At the same time that poets were searching for new subject matter and poetic techniques, profound political and social changes were transforming the world. The enormous destruction of the first World War convinced many writers that Western literary, political, and religious heritage was bankrupt. Young writers, such as Pound and William Carlos Williams, lost faith in the nineteenth-century idea that scientific and economic progress was creating a better world. The writers' loss of belief in scientific and economic progress was not shared by the general public. As a result, many writers, especially poets, became alienated from the mainstream of society.

In America, the separation between poets and society increased because of the fragmented nature of our social structure. The constant changes and tremendous variety of modern life meant that poets could no longer depend on a stable public mythology—that is, on stories and symbols which are not only commonly understood by all readers but also meaningful to them. Since the years following the first World War, many poets and other contemporary writers have rejected Western traditions. As a result, some poets have invented private mythologies, which can be understood only after much study.

The modern study of psychology has also had its effect on poetry, for it contributed to an emphasis on the nonlogical, on images connected by associations rather than by rational patterns. Imagery was intended to evoke certain emotional responses in the reader. Instead of direct statement, which many poets feel will deaden the impact of what they are trying to communicate, a kind of personal and emotional shorthand has been evolved.

The use of an indirect "emotional shorthand" was particularly characteristic of several important poets who came to prominence in what is commonly considered the most creative period in the history of American poetry—the years between the beginning of the first World War and the beginning of the Depression of the thirties. Poets such as Wallace Stevens, Marianne Moore, and Hart Crane are among those who were most strongly influenced by psychology.

During the Depression, many poets became actively involved in political causes. Kenneth Fearing and Muriel Rukeyser, for example, called public attention to the effects of social injustice on the individual. Other poets, notably Benét and Archibald Mac-Leish, wrote against the rise of Fascism in Europe.

After the second World War, new trends in American poetry became noticeable. The war itself provided a subject that both poet and reader had experienced: both had been affected by the same disruptions of individual life and of society. The war poems of Randall Jarrell point out the savagery of armed conflict and its effects on the human spirit. Richard Eberhart and Peter Viereck recapture the pity of death brought about by the war and in a larger sense by the human condition.

In the postwar society, an autobiographical form of poetry came into prominence. The so-called confessional poets told about events in their lives and how these events affected them. Because the poets usually gave specific details of these events—rather than expressing them symbolically—this type of poetry had a more direct impact than much of previous American poetry. The confessional poems of writers such as Robert Lowell and Theodore Roethke have influenced numerous younger poets, especially Allen Ginsberg, Anne Sexton, and W. D. Snodgrass.

For the most part, other poets of the postwar period can still be divided into those "groups" apparent at the beginning of this century: the traditionalists and the experimentalists. The traditionalists, led by Richard Wilbur, emphasize technical skill and write poems in complex stanza forms and rhythms. Western literary and religious heritage, they feel, still has relevance—if only to point out the ironies of modern life. They make complicated webs of allusion to this heritage, as well as to the new discoveries of anthropology, psychology, and the physical sciences.

The current experimentalists, like their early twentieth-century predecessors, work with free verse, but often attempt to give it order and shape by different theories. One group—the Projectivists, or Black Mountain poets—believes that verse should be written in "breath units"; that is, it should be shaped by the "breathing of the man who writes, at the moment that he writes. . . ." The Projectivist poets have been influenced by the technical experiments of Pound and Williams. The experimentalists—for example, Denise Levertov—tend to choose less personal subject matter than the confessional poets, and to comment more directly on modern life than the traditionalists do.

Edwin Arlington Robinson

[1869–1935]

E. A. Robinson was born in Head Tide, Maine, and spent his youth in Gardiner, Maine. After graduating from high school, he remained at home for four years, reading books and writing verse that publishers continually rejected. In 1891, Robinson entered Harvard University, but he remained there for only two years. His father's death and his family's loss of most of their inheritance in a stock market panic forced him to leave Harvard and return home before obtaining a degree.

He left Maine again after his mother's death in 1896 and went to New York City, where he held a series of low-paying jobs. In 1905 President Theodore Roosevelt, impressed by Robinson's book of poems, *The Children of the Night*, appointed him to a clerkship in the New York Customs House. This was the first time that the poet had a steady job that enabled him both to eat and to write. His salary was small, and it was not until the 1920's, when he was in his fifties, that he was able to live comfortably without outside help.

For most of his life, Robinson's lack of money was paralleled by the lack of recognition given to his subtle, carefully constructed poems. He paid for the publication of his first two books of poems, and his third book was subsidized by friends from Gardiner. Ironically, when Robinson did achieve success, it came like a sudden cloudburst—with three Pulitzer prizes for poetry in the 1920's. During his later years, he was regarded by many as America's greatest living poet.

Considering Robinson's own frustrating struggles for success, it is not surprising that many of his best poems are about failures. In psychological portraits drawn with deep irony, he presented the misfits of society—men such as Miniver Cheevy, who dreamed and drank his way through dreary reality, and Richard Cory, whose outside glitter hid his inner darkness. His character portraits were often based on people he had known in Gardiner (called Tilbury Town in his poems). The best of these portraits are timeless because they illuminate enduring problems in the lives of men.

Robinson stands midpoint between nineteenth- and twentieth-century poets. He wrote in traditional nineteenth-century forms, such as the sonnet and the dramatic monologue, but he also opened new paths by making his poems realistic and by using colloquial diction to capture American speech rhythms. His poems contain a deeply felt criticism of the desire for power and material things, which Robinson believed characterized modern life.

Mr. Flood's Party

Old Eben Flood, climbing alone one night
Over the hill between the town below
And the forsaken upland hermitage
That held as much as he should ever know
On earth again of home, paused warily.   5
The road was his with not a native near;
And Eben, having leisure, said aloud,
For no man else in Tilbury Town to hear:

"Well, Mr. Flood, we have the harvest moon
Again, and we may not have many more;   10
The bird is on the wing, the poet° says,
And you and I have said it here before.
Drink to the bird." He raised up to the light
The jug that he had gone so far to fill,
And answered huskily: "Well, Mr. Flood,   15
Since you propose it, I believe I will."

Alone, as if enduring to the end
A valiant armor of scarred hopes outworn,
He stood there in the middle of the road

11. **the poet:** Edward FitzGerald, who translated *The Rubáiyát of Omar Khayyám*. The phrase "The bird is on the wing" is a quotation from the *Rubáiyát:* "The Bird of Time has but a little way / To flutter—and the Bird is on the Wing."

Like Roland's° ghost winding° a silent horn.°   20
Below him, in the town among the trees,
Where friends of other days had honored him,
A phantom salutation of the dead
Rang thinly till old Eben's eyes were dim.

Then, as a mother lays her sleeping child   25
Down tenderly, fearing it may awake,
He set the jug down slowly at his feet
With trembling care, knowing that most things break;
And only when assured that on firm earth
It stood, as the uncertain lives of men   30
Assuredly did not, he paced away,
And with his hand extended paused again:

"Well, Mr. Flood, we have not met like this
In a long time; and many a change has come
To both of us, I fear, since last it was   35
We had a drop together. Welcome home!"
Convivially returning with himself,
Again he raised the jug up to the light;
And with an acquiescent quaver said:
"Well, Mr. Flood, if you insist, I might.   40

"Only a very little, Mr. Flood—
For auld lang syne.° No more, sir; that will do."
So, for the time, apparently it did,
And Eben evidently thought so too;
For soon amid the silver loneliness   45
Of night he lifted up his voice and sang,
Secure, with only two moons listening,
Until the whole harmonious landscape rang—

---

20. Roland: an officer of the French king Charlemagne and the legendary hero of the medieval French epic, *The Song of Roland.* Roland possessed a horn with which he could summon help, but in a battle against the Saracens at Roncesvalles, Spain, he was too proud to blow the horn, even though his forces were greatly outnumbered. When he finally did sound for help, it was too late, and all his troops were killed. **winding:** blowing. **a silent horn:** Mr. Flood's jug is compared to Roland's horn. **42. For . . . syne:** for old times.

"For auld lang syne." The weary throat gave out,
The last word wavered; and the song being done,   50
He raised again the jug regretfully
And shook his head, and was again alone.
There was not much that was ahead of him,
And there was nothing in the town below—
Where strangers would have shut the many doors   55
That many friends had opened long ago.

Meaning and Method

1. Which words in the opening stanza establish the mood of the poem? How does this mood contrast with what a reader would expect from the title?
2. How do the setting and time of year reflect or symbolize Mr. Flood's state in life. What are the connotations of *forsaken upland hermitage* (line 3)?
3. Mr. Flood talks to himself in the second, fifth, and sixth stanzas. Which words or phrases in these stanzas indicate that Mr. Flood has had some education? that he has good manners?
4. How is Mr. Flood like "Roland's ghost winding a silent horn"? Why is the imagery so appropriate? What are the similarities between Roland and his horn and Mr. Flood and his jug of liquor? What images in lines 13 and 14 and in line 18 prepare you for this simile in line 20?
5. What is Mr. Flood's attitude toward the past? toward the present? toward the future? Which words or phrases in the fourth stanza indicate that Mr. Flood has been disillusioned by life?
6. We are told that Mr. Flood was once honored in the town. Do you think that the change of attitude toward him was caused by his actions? by the fact that he has outlived his time? by both? by something else?
7. Why do you think Mr. Flood drinks? Do you think he is comical? tragic? dignified? pathetic? a combination of these?

Composition and Discussion

1. Is this simply a story of an old man, or is Eben Flood a symbol—a symbol of old age and loneliness, a symbol of the uncertainties of life? Explain your reasons for reaching your decision.
2. Write an obituary of Mr. Flood as it might have appeared in the *Tilbury Town Gazette*.

Cliff Klingenhagen

Cliff Klingenhagen had me in to dine
With him one day; and after soup and meat,
And all the other things there were to eat,
Cliff took two glasses and filled one with wine
And one with wormwood.° Then, without a sign   5
For me to choose at all, he took the draught°
Of bitterness himself, and lightly quaffed
It off, and said the other one was mine.

And when I asked him what the deuce he meant
By doing that, he only looked at me   10
And smiled, and said it was a way of his.
And though I know the fellow, I have spent
Long time a-wondering when I shall be
As happy as Cliff Klingenhagen is.

5. **wormwood:** a bitter liquid made from an herb; anything very bitter. 6.
draught (draft): drink.

Meaning and Method

1. How do you know that Cliff Klingenhagen is comparatively affluent?
2. How does wormwood differ from wine? What do you think the wormwood symbolizes? Why does Cliff drink it?
3. What is Cliff's attitude toward life? Is he realistic? pessimistic? both? something else? Why does the speaker feel that Cliff is a happy man?
4. In dramatic literature, a *foil* is a person who, by being presented as a contrast, serves to enhance or set off the qualities of another person. In what way is the speaker a foil? Do you think the story would have been equally effective if the speaker had not been personally involved in it? Why or why not?
5. Why are the colloquial phrases appropriate for the poem?
6. This poem, an "Italian" sonnet, is divided into an octave—the first eight lines—and a sestet—the last six lines. Usually the division between the octave and the sestet in an Italian sonnet marks a change, either in tone or thought. Is there a change of this sort in "Cliff Klingenhagen"? Explain.

"Cliff Klingenhagen" from *The Children of the Night* by Edwin Arlington Robinson (1897). Reprinted by permission of Charles Scribner's Sons.

Bewick Finzer

Time was when his half million drew
    The breath of six percent;
But soon the worm of what-was-not
    Fed hard on his content;
And something crumbled in his brain   5
    When his half million went.

Time passed, and filled along with his
    The place of many more;
Time came, and hardly one of us
    Had credence to restore,   10
From what appeared one day, the man
    Whom we had known before.

The broken voice, the withered neck,
    The coat worn out with care,
The cleanliness of indigence,°   15
    The brilliance of despair,
The fond imponderable° dreams
    Of affluence—all were there.

Poor Finzer, with his dreams and schemes,
    Fares hard now in the race,   20
With heart and eye that have a task
    When he looks in the face
Of one who might so easily
    Have been in Finzer's place.

He comes unfailing for the loan   25
    We give and then forget;
He comes, and probably for years
    Will he be coming yet—
Familiar as an old mistake,
    And futile as regret.   30

15. **indigence:** poverty. 17. **imponderable:** incapable of being estimated.

Meaning and Method

1. What physical changes occurred in Finzer after he lost his money? How did his way of living change? Did he adjust to his changed circumstances?
2. What does the use of the similes in lines 29 and 30 show about the speaker's attitude toward Finzer?
3. Is Finzer a type, that is, a person who has the characteristics of a group or class, or is he an individual? In your answer, comment particularly on the third stanza.
4. As in "Cliff Klingenhagen," the narrator is personally involved in the story he tells. Where in the poem does he indicate his personal involvement? What do we learn about the narrator from his reaction to Finzer?

Composition

Write a composition discussing the role money should play in one's life. Should it be the dominant value in life? one of many values? not a value at all?

Reuben Bright

Because he was a butcher and thereby
Did earn an honest living (and did right),
I would not have you think that Reuben Bright
Was any more a brute than you or I;
For when they told him that his wife must die,   5
He stared at them, and shook with grief and fright,
And cried like a great baby half that night,
And made the women cry to see him cry.

And after she was dead, and he had paid
The singers and the sexton and the rest,   10
He packed a lot of things that she had made
Most mournfully away in an old chest
Of hers, and put some chopped-up cedar boughs
In with them, and tore down the slaughterhouse.

Meaning and Method

1. What are the connotations of *butcher* (line 1) and of *brute* (line 4)? What kind of man do most people expect a butcher to be? Does Reuben Bright fit this image?
2. The cedar is a tree with fragrant wood of remarkable durability; its wood is frequently used to make chests and closets. What does Bright's placing of the cedar boughs into the chest he packed show about his attitude toward his wife's death?
3. Why does Bright tear down the slaughterhouse? Consider the relationship between the slaughterhouse and the fact that "his wife *must* die" (line 5).
4. In what words of the first four lines is the /b/ sound used? What kind of sound is it? Is it harsh? pleasant? violent? Why is it used? Why is the /b/ sound dropped in the rest of the poem?
5. What is the theme of the poem?

Composition

1. Do you know anyone who behaves in a way that his occupation would not lead you to expect? If so, write a short composition comparing the type of man or woman you would expect to hold a certain job and the actual person you know.
2. Write a character sketch—humorous or serious—of a person named Serena Silver, Fretful Plagiary, Benjamin Backbite, Squire Allworthy, or any other name which you think has interesting and/or humorous connotations.

Edgar Lee Masters

[1869–1950]

Like Robinson, Edgar Lee Masters created a fictional community—Spoon River—that was based on the town in which he grew up—Lewiston, Illinois. Masters wanted to characterize small-town people in verse, for he saw in their lives

> Tragedy, comedy, valor and truth,
> Courage, constancy, heroism, failure—
> All in the loom, and oh, what patterns! *

The *Spoon River Anthology* (1915) was his response to this desire. The *Anthology* is a collection of poems in which more than two hundred inhabitants of the town speak from their graves about their lives. The characterizations gave a remarkably accurate account of Midwestern life. As one critic wrote of these poems when the book first appeared: "It was as though thousands of restless, defeated, anonymous souls had suddenly found their voices."

Masters conceived the idea of writing an anthology of Midwestern life from reading a copy of *Epigrams from the Greek Anthology*. The *Greek Anthology* was a collection of short poems, many of them epitaphs, tracing the life of a man. Masters abandoned the traditional poetic forms of his model to write free-verse epitaphs for his *Anthology*.

The poet was well acquainted with small-town life. He was born in Garnett, Kansas, and lived most of his boyhood years in small towns in southern Illinois, notably Lewiston. He studied for a year at Knox College before returning to Lewiston to practice law with his father. After a year in his father's office, he went to Chicago, where he became a successful lawyer. But from childhood, Masters's real interest was literature and not law. Before he left Lewiston, he had written numerous poems and plays, and this avocation consumed most of his spare time while he was in Chicago.

The *Spoon River Anthology* brought him nation-wide recognition. Several years after the *Anthology's* publication, Masters aban-

---

* Lines fom "Petit the Poet" from *Spoon River Anthology* by Edgar Lee Masters, copyright 1915, 1942 by Edgar Lee Masters. Reprinted by permission of Mrs. Edgar Lee Masters.

doned his law practice to become a professional writer. Although he was a prolific writer of verse as well as of fiction and biography, his later efforts never equaled the success of the *Anthology*. Like the people of Spoon River, Masters seemed to find his voice suddenly and lose it just as quickly.

The Hill

Where are Elmer, Herman, Bert, Tom and Charley,
The weak of will, the strong of arm, the clown, the boozer,
    the fighter?
All, all, are sleeping on the hill.

One passed in a fever,
One was burned in a mine,   5
One was killed in a brawl,
One died in a jail,
One fell from a bridge toiling for children and wife—
All, all are sleeping, sleeping, sleeping on the hill.

Where are Ella, Kate, Mag, Lizzie and Edith,   10
The tender heart, the simple soul, the loud, the proud,
    the happy one?—
All, all, are sleeping on the hill.

One died in shameful childbirth,
One of a thwarted love,
One at the hands of a brute in a brothel,   15
One of a broken pride, in the search for heart's desire,
One after life in faraway London and Paris
Was brought to her little space by Ella and Kate and Mag—
All, all are sleeping, sleeping, sleeping on the hill.

Where are Uncle Isaac and Aunt Emily,   20
And old Towny Kincaid and Sevigne Houghton,

And Major Walker who had talked
With venerable men of the revolution?—
All, all, are sleeping on the hill.

They brought them dead sons from the war,   25
And daughters whom life had crushed,
And their children fatherless, crying—
All, all are sleeping, sleeping, sleeping on the hill.

Where is Old Fiddler Jones
Who played with life all his ninety years,   30
Braving the sleet with bared breast,
Drinking, rioting, thinking neither of wife nor kin,
Nor gold, nor love, nor heaven?
Lo! He babbles of the fish frys of long ago,
Of the horse races of long ago at Clary's Grove,   35
Of what Abe Lincoln said
One time at Springfield.

Meaning and Method

1. "The Hill," the opening poem of the *Spoon River Anthology,* is
   a variation of the traditional *ubi sunt* theme. *Ubi sunt* are the Latin
   words for "where are," and probably the most famous example in
   English is from Dante Gabriel Rossetti's translation of the French
   poet Villon's line, "But where are the snows of yesteryear"? The
   theme expresses the mutability of all things in nature.

   How does the use of proper names make the *ubi sunt* theme more
   realistic? How does the use of abstract types, such as "the clown"
   and "the fighter," make the theme universal? How does the last line
   of each stanza but the final one suggest the universality of Masters's
   theme?
2. Look at the various ways people die in the poem. Do these suggest
   that Masters's outlook on life was optimistic or pessimistic?
3. "The Hill" is written in free verse; that is, verse that does not have
   any regular meter or line length. However, the poem follows specific
   patterns. Analyze the first six stanzas. What similarities are there
   between the form of stanzas 1, 3, and 5? between 2, 4, and 6?
4. Fiddler Jones is the only person whose life is discussed in detail.
   Why do you think he received more attention than Major Walker,
   "who had talked / With venerable men of the revolution"? How
   do the lives of these two men seem to contrast?

Fiddler Jones

The earth keeps some vibration going
There in your heart, and that is you.
And if the people find you can fiddle,
Why, fiddle you must, for all your life.
What do you see, a harvest of clover?   5
Or a meadow to walk through to the river?
The wind's in the corn; you rub your hands
For beeves° hereafter ready for market;
Or else you hear the rustle of skirts
Like the girls when dancing at Little Grove.   10
To Cooney Potter a pillar of dust
Or whirling leaves meant ruinous drought;
They looked to me like Red-Head Sammy
Stepping it off, to "Toor-a-Loor."
How could I till my forty acres   15
Not to speak of getting more,
With a medley of horns, bassoons, and piccolos
Stirred in my brain by crows and robins
And the creak of a windmill—only these?
And I never started to plow in my life   20
That some one did not stop in the road
And take me away to a dance or picnic.
I ended up with forty acres;
I ended up with a broken fiddle—
And a broken laugh, and a thousand memories,   25
And not a single regret.

8. beeves: alternative plural of beef.

Meaning and Method

1. In his monologue, Fiddler Jones notes the way different persons
react to the same thing. What contrasting reactions to a field, the
wind, and a pillar of dust does he describe, respectively, in (a) line
5 and line 6; (b) lines 7 and 8 and lines 9 and 10; (c) lines 11 and
12 and lines 13 and 14? What is he saying about himself by means
of these contrasts?

"Fiddler Jones" from *Spoon River Anthology* by Edgar Lee Masters, copyright 1915,
1942 Edgar Lee Masters. Reprinted by permission of Mrs. Edgar Lee Masters.

2. How does Jones differ from others in the farm community? Is he, in his way, as close to nature as they are? Did he choose his way of life? Was he forced into it? neither? both? Was he a success or failure in his own estimation?

3. *Diction* may be poetic or colloquial, journalistic or scholarly, formal or informal. How would you characterize the diction of the speaker? Would the poet's diction have been equally appropriate if he had had Jones use the word *violin* instead of *fiddle?*

Composition

Write a monologue in which Fiddler Jones speaks of other men with a different attitude, perhaps anger, bitterness, or envy. Or write a monologue in which you attempt to explain your reasons for a specific choice—of a type of automobile, a sport, baseball team, a favorite movie, a future career—to an imaginary other person who offers unspoken disagreements.

George Gray

I have studied many times
The marble which was chiseled for me—
A boat with a furled sail at rest in a harbor.
In truth it pictures not my destination
But my life.   5
For love was offered me and I shrank from its disillusionment;
Sorrow knocked at my door, but I was afraid;
Ambition called to me, but I dreaded the chances.
Yet all the while I hungered for meaning in my life.
And now I know that we must lift the sail   10
And catch the winds of destiny
Wherever they drive the boat.
To put meaning in one's life may end in madness,
But life without meaning is the torture
Of restlessness and vague desire—   15
It is a boat longing for the sea and yet afraid.

Meaning and Method

1. Characterize George Gray. Compare his life with that of Fiddler Jones, as described in the last stanza of "The Hill" (page 15).
2. Why does the statue on his grave—a boat at rest in a harbor—more accurately describe his life than his present state?
3. What attitude toward life is suggested in lines 13–15? Why is madness better than a life without meaning?

Lucinda Matlock

I went to the dances at Chandlerville,
And played snap-out at Winchester.
One time we changed partners,
Driving home in the moonlight of middle June,
And then I found Davis.   5

We were married and lived together for seventy years,
Enjoying, working, raising the twelve children,
Eight of whom we lost
Ere I had reached the age of sixty.
I spun, I wove, I kept the house, I nursed the sick,   10
I made the garden, and for holiday
Rambled over the fields where sang the larks,
And by Spoon River gathering many a shell,
And many a flower and medicinal weed—
Shouting to the wooded hills, singing to the green valleys.   15
At ninety-six I had lived enough, that is all,
And passed to a sweet repose.
What is this I hear of sorrow and weariness,
Anger, discontent, and drooping hopes?
Degenerate sons and daughters.   20
Life is too strong for you—
It takes life to love Life.

Meaning and Method

1. Was Lucinda's life commonplace or unusual? happy or unhappy? How do you know?

2. Why does Lucinda call the sons and daughters of Spoon River "degenerate"? Is life "too strong" for them because they will not accept it as it is? How does her attitude toward life contrast with their attitudes?

3. When a common noun is capitalized, it usually means that the author is speaking about a generalized or abstract quality rather than about a specific thing. For example, a poet may note the beauty of a specific rose, but when he discusses Beauty, he is referring to an overall quality which single objects of beauty reflect. Considering this, explain the difference between "life" and "Life" (line 22).

4. Point out repetitions of the liquid /l/ and the soft /s/ sounds throughout the poem. Considering Lucinda's character and attitude, why are the repetitions of these sounds appropriate?

5. What does Lucinda Matlock feel about the death of her children (lines 7–9) and about her own death (line 16)? What is the tone of the poem? Is it emotional? matter-of-fact?

Composition

1. Write a short reply to Lucinda from the point of view of one of the "degenerate" sons or daughters explaining why the type of life she led is not satisfactory. Or explain why you feel that "sorrow and weariness, / Anger, discontent, and dropping hopes" are appropriate responses to modern life.

2. Write a short description of the life of a modern housewife. How does the modern housewife's life differ from Lucinda's? State your position in your topic sentence.

James Weldon Johnson
[1871–1938]

The variety of careers at which James Weldon Johnson was successful is astonishing. Johnson, who received his B.A. and M.A. from Atlanta University, was the principal of a school in Jacksonville, Florida (his home town), and was the first black lawyer to be admitted to the bar in Florida after Reconstruction. He was also the editor of America's first Negro daily newspaper.

Just after the turn of the century, Johnson went to New York City and collaborated with his brother in writing songs and musical comedies. His interest in music led to a career in the foreign service. Johnson supported President Theodore Roosevelt's bid for a second term, and he and his brother wrote the President's campaign song. Roosevelt, in turn, appointed Johnson as a United States consul in Venezuela, and Johnson later served as a consul in Nicaragua.

While in the diplomatic corps, Johnson wrote a novel, *The Autobiography of an Ex-Colored Man* (1912). This novel was followed by two collections of his poetry: *Fifty Years and Other Poems* (1917) and *God's Trombones* (1927). He also wrote his own autobiography, *Along the Way* (1933).

From 1916 to 1930, Johnson held positions as field secretary and general secretary in the National Association for the Advancement of Colored People. When he retired as general secretary, he became professor of creative literature at Fisk University in Nashville, Tennessee, and in 1934 visiting professor of literature at New York University.

Johnson often found his inspiration in Negro spirituals and sermons, and his collections of these were influential in arousing public appreciation of such rich veins of literature. His best-known poems "capture the charm of the folk speech." Johnson's poems are deeply imbued with the vigorous rhythm and colorful imagery that give Negro folk songs their distinctive quality.

O Black and Unknown Bards

O black and unknown bards of long ago,
How came your lips to touch the sacred fire?
How, in your darkness, did you come to know
The power and beauty of the minstrel's lyre?
Who first from midst his bonds lifted his eyes?   5
Who first from out the still watch, lone and long,
Feeling the ancient faith of prophets rise
Within his dark-kept soul, burst into song?

Heart of what slave poured out such melody
As "Steal away to Jesus"? On its strains   10
His spirit must have nightly floated free,
Though still about his hands he felt his chains.
Who heard great "Jordan roll"? Whose starward eye
Saw chariot "swing low"? And who was he
That breathed that comforting, melodic sigh,   15
"Nobody knows de trouble I see"?

What merely living clod, what captive thing,
Could up toward God through all its darkness grope,
And find within its deadened heart to sing
These songs of sorrow, love and faith, and hope?   20
How did it catch that subtle undertone,
That note in music heard not with the ears?
How sound the elusive reed so seldom blown,
Which stirs the soul or melts the heart to tears.

Not that great German master in his dream   25
Of harmonies that thundered amongst the stars
At the creation,° ever heard a theme
Nobler than "Go down, Moses." Mark its bars

25–27. **great . . . creation:** perhaps a reference to either Beethoven or Haydn, both of whom wrote musical works about the Creation.

"O Black and Unknown Bards" from *Saint Peter Relates an Incident* by James Weldon Johnson, copyright 1917, 1921, 1935 by James Weldon Johnson, 1962 by Grace Nail Johnson. Reprinted by permission of The Viking Press, Inc.

How like a mighty trumpet-call they stir
The blood. Such are the notes that men have sung   30
Going to valorous deeds; such tones there were
That helped make history when Time was young.

There is a wide, wide wonder in it all,
That from degraded rest and servile toil
The fiery spirit of the seer should call   35
These simple children of the sun and soil.
O black slave singers, gone, forgot, unfamed,
You—you alone, of all the long, long line
Of those who've sung untaught, unknown, unnamed,
Have stretched out upward, seeking the divine.   40

You sang not deeds of heroes or of kings;
No chant of bloody war, no exulting paean°
Of arms-won triumphs; but your humble strings
You touched in chord with music empyrean.°
You sang far better than you knew; the songs   45
That for your listeners' hungry hearts sufficed
Still live—but more than this to you belongs:
You sang a race from wood and stone to Christ.

42. **paean** (pē′ən): a joyously exultant song or hymn of praise, tribute, thanksgiving, or triumph. 44. **empyrean** (em′pə·rē′ən): reaching the highest, where God and his angels reside.

Meaning and Method

1. Why is the speaker surprised that the black bards of long ago were inspired to sing? What types of songs did they sing?
2. What is "That note in music heard not with the ears" (line 22)? What phrase or phrases in lines 23 and 24 could be used to answer this question?
3. How were the songs of the black bards different from those of other bards—that is, from poets who sang of the deeds of a people or nation? In your answer, consider lines 37–44.
4. According to the speaker in line 48, what is the greatest accomplishment of the black bards?
5. Find several instances in the text in which the poet uses words that contrast darkness with light, and being earthbound with rising spiritually. Why is this method appropriate to the theme?

6. A *rhetorical question* is a question asked only to achieve an effect; as a rule the answer is implied. Are the questions in the first three stanzas primarily rhetorical questions? If so, what effect do you think the poet intended to achieve by using these questions?

Go Down Death (A Funeral Sermon)

Weep not, weep not,
She is not dead;
She's resting in the bosom of Jesus.
Heart-broken husband—weep no more;
Grief-stricken son—weep no more;   5
She's only just gone home.

Day before yesterday morning,
God was looking down from his great, high heaven,
Looking down on all his children,
And his eye fell on Sister Caroline,   10
Tossing on her bed of pain.
And God's big heart was touched with pity,
With the everlasting pity.

And God sat back on his throne,
And he commanded that tall, bright angel standing at his
      right hand: 15
Call me Death!
And that tall, bright angel cried in a voice
That broke like a clap of thunder:
Call Death!—Call Death!
And the echo sounded down the streets of heaven   20
Till it reached away back to that shadowy place,
Where Death waits with his pale, white horses.

And Death heard the summons,
And he leaped on his fastest horse,

"Go Down Death" from *God's Trombones* by James Weldon Johnson, copyright 1927 by The Viking Press, Inc., 1935 by Grace Nail Johnson. Reprinted by permission of The Viking Press, Inc.

Pale as a sheet in the moonlight.   25
Up the golden street Death galloped,
And the hoof of his horse struck fire from the gold,
But they didn't make no sound.
Up Death rode to the Great White Throne,
And waited for God's command.   30

And God said: Go down, Death, go down,
Go down to Savannah, Georgia,
Down in Yamacraw,
And find Sister Caroline.
She's borne the burden and heat of the day,   35
She's labored long in my vineyard,
And she's tired—
She's weary—
Go down, Death, and bring her to me.

And Death didn't say a word,   40
But he loosed the reins on his pale, white horse,
And he clamped the spurs to his bloodless sides,
And out and down he rode,
Through heaven's pearly gates,
Past suns and moons and stars;   45
On Death rode,
And the foam from his horse was like a comet in the sky;
On Death rode,
Leaving the lightning's flash behind;
Straight on down he came.   50

While we were watching round her bed,
She turned her eyes and looked away,
She saw what we couldn't see;
She saw Old Death. She saw Old Death
Coming like a falling star.   55
But Death didn't frighten Sister Caroline;
He looked to her like a welcome friend.
And she whispered to us: I'm going home,
And she smiled and closed her eyes.

And Death took her up like a baby,   60
And she lay in his icy arms,
But she didn't feel no chill.
And Death began to ride again—
Up beyond the evening star,
Out beyond the morning star,   65
Into the glittering light of glory,
On to the Great White Throne.
And there he laid Sister Caroline
On the loving breast of Jesus.

And Jesus took his own hand and wiped away her tears,   70
And he smoothed the furrows from her face,
And the angels sang a little song,
And Jesus rocked her in his arms,
And kept a-saying: Take your rest,
Take your rest, take your rest.   75

Weep not—weep not,
She is not dead;
She's resting in the bosom of Jesus.

Meaning and Method

1. In the preacher's view, what is God like? What is Death like? Is Death frightening? Why or why not? Why is Death's "pale, white horse" more fitting to the preacher's idea of death than a black horse would have been?
2. What kind of woman was the dead person? What kind of life had she led?
3. The preacher attempts to console the mourners by indicating that the heavenly life of the dead woman will be more satisfying than her earthly life was. Which words or phrases convey this attitude? Do you think his method would be successful in consoling the mourners?
4. What is personified in this poem? Is the use of personification suitable to the speaker's theme?
5. Notice the similes in lines 18, 25, 47, 55, 57, and 60. Why does the poet use comparisons within the experiences of those listening to the sermon?

Ezra Pound

One of the most controversial and original of modern poets, Ezra Loomis Pound was born in Hailey, Idaho, in 1885. When he was fifteen, he entered the University of Pennsylvania; at seventeen, he registered there as a "special student"—that is, one not seeking a degree—because he wanted "to avoid irrelevant subjects."

Despite his iconoclastic approach to education, by the time he was twenty-one, Pound had earned a B.A. from Hamilton College and an M.A. from the University of Pennsylvania. The scholarly poet, a specialist in Renaissance literature, then had a short-lived career as a college teacher. He was dismissed from his position at Wabash College in Indiana for being too bohemian. Pound became an expatriate, settling in London and later in Paris, where he was a central figure in the avant-garde literary world.

By 1920, Pound had written a number of distinctive books of verse, notably *Personae* (1909), and had done translations from such diverse languages as Chinese, Greek, and Italian. The poet T. S. Eliot called Pound's poetic sequence *Hugh Selwyn Mauberley* (1920) "a document of an epoch." And, according to the poet Carl Sandburg, Pound had done the "most of living men to incite new impulses in poetry." This incitement took two forms, often both at the same time: theorizing about poetry and directly influencing other poets.

His most important theoretical contribution was in the formation of the principles of Imagism, which emphasized the use of precise, concentrated, yet connotive images that, according to Pound, would present "an intellectual and emotional complex in an instant of time." This concept of poetry, although widely accepted today, was revolutionary in an age of ornate, vague, romantic writing. Pound's dictum—"make it new"—became the doctrine of the age.

Personally, Pound acted as a one-man entrepreneur and critic for talented and unconventional writers. He was instrumental in having the works of James Joyce, the Irish novelist, published. He influenced the poetry of William Butler Yeats and William Carlos Williams, and when Robert Frost's second book of verse appeared, Pound praised it highly. Perhaps his most important influence was on T. S. Eliot, who is now generally recognized as one of the great poets of the century. Pound literally forced the American magazine, *Poetry*, of which he was the European correspondent, to publish Eliot's earliest work, and he found a publisher for Eliot's first volume of poetry. Eliot publicly acknowledged his literary and personal debt to Pound.

During and after the 1920's, Pound's original and rebellious mind and spirit took less benevolent paths, and he suffered from mental illness. The poet became obsessed with economic theories and was strongly attracted to Fascism. In 1924, he moved to Rapallo, Italy, where he subsequently became an active supporter of Mussolini. During the second World War, he broadcasted anti-American propaganda for the Italian government. After the war, he was indicted for treason by the United States government, but before he was tried, he was declared insane and was committed to St. Elizabeth's Hospital in Washington, D.C.

Even while hospitalized he was the center of controversy. In February 1949, he was awarded the Bollingen prize for the best poetry by an American citizen published during the year in the United States. Although there were many protests, he eventually received the prize. In 1958, he was released in the custody of his daughter and returned to Rapallo.

Pound's place as a poet has not been fully appraised. One reason for this is that his major work, *The Cantos*—a series of poems begun in 1917 and presently having more than one hundred parts— is packed with allusions to works in many languages and more often than not is obscure. Some critics feel that over it "there hangs a dismal mist of unresolved confusion." Others think that it is one of the "great works of poetry of our time." Whatever the final outcome of the controversy, it is already clear that Pound is a major figure in the history of modern literature.

The River Merchant's Wife: A Letter

While my hair was still cut straight across my forehead
I played about the front gate, pulling flowers.
You came by on bamboo stilts, playing horse,

You walked about my seat, playing with blue plums.
And we went on living in the village of Chokan: 5
Two small people, without dislike or suspicion.

At fourteen I married my Lord you.
I never laughed, being bashful.
Lowering my head, I looked at the wall.
Called to, a thousand times, I never looked back.   10

At fifteen I stopped scowling,
I desired my dust to be mingled with yours
Forever and forever and forever.
Why should I climb the look out?

At sixteen you departed,   15
You went into far Ku-to-yen, by the river of swirling eddies,
And you have been gone five months.
The monkeys make sorrowful noise overhead.
You dragged your feet when you went out.
By the gate now, the moss is grown, the different mosses,   20
Too deep to clear them away!
The leaves fall early this autumn, in wind.
The paired butterflies are already yellow with August
Over the grass in the West garden;
They hurt me. I grow older.   25
If you are coming down through the narrows of the
      river Kiang,
Please let me know beforehand,
And I will come out to meet you
            As far as Cho-fu-Sa.

*A free translation from
the Chinese poet Rihaku (eighth century)*

Meaning and Method

1. This poem is a subdued love letter. Which lines in particular do you think show the speaker's love for her husband? Which lines indicate his love for her?
2. Why do the "paired butterflies" (line 23) hurt the speaker?
3. What is the speaker's mood? How does the description in lines 18–24 reflect this mood?

In a Station of the Metro

The apparition of these faces in the crowd;
Petals on a wet, black bough.

Meaning and Method

1. The poem is based on the comparison of faces in a subway with petals on a bough. The Metro is the Paris subway.

   What are the connotations of *apparition* (line 1)? What does the use of this word suggest about the speaker's attitude toward "these faces in the crowd"? What associations or images does the line "Petals on a wet, black bough" call to mind? What does the speaker's use of this image show about his attitude toward the faces in the crowd?

2. The major point of the Imagist movement, of which Pound was a leader, was to advocate the use of concrete, precise images. How does this qualify as an Imagist poem?

Composition

1. Pound has said that this is a "hokku-like poem." Which of the following characteristics of hokku, or haiku, do you find in the poem?
   (a) reliance of suggestion through images and symbols.
   (b) creation of a single mood.
   (c) a conciseness that forces the reader to make his own connections between thoughts and images.

   Write a short composition in which you support your answers to this question.

2. Write a two- or three-line poem in which you begin with vague words and end up with concrete, precise images.

Amy Lowell

[1874–1925]

Wealth, social prominence, and intellectual interests—these were the birthright of Amy Lowell. Her grandfather founded the cotton-mill town of Lowell, Massachusetts, and her grandfather's cousin, James Russell Lowell, was a famous poet and diplomat. One of her brothers became president of Harvard, and many lesser-known Lowells had distinguished careers as lawyers, judges, and scholars.

Miss Lowell did not "discover" that poetry was her "natural mode of expression" until she was twenty-eight. She then carefully studied the works and techniques of other poets for years before allowing any of her poems to be published. It was not until 1912 that her first book of poetry, A Dome of Many-Colored Glass, appeared. This initial volume imitated techniques of conventional nineteenth-century poets.

In 1913, she went to England and met Ezra Pound, who had founded the Imagist movement. Miss Lowell joined the Imagists and subsequently became the leader and main spokesman for this group in both America and England. Pound, who eventually left the movement, referred to Miss Lowell and her theories as "Amygism" because of the influence she had on the other poets in the group.

Imagism, as Amy Lowell interpreted it, meant discarding the trite and worn-out poetic conventions of the past century and returning to the language of ordinary speech. She wrote in and helped to popularize free verse, a form that approximates the rhythms of everyday speech. An Imagist poem, she decreed, should create an impression or emotion through the use of sharp, clear sensory images. Her poetry illustrated these theories. They had an "enameled" quality—a brightly hued series of images that combined to produce a single final effect.

In retrospect, her technical experiments and her influence on modern poetry seem to overshadow her own work. However, many of the poems in her later books—Sword Blades and Poppy Seeds (1914), Men, Women, and Ghosts (1916), and the Pulitzer prize winning What's O'Clock? (1925)—are still justly praised. Her best writing is noted for the variety and concreteness of sensory impressions, particularly of color and sound, and for her skill in conveying moods through images.

Patterns

I walk down the garden-paths,
And all the daffodils
Are blowing, and the bright blue squills.°
I walk down the patterned garden-paths
In my stiff, brocaded gown.   5
With my powdered hair and jeweled fan,
I too am a rare
Pattern. As I wander down
The garden-paths.

My dress is richly figured,   10
And the train
Makes a pink and silver stain
On the gravel, and the thrift°
Of the borders.
Just a plate of current fashion,   15
Tripping by in high-heeled, ribboned shoes.
Not a softness anywhere about me,
Only whalebone and brocade.
And I sink on a seat in the shade
Of a lime tree. For my passion   20
Wars against the stiff brocade.
The daffodils and squills
Flutter in the breeze
As they please.
And I weep;   25
For the lime tree is in blossom
And one small flower has dropped upon my bosom.

3. **squills:** plants of the lily family. 13. **thrift:** a tufted herb with white or pink flowers.

And the plashing° of waterdrops
In the marble fountain
Comes down the garden-paths.   30
The dripping never stops.
Underneath my stiffened gown
Is the softness of a woman bathing in a marble basin,
A basin in the midst of hedges grown
So thick, she cannot see her lover hiding,   35
But she guesses he is near,
And the sliding of the water
Seems the stroking of a dear
Hand upon her.
What is Summer in a fine brocaded gown!   40
I should like to see it lying in a heap upon the ground.
All the pink and silver crumpled upon the ground.

I would be the pink and silver as I ran along the paths,
And he would stumble after.
Bewildered by my laughter.   45
I should see the sun flashing from his sword-hilt and
    the buckles on his shoes.
I would choose
To lead him in a maze along the patterned paths,
A bright and laughing maze for my heavy-booted lover,
Till he caught me in the shade,   50
And the buttons of his waistcoat bruised my body as he
    clasped me,
Aching, melting, unafraid.
With the shadows of the leaves and the sundrops
And the plopping of the waterdrops,
All about us in the open afternoon—   55
I am very like to swoon
With the weight of this brocade,
For the sun sifts through the shade.

Underneath the fallen blossom
In my bosom,
Is a letter I have hid.   60

28. plashing: splashing lightly.

It was brought to me this morning by a rider from the Duke.
"Madam, we regret to inform you that Lord Hartwell
Died in action Thursday se'n-night." °
As I read it in the white, morning sunlight,   65
The letters squirmed like snakes.
"Any answer, Madam?" said my footman,
"No," I told him.
"See that the messenger takes some refreshment.
No, no answer."   70
And I walked into the garden,
Up and down the patterned paths,
In my stiff, correct brocade.
The blue and the yellow flowers stood up proudly in the sun,
Each one.   75
I stood upright too,
Held rigid to the pattern
By the stiffness of my gown.
Up and down I walked,
Up and down.   80

In a month he would have been my husband.
In a month, here, underneath this lime,
We would have broke the pattern;
He for me, and I for him,
He as Colonel, I as Lady,   85
On this shady seat.
He had a whim
That sunlight carried blessing.
And I answered, "It shall be as you have said."
Now he is dead.   90

In Summer and in Winter I shall walk
Up and down
The patterned garden-paths
In my stiff, brocaded gown.
The squills and daffodils   95
Will give place to pillared roses, and to asters, and to snow.
I shall go

64. se'n-night: an abbreviation of seven-night; *that is,* a week ago.

Up and down,
In my gown.
Gorgeously arrayed,   100
Boned and stayed.
And the softness of my body will be guarded from embrace
By each button, hook, and lace.
For the man who should loose me is dead,
Fighting with the Duke in Flanders,°   105
In a pattern called war.
Christ! What are patterns for?

105. **Flanders:** now part of Belgium, but formerly part of France. In the early eighteenth century, the Duke of Marlborough won a famous victory there.

Meaning and Method

1. The poem is set in eighteenth-century England, a time when many gardens were laid out according to a formal pattern. It was also a period of formality in art, in manners, and in dress.

   In what ways do the speaker and her life also form patterns? Who or what has decided the patterns? Are the patterns natural? Does the speaker accept the rigid pattern of her life, or does she protest against them? both? In your answer, take lines 4–6 and lines 20–25 into consideration.

2. In lines 15–18, the speaker describes herself as she looks to an outsider. How does her impression of her "true" self—described in the imaginary incidents in lines 32–55—contrast with the outsider's view? Why is the metaphor in lines 32 and 33 a particularly apt one to describe this contrast?

3. In lines 60–70, the speaker describes the news that has sent her walking in the garden. What has happened? Does she react to the news like her "true" self or like a pattern? both? How do lines 60–70 explain the reasons for her moods in the previous lines?

4. In lines 91–103 what type of life does the speaker see stretching before her? Is she resigned to her future position? Is she rebellious? Does she show both attitudes?

5. In what ways is war similar to the other patterns the speaker has described? What does the speaker's question in the last line reveal about her attitude toward the conventions of society?

6. *Tone* is the speaker's attitude toward a subject. What is the tone in lines 15–18? lines 47–52? Is the dominant tone of the poem one of anger? self-control? something else? Is the tone of the last line similar to or different from the tone in most of the poem?

7. Find several images that emphasize hardness and several images that emphasize softness. In general, which images describe natural things? Which describe products of society? How does the contrast or alternation of these types of images emphasize the theme of the poem?

8. A *dramatic monologue* is a poem in which a speaker talks about his or her conflicts to a silent listener. Is this poem a dramatic monologue? Why or why not? Are the events in the poem ordered in chronological fashion—that is, according to the way they happened in time—or do they follow a psychological pattern? Explain your answer.

9. In an Imagist manifesto published in an American anthology of Imagist poets in 1915, Amy Lowell and another poet, Richard Aldington, set down some principles that Imagist poets followed. Among these principles were the following:

   (a) to use common language precisely—without undue ornament.
   (b) to have variety in rhythm, as in free verse.
   (c) to present sharp images and to produce firm and clear poetry.

   Give examples to show how Amy Lowell upheld these principles in this poem.

Language: Onomatopoeia

In line 28, when the speaker talks of the *"plashing* of the water-drops," she is using an *onomatopoeic* word, that is, a word which imitates sound. What word imitates a sound in line 54?

What sounds do the following words imitate:

1. cackle	5. tweet
2. neigh	6. buzz
3. hiss	7. pop
4. swish	8. snicker

Composition

At one time or another, everyone has felt an urge to *break the pattern*. Write a composition mentioning some patterns you think should be changed. These constraints might be found in school, in politics, in social conventions, etc. Give reasons why you think the changes are necessary and suggest benefits that would follow from the changes.

Meeting-House * Hill

I must be mad, or very tired,
When the curve of a blue bay beyond the railroad track
Is shrill and sweet to me like the sudden springing of a tune,
And the sight of a white church above thin trees in a city
   square
Amazes my eyes as though it were the Parthenon.°   5
Clear, reticent, superbly final,
With the pillars of its portico° refined to a cautious elegance,
It dominates the weak trees,
And the shot of its spire
Is cool and candid,   10
Raising into an unresisting sky.

Strange meeting house
Pausing a moment upon a squalid hilltop.
I watch the spire sweeping the sky,
I am dizzy with the movement of the sky;   15
I might be watching a mast
With its royals° set full
Straining before a two-reef breeze.°
I might be sighting a tea clipper,°
Tacking° into the blue bay,   20
Just back from Canton
With her hold full of green and blue porcelain
And a Chinese coolie leaning over the rail
Gazing at the white spire
With dull, sea-spent eyes.   25

* Meeting House: a Quaker place of worship. 5. Parthenon: a Greek temple to the goddess Athena. The white-marble structure, which is surrounded by columns, stands on the top of the Acropolis, a hill in Athens, and dominates the city. 7. portico: a porch with a roof supported by columns. 17. royals: sails located next to the top of each mast of a ship; they are used to catch light breezes. 18. two-reef breeze: a breeze that requires the sails to be pulled in twice so they can catch all the wind possible. 19. tea clipper: a large, fast sailing vessel used to transport freight on long voyages—for example, tea between China (Canton) and America. 20. Tacking: veering to one side to take advantage of a side wind.

"Meeting-House Hill" from The Complete Poetical Works of Amy Lowell, copyright 1955 by Houghton Mifflin Company. Reprinted by permission of the publisher.

Meaning and Method

1. In the first stanza, the speaker describes her reactions and emotions as she catches a glimpse of the town's meeting house and the bay as if for the first time. What are her reactions as she "sees" the church and the bay?
2. What words or phrases in the first stanza prepare the reader for the comparison of the church's spire to a ship's mast in stanza 2? How does line 14 serve as a transitional idea? Does the comparison strike you as apt or strange? both? In your answer, mention the words of motion referring either to the meeting house or to the ship, and the connotations of *tea clipper*.
3. How does the description of the coolie in lines 24 and 25 reflect the mood of the speaker in the poem? The coolie looks with "sea-spent eyes"; does he see something different from the narrator? Why does the poet use *coolie* instead of *sailor*?
4. Which images give you a concrete, visual impression of the real and imaginary scenes the speaker sees?

Language: Specialized Vocabularies

Many professions have specialized vocabularies that are used primarily among the members of a profession or group. In this poem, Amy Lowell employs a nautical vocabulary in using such terms as "royals," "two-reef breeze," and "tacking."

Look up the following words and give their meaning and the professions with which they are associated:

1. fade-out
2. fair ball
3. to ghost
4. pica
5. twofers

Composition

Write a paragraph about a specific object—for example, a cloud, a tree, a building, or a street. In the paragraph, tell what you might think them to be if you were in an imaginative mood. Your paragraph may be humorous or serious, but you should attempt to use concrete, visual images in your descriptions.

Solitaire

When night drifts along the streets of the city,
And sifts down between the uneven roofs,
My mind begins to peek and peer.
It plays at ball in odd, blue Chinese gardens,
And shakes wrought° dice-cups in Pagan temples   5
Amid the broken flutings of white pillars.
It dances with purple and yellow crocuses in its hair,
And its feet shine as they flutter over drenched grasses.
How light and laughing my mind is,
When all good folk have put out their bedroom candles,   10
And the city is still.

5. **wrought:** hammered or beaten into shape; usually delicately and elborately made.

Meaning and Method

1. How does the real place and time of day contrast with the places and atmospheres the speaker imagines?
2. The major figure of speech in this poem is personification. Which words—especially verbs—carry out the personification of the speaker's mind?
3. What is the effect of personifying the mind? Would the effect be different had the speaker used *I* instead of *mind?*

Composition

Write a short composition entitled "Solitaire" in which you describe the time of day you like best and the real or imagined things you see when you are alone at that time.

"Solitaire" from *The Complete Poetical Works of Amy Lowell,* copyright 1955 by Houghton Mifflin Company. Reprinted by permission of the publisher.

H. D.

[1886–1961]

The initials which Hilda Doolittle used as her poetic signature evoke an atmosphere of elusiveness, a quality found in many of her poems. Her poems have been called "chiseled," "frozen," and "static." Yet they are far from dead; passion and intensity underlie the polished jewellike surfaces.

H. D. was born in Bethlehem, Pennsylvania, and grew up in Philadelphia, where her father was a professor of astronomy. She attended Bryn Mawr College until poor health forced her to leave. In 1911, she went to London, met Ezra Pound, and became an enthusiastic proponent of Imagism. While in England, she married the English writer Richard Aldington, and, except for a short time in California, she lived abroad for the rest of her life.

Throughout her life, she loved Greek poetry, both in subject and style, and she often strove to write in the Greek tradition. Her poems are notable for a combination of strongly sensual images and a classical conciseness and restraint.

Pear Tree

Silver dust
lifted from the earth,
higher than my arms reach,
you have mounted,
O silver,   5
higher than my arms reach,
you front us with great mass;

no flower ever opened
so staunch a white leaf,
no flower ever parted silver   10
from such rare silver;

O white pear,
your flower-tufts
thick on the branch
bring summer and ripe fruits   15
in their purple hearts.

Meaning and Method

1. Is the speaker addressing a pear tree in blossom or after the fruit
   has appeared?
2. What words or phrases appealing to the senses does the speaker use
   to describe the pear tree?
3. What does the use of the italicized words in the following phrases
   indicate about the speaker's attribute toward the tree: (a) *lifted*
   from the earth; (b) *higher* than my arms reach; (c) you have
   mounted? What is the effect of the use of apostrophe (lines 5 and
   12)?
4. Does the poem suggest that the pear tree is a form of deity? For
   example, why does the speaker say that the pear will "bring summer
   and ripe fruits"? Is the speaker's attitude toward it one of adoration
   (see lines 3 and 6)? Does the tree symbolize fertility?

The Garden

1

You are clear,
O rose, cut in rock;
Hard as the descent of hail.

I could scrape the color
From the petals,   5
Like spilt dye from a rock.

If I could break you
I could break a tree.

"The Garden" from *The Sea Garden* by Hilda Doolittle. London: Constable Publishers, 1916. Reprinted by permission of the publisher.

If I could stir
I could break a tree—   10
I could break you.

2

O wind, rend open the heat,
Cut apart the heat,
Rend it to tatters.

Fruit cannot drop   15
Through this thick air;
Fruit cannot fall into heat
That presses up and blunts
The points of pears,
And rounds the grapes.   20

Cut the heat:
Plow through it,
Turning it on either side
Of your path.

Meaning and Method

1. How does the picture of roses presented in lines 1–11 differ from the usual description?
2. What words or phrases in Part 1 indicate that the speaker feels incapable of any action? that she feels the world around her weighs her down or prevents any action on her part?
3. What words or phrases in Part 2 make the heat seem solid? Why does the speaker want the wind to cut through the heat?
4. The speaker's mood in lines 12–24 seems to be one of passionate desperation. She seems to feel an oppressiveness of nature, against which she cries out. Which words or phrases in the poem substantiate this interpretation?

Language: Specific Verbs

Much of the effect of this poem is created by H. D.'s use of specific verbs—that is, verbs which signify precise actions. Among the specific verbs used in the poem are "scrape" (line 4), "rend" (line 12), "cut" (line 13), "presses up and blunts" (line 18), "rounds" (line 20), and "plow" (line 22).

The verb "run" is a general verb. Look up the following synonyms of "run" and point out how they are more specific than the general word.

1. canter	3. jog	5. sprint
2. gallop	4. lope	6. trot

Composition

Write a free verse, Imagist poem about a specific object, such as a tree, an apple, or a vacant lot.

William Carlos Williams
[1883–1963]

In his *Autobiography*, William Carlos Williams indirectly answered a question he must have been asked scores of times: How can a busy pediatrician also be a prolific, avant-garde poet? His answer was that the "poet's business" is "to write particularly, as a physician works," and "in the particular, to discover the universal." (Or, as he said at another time: "No ideas but in things.") Following his own prescription, Williams wrote poems in which he described "things" specifically, and yet he connected them to a larger scheme: for example, a poem precisely describing a landscape hovering between winter and spring is also a comment on the cycle of dying and rebirth in man and nature.

William Carlos Williams was born in Rutherford, New Jersey, and attended private schools in New York City and in Switzerland. He studied medicine at the University of Pennsylvania (where he met Ezra Pound) and did graduate work in pediatrics at the University of Leipzig in Germany. Williams subsequently returned to America and settled in his home town. Later he explained that he had given up traveling because "I never saw anything outside to equal what I was going through in my innards."

Williams's major work is *Paterson*, a series of poems forming an impressionistic history of this industrial New Jersey town. The poems expressed Williams's disgust for the tawdry commercialism that dominated the American way of life. At the same time, the poet was able to perceive a sense of beauty and vitality in the squalor of the city and, by extension, in America itself.

The best of Williams's poems are distinguished by their graphic images, reflecting both his lifelong interest in painting and the influence of Pound and the Imagists. He attempted to present objectively his observations of sensory experience, and his free verse captured the rhythms and the colloquial conversational tone of everyday speech. Both in theme and in style, Williams is "in the American grain."

Classic Scene

A power-house
in the shape of
a red brick chair
90 feet high

on the seat of which   5
sit the figures
of two metal
stacks—aluminum—

commanding an area
of squalid shacks   10
side by side—
from one of which

buff smoke streams while under
a gray sky
the other remains   15

passive today—

Meaning and Method

1. The phrase "classic scene" suggests a traditional, harmonious picture. Such a picture would have formal and austere buildings of
marble, decorated with statues, arranged in the balanced style of
ancient Greece and Rome, and set against a background of nature.
What parts, if any, of the picture Williams draws are reminiscent
of a classic scene? What parts are different? Do you think Williams
meant his title seriously? ironically? both?
2. Williams combines realistic detail with imaginative metaphor. What
specific details did he use to describe the powerhouse? What metaphor did he use, and what does it connote?
3. The poet's use of free verse gives the impression of a slowly unfolding picture. Each detail seems to add a surprising addition to the
picture that had previously formed in the reader's mind. Find

several examples of this technique; in each case explain the contrast between the original picture and the image created by the additional phrase on the next line.

4. In your opinion, what is the poet's attitude toward the scene he describes? toward modern life in general?

Nantucket *

Flowers through the window
lavender and yellow

changed by white curtains—
Smell of cleanliness—

Sunshine of late afternoon—   5
On a glass tray

a glass pitcher, the tumbler
turned down, by which

a key is lying—And the
immaculate white bed   10

* Nantucket: an island off the coast of Massachusetts. It is a popular summer resort.

Meaning and Method

1. Which details give an impression of light? of cleanliness?
2. Why does it seem that the speaker is seeing the room for the first time? Why does the reader get the impression that the room described is a room in a hotel or the guest room in a private house?

Composition

Write a composition describing a room in another season—winter, for example. Present the specific details objectively, so that the reader will think he is "seeing" a still-life painting.

This Is Just to Say

I have eaten
the plums
that were in
the icebox

and which   5
you were probably
saving
for breakfast.

Forgive me
they were delicious   10
so sweet
and so cold

Meaning and Method

1. To whom do you think the speaker is writing? Is he really apologizing for eating the plums? What is the tone of the poem?
2. Why are the language and the form of the poem appropriate?
3. Is this poem a simple message saying that the speaker has eaten the plums in the icebox, or is it a poem that attempts to show there may be a special quality in seemingly ordinary things? Give reasons for your answer.

Spring and All
(By the road to the contagious hospital)

By the road to the contagious hospital
under the surge of the blue
mottled clouds driven from the
northeast—a cold wind. Beyond, the

waste of broad, muddy fields   5
brown with dried weeds, standing and fallen

patches of standing water
the scattering of tall trees

All along the road the reddish
purplish, forked, upstanding, twiggy   10
stuff of bushes and small trees
with dead, brown leaves under them
leafless vines—

Lifeless in appearance, sluggish
dazed spring approaches—   15

They enter the new world naked,
cold, uncertain of all
save that they enter. All about them
the cold, familiar wind—

Now the grass, tomorrow   20
the stiff curl of wildcarrot leaf
One by one objects are defined—
It quickens: clarity, outline of leaf

But now the stark dignity of
entrance—Still, the profound change   25
has come upon them: rooted, they
grip down and begin to awaken

Meaning and Method

1. What are the connotations of *contagious hospital* (line 1)? How
   are these connotations relevant to the portrayal of winter in the
   poem?
2. What words or phrases give an impression of the static barrenness
   of winter? How does spring approach, transforming this barrenness?
   (See lines 4–15.)
3. Who are "they" in line 16? Who or what is "It" in line 23? Why may
   their "entrance" be said to have a "stark dignity" (line 24)? What
   transformations are described in lines 22 and 23 and 26 and 27?

4. Williams uses sound patterns to emphasize the impression of the dullness and sluggishness of winter. For example, if you say the letter /s/ and then the words "sand" and "and," you will see that the /s/ sound is a long sound that in effect slows the pace of a word. Find several examples of the repetition of the /s/ sound and of the /u/ sound as in "dull."

In Chains

When blackguards and murderers
under cover of their offices
accuse the world of those villainies
which they themselves invent to
torture it—we have no choice   5
but to bend to their designs,
buck them or be trampled while
our thoughts gnaw, snap and bite
within us helplessly—unless
we learn from that to avoid   10
being as they are, how love
will rise out of its ashes if
we water it, tie up the slender
stem and keep the image of its
lively flower chiseled upon our minds.   15

Meaning and Method

1. Who are the "blackguards and murderers" the speaker mentions in line 1? Are they politicians? businessmen? military leaders? some other group? How does the word "offices" (line 2) limit the interpretation of line 1?

2. What does the speaker see as the result of the actions of those in power on us and on the world? How can we avoid being like the "blackguards and murderers"?

3. Why is a flower an appropriate image for love? What words extend the metaphor?

Composition and Discussion

In the poem, Williams laments that the ordinary person is helpless to fight against or to change the "establishment." In a composition or a discussion, give reasons why you agree or disagree with Williams's appraisal of man's condition in modern society. Mention whether or not you think love is the solution to the domestic problems facing the United States today. Will it solve the foreign problems?

Robert Frost

[1874–1963]

When Robert Frost was poet-in-residence at Amherst College in Massachusetts, he defined his job as "being a sort of poetic radiator." This statement was typical of Frost's public remarks and resembled the colloquial speech of the New England farm folk who people his poems. Both his poems and statements contributed to the image that slowly became fixed in the minds of the admiring American public: Frost the New England farmer-poet, weathered like granite but not beaten, a rugged independent spirit rooted in folk traditions.

The image, however, like many of Frost's poems, is somewhat deceptive. Although his father was an eighth-generation New Englander, Frost himself was born in San Francisco and lived there until his father's death in 1885. From San Francisco, his Scottish-born mother, a teacher, moved not to rural New England, but to a mill town—Lawrence, Massachusetts.

Frost attended Dartmouth and Harvard and although he was not graduated from either, he showed himself to be an exceptionally good student of Greek and Roman classical literature. After Frost left Harvard, he worked at several jobs, such as newspaper editor, teacher, and, eventually, farmer. He spent eleven years farming the poor, rocky soil of New Hampshire. Farming, however, was his avocation; he was primarily a struggling poet. As much as he could, he arranged his farm chores to give him time for writing: he even milked his cows at midnight.

It wasn't until he was thirty-nine that he became a successful poet, and then this American writer had to go to England to find appreciation of his talent. The once-neglected poet subsequently lived to be inundated with honors: he won the Pulitzer prize for poetry four times, as well as scores of other literary prizes, and saw himself commonly accepted as a great poet—America's "national poet"—in his own lifetime. This man who had never earned a college degree became a lecturer sought after by colleges, and he won so many honorary degrees that he had the colored hoods signifying these honors sewn into a patchwork quilt.

In order to achieve a colloquial effect, Frost developed a loose blank verse that kept the music inherent in the metered lines while giving the impression of normal speech. "We must write with the ear to the speaking voice," he had said, and he trimmed the excesses from "the language really used by men" without losing the easy flow of speech. In his subjects, too, he took realistic people and situations and strove to present their essential, complex qualities. Art, he once said, "strips life to form," and poetry "ends in a clarification of life."

Stopping by Woods on a Snowy Evening

Whose woods these are I think I know.
His house is in the village though;
He will not see me stopping here
To watch his woods fill up with snow.

My little horse must think it queer   5
To stop without a farmhouse near
Between the woods and frozen lake
The darkest evening of the year.

He gives his harness bells a shake
To ask if there is some mistake.   10
The only other sound's the sweep
Of easy wind and downy flake.

The woods are lovely, dark and deep.
But I have promises to keep,
And miles to go before I sleep,   15
And miles to go before I sleep.

Meaning and Method

1. What is implied by the fact that the "owner" of the woods lives "in the village"? Why might the speaker feel uneasy at being seen by the owner, as he indicates in lines 3 and 4?
2. Why might the horse "think it queer" that the speaker stops? Why does the speaker stop? How does his attitude toward the woods contrast with that of the owner and the horse?

"Stopping by Woods on a Snowy Evening" from Complete Poems of Robert Frost, copyright 1923, 1930, 1939 by Holt, Rinehart and Winston, Inc., copyright 1942, 1951, © 1958 by Robert Frost. Reprinted by permission of the publisher.

3. Why might the horse be interpreted as a symbol of the practical side of life? of a life of action? What are the connotations of *harness bells* (line 9), and of *easy wind and downy flake* (line 12)? What contrast between two ways of life do the contrasting sounds of the bells and the weather symbolize?

4. How do you know that the speaker regrets leaving the scene? Why does he finally go on? How does his action represent a choice of a way of life?

5. Some critics have interpreted the woods as a symbol of death. What words or phrases would support such an interpretation? If the woods are a symbol of death, how might the last stanza be interpreted as a choice between life and death? Is the interpretation of the woods as a symbol of death valid? Is it better to say the woods symbolize a desire to escape from responsibility? Why?

6. The poet and critic John Ciardi has noted that Frost used a very difficult rhyme scheme in this poem. He pointed out that each four-line stanza contains three rhyming sounds and that the unrhymed sound in each stanza is used as a rhymed sound in the next stanza. The result is that one stanza seems tightly connected to the next.

Show how Frost followed this pattern in the first three stanzas. How is the last stanza both similar to and different from the others? Why might Frost have wanted to create an interlocking effect? How might the very difficulty and tightness of the rhyme scheme reflect the poem's theme?

7. What is the effect of the number of long vowels and the repetition of such sounds as /o/ and /s/?

8. What is the effect of the repetition in the last stanza? What would you say is the theme or meaning of the poem?

Mending Wall

Something there is that doesn't love a wall,
That sends the frozen-ground-swell under it,
And spills the upper boulders in the sun;
And makes gaps even two can pass abreast.

The work of hunters is another thing: 5
I have come after them and made repair
Where they have left not one stone on a stone,
But they would have the rabbit out of hiding,
To please the yelping dogs. The gaps I mean,
No one has seen them made or heard them made,   10
But at spring mending-time we find them there.
I let my neighbor know beyond the hill;
And on a day we meet to walk the line
And set the wall between us once again.
We keep the wall between us as we go.   15
To each the boulders that have fallen to each.
And some are loaves and some so nearly balls
We have to use a spell to make them balance:
"Stay where you are until our backs are turned!"
We wear our fingers rough with handling them.   20
Oh, just another kind of outdoor game,
One on a side. It comes to little more:
There where it is we do not need the wall:
He is all pine and I am apple orchard.
My apple trees will never get across   25
And eat the cones under his pines, I tell him.
He only says, "Good fences make good neighbors."
Spring is the mischief in me, and I wonder
If I could put a notion in his head:
"Why do they make good neighbors? Isn't it   30
Where there are cows? But here there are no cows.
Before I built a wall I'd ask to know
What I was walling in or walling out,
And to whom I was like to give offense.
Something there is that doesn't love a wall,   35
That wants it down." I could say "Elves" to him,
But it's not elves exactly, and I'd rather
He said it for himself. I see him there
Bringing a stone grasped firmly by the top
In each hand, like an old-stone savage armed.   40
He moves in darkness as it seems to me,
Not of woods only and the shade of trees.

He will not go behind his father's saying,
And he likes having thought of it so well
He says again, "Good fences make good neighbors."   45

Meaning and Method

1. According to the speaker in lines 1–11, what are two of the ways a stone wall between farms gets broken down? What is the "something" that doesn't love a wall? Is it human? an aspect of nature? What is implied about the "something" in lines 36 and 37?
2. Describe the process by which the wall is rebuilt. (See lines 12–19.) Does the process of rebuilding show that the men are "good neighbors"? What is the speaker's attitude toward his task? In your answer, attempt to define the speaker's tone in lines 17–21, and restate these lines in your own words.
3. According to lines 21–26, when does the speaker feel a wall is unnecessary? Why does he continue to repair the wall despite this feeling?
4. What do you think the neighbor means when he says, "Good fences make good neighbors" (line 27)? What reasons does the speaker give in lines 28–36 for questioning this assertion?
5. Explain lines 38–42. Comment on the connotations of *darkness* (line 41) and of *like an old-stone savage armed* (line 40). How is the speaker's neighbor like an "old-stone savage"?
6. Compare and contrast the characters of the speaker and his neighbor. For example, which one is more traditional? more questioning? more imaginative? Which one shows a sense of humor? a playful spirit? a dour, rigid nature? What is the speaker's attitude toward his neighbor?

Composition

1. If you were a member of the United Nations arguing about whether enforced international boundaries should be kept, would you support the view that "Good fences make good neighbors" or the view that "Something there is that doesn't love a wall"? Or would you argue that both statements are sometimes true?

In a composition explain and defend your point of view. Give real or imagined examples to support your stand.

2. Frost read this poem in Russia shortly after the wall dividing East Berlin from West Berlin had been erected in 1961 by the East Germans. In a composition, explain what his reading of the poem indicated about his attitude toward the Berlin Wall.

Fire and Ice

Some say the world will end in fire,
Some say in ice.
From what I've tasted of desire
I hold with those who favor fire.
But if it had to perish twice,   5
I think I know enough of hate
To say that for destruction ice
Is also great
And would suffice.

Meaning and Method

1. What do the emotions that the speaker has had tell you about his character or personality?
2. The poet uses the word "fire" in line 1 and the word "desire" in line 3. And the word "hate" in line 6 is used in conjunction with the word "ice" in line 7.

   How is desire like fire? How is hate like ice? What are some other connotations of the words *fire* and *ice*?
3. What emotions—those of the intellect or of the flesh—do you associate with destruction by fire? with destruction by ice? Why?

Nothing Gold Can Stay

Nature's first green is gold,
Her hardest hue to hold.
Her early leaf's a flower;
But only so an hour.
Then leaf subsides to leaf.   5
So Eden sank to grief,
So dawn goes down to day.
Nothing gold can stay.

Meaning and Method

1. In lines 1–4, the speaker states two paradoxes: (1) that "Nature's first *green* is *gold*" and that "Her early *leaf's* a *flower*." To what actual event is the speaker referring? What are the connotations of *green* and of *gold?* the connotations of *leaf* and of *flower?*
2. What do an "early leaf," "Eden," and "dawn" have in common? Do they last for a long or a short time?
3. What words or phrases indicate that the speaker regrets that "Nothing gold can stay"? In your answer, explain what the speaker means by lines 5 and 7. In the speaker's view, do leaves, Eden, and dawn fulfill their early promise?
4. What do you think "gold" symbolizes in this poem? What statement is the poet making about life?

The Gift Outright

The land was ours before we were the land's.
She was our land more than a hundred years
Before we were her people. She was ours
In Massachusetts, in Virginia,
But we were England's, still colonials,   5
Possessing what we still were unpossessed by,
Possessed by what we now no more possessed.
Something we were withholding made us weak
Until we found out that it was ourselves
We were withholding from our land of living,   10
And forthwith found salvation in surrender.
Such as we were we gave ourselves outright
(The deed of gift was many deeds of war)
To the land vaguely realizing° westward,
But still unstoried, artless, unenhanced,   15
Such as she was, such as she would become.

14. **realizing:** becoming itself.

Meaning and Method

1. At what time in American history was the land "ours before we were the land's"? What is meant by the paradoxes in lines 6 and 7? Why did the land not possess us? What other land had we once possessed and still longed for?
2. Why were we "weak" (line 8), in the speaker's view? How did we finally "surrender" (line 11) historically? According to the speaker, why was our surrender paradoxically our "salvation"?
3. How was the land different at the time we "gave ourselves outright"? Did we give ourselves only once and at that time only?
4. Is the poet saying total commitment is necessary for full development? necessary some of the time only?

Language: The Use of Synecdoche, a Figure of Speech

In line 4, *Massachusetts* and *Virginia* stand for all thirteen of the original colonies. Here the poet is using a figure of speech called *synecdoche* (sĭ·nek'də·kē), in which a part is used for the whole or the whole is used to represent the part.

Explain the use of synecdoche in the following sentences:

1. Give us this day our daily bread.
2. There are fifty sails in the harbor.
3. The company employed two hundred hands.

Composition and Discussion

1. Many people have different ideas of patriotism. Some feel that in order to be patriotic you cannot criticize a government publicly. Others maintain that criticism of a government is patriotic because it might help prevent a disaster for the country.

What is your attitude toward patriotism and criticism of your government? In a composition, explain your viewpoint with as many examples as possible.

2. Robert Frost recited this poem at the Presidential inauguration of John F. Kennedy on January 20, 1961. In a discussion, compare what Frost meant by commitment with Kennedy's statement, "Ask not what your country can do for you—ask what you can do for your country."

3. In Frost's "An Extemporaneous Talk for Students" (delivered at the twenty-eighth annual commencement of Sarah Lawrence College June 7, 1956), he said, "This poem is my story of the Revolutionary

War. The dream was to occupy the land with character—that's another way to put it—to occupy a new land with character."

In a brief composition, explain what you think Frost meant by "character." Does the United States today retain the character Frost mentioned?

The Death of the Hired Man

Mary sat musing on the lamp flame at the table
Waiting for Warren. When she heard his step
She ran on tiptoe down the darkened passage
To meet him in the doorway with the news
And put him on his guard. "Silas is back."   5
She pushed him outward with her through the door
And shut it after her. "Be kind," she said.
She took the market things from Warren's arms
And set them on the porch, then drew him down
To sit beside her on the wooden steps.   10

"When was I ever anything but kind to him?
But I'll not have the fellow back," he said.
"I told him so last haying, didn't I?
'If he left then,' I said, 'that ended it.'
What good is he? Who else will harbor him   15
At his age for the little he can do?
What help he is there's no depending on.
Off he goes always when I need him most.
He thinks he ought to earn a little pay,
Enough at least to buy tobacco with,   20
So he won't have to beg and be beholden.
'All right,' I say, 'I can't afford to pay
Any fixed wages, though I wish I could.'
'Someone else can.' 'Then someone else will have to.'
I shouldn't mind his bettering himself   25

If that was what it was. You can be certain,
When he begins like that, there's someone at him
Trying to coax him off with pocket money—
In haying time, when any help is scarce.
In winter he comes back to us. I'm done."   30

"Sh! not so loud; he'll hear you," Mary said.

"I want him to; he'll have to soon or late."

"He's worn out. He's asleep beside the stove.
When I came up from Rowe's I found him here,
Huddled against the barn door fast asleep,   35
A miserable sight, and frightening, too—
You needn't smile—I didn't recognize him—
I wasn't looking for him—and he's changed.
Wait till you see."

       "Where did you say he'd been?"

"He didn't say. I dragged him to the house,   40
And gave him tea and tried to make him smoke.
I tried to make him talk about his travels.
Nothing would do: he just kept nodding off."

"What did he say? Did he say anything?"

"But little."

       "Anything? Mary, confess   45
He said he'd come to ditch the meadow° for me."

"Warren!"

       "But did he? I just want to know."

"Of course he did. What would you have him say?
Surely you wouldn't grudge the poor old man

46. **ditch the meadow:** drain the meadow by digging ditches.

Some humble way to save his self-respect.   50
He added, if you really care to know,
He meant to clear the upper pasture, too.
That sounds like something you have heard before?
Warren, I wish you could have heard the way
He jumbled everything. I stopped to look   55
Two or three times—he made me feel so queer—
To see if he was talking in his sleep.
He ran on Harold Wilson—you remember—
The boy you had in haying four years since.
He's finished school, and teaching in his college.   60
Silas declares you'll have to get him back.
He says they two will make a team for work:
Between them they will lay this farm as smooth!
The way he mixed that in with other things.
He thinks young Wilson a likely lad, though daft   65
On education—you know how they fought
All through July under the blazing sun,
Silas up on the cart to build the load,
Harold along beside to pitch it on."

"Yes, I took care to keep well out of earshot."   70

"Well, those days trouble Silas like a dream.
You wouldn't think they would. How some things linger!
Harold's young college boy's assurance piqued him.
After so many years he still keeps finding
Good arguments he sees he might have used.   75
I sympathize. I know just how it feels
To think of the right thing to say too late.
Harold's associated in his mind with Latin.
He asked me what I thought of Harold's saying
He studied Latin like the violin   80
Because he liked it—that an argument!
He said he couldn't make the boy believe
He could find water with a hazel prong°—
Which showed how much good school had ever done him.

83. find . . . prong: a reference to the belief that a forked hazel twig, held by
someone walking back and forth, will bend down when water is underneath it.

He wanted to go over that. But most of all   85
He thinks if he could have another chance
To teach him how to build a load of hay—"

"I know, that's Silas' one accomplishment.
He bundles every forkful in its place,
And tags and numbers it for future reference,   90
So he can find and easily dislodge it
In the unloading. Silas does that well.
He takes it out in bunches like big birds' nests
You never see him standing on the hay
He's trying to lift, straining to lift himself."   95

"He thinks if he could teach him that, he'd be
Some good perhaps to someone in the world.
He hates to see a boy the fool of books.
Poor Silas, so concerned for other folk,
And nothing to look backward to with pride,   100
And nothing to look forward to with hope,
So now and never any different."

Part of a moon was falling down the west,
Dragging the whole sky with it to the hills.
Its light poured softly in her lap. She saw it   105
And spread her apron to it. She put out her hand
Among the harplike morning-glory strings,
Taut with the dew from garden bed to eaves,
As if she played unheard some tenderness
That wrought on him beside her in the night.   110
"Warren," she said, "he has come home to die:
You needn't be afraid he'll leave you this time."

"Home," he mocked gently.

                    "Yes, what else but home?
It all depends on what you mean by home.
Of course he's nothing to us, any more   115
Than was the hound that came a stranger to us
Out of the woods, worn out upon the trail."

"Home is the place where, when you have to go there,
They have to take you in."

          "I should have called it
Something you somehow haven't to deserve."   120

Warren leaned out and took a step or two,
Picked up a little stick, and brought it back
And broke it in his hand and tossed it by.
"Silas has better claim on us you think
Than on his brother? Thirteen little miles   125
As the road winds would bring him to his door.
Silas has walked that far no doubt today.
Why didn't he go there? His brother's rich,
A somebody—director in the bank."

"He never told us that."   130

          "We know it though."

"I think his brother ought to help, of course.
I'll see to that if there is need. He ought of right
To take him in, and might be willing to—
He may be better than appearances.
But have some pity on Silas. Do you think   135
If he'd had any pride in claiming kin
Or anything he looked for from his brother,
He'd keep so still about him all this time?"

"I wonder what's between them."

          "I can tell you.
Silas is what he is—we wouldn't mind him—   140
But just the kind that kinsfolk can't abide.
He never did a thing so very bad.
He don't know why he isn't quite as good
As anybody. Worthless though he is,
He won't be made ashamed to please his brother."   145

"*I* can't think Si ever hurt anyone."

"No, but he hurt my heart the way he lay
And rolled his old head on that sharp-edged chair back.
He wouldn't let me put him on the lounge.
You must go in and see what you can do.   150
I made the bed up for him there tonight.
You'll be surprised at him—how much he's broken.
His working days are done; I'm sure of it."

"I'd not be in a hurry to say that."

"I haven't been. Go, look, see for yourself.   155
But, Warren, please remember how it is:
He's come to help you ditch the meadow.
He has a plan. You mustn't laugh at him.
He may not speak of it, and then he may.
I'll sit and see if that small sailing cloud   160
Will hit or miss the moon."

                    It hit the moon.
Then there were three there, making a dim row,
The moon, the little silver cloud, and she.

Warren returned—too soon, it seemed to her,
Slipped to her side, caught up her hand and waited.   165

"Warren?" she questioned.

                    "Dead," was all he answered.

Meaning

1. Relate in your own words the story told in the poem. What is the
   setting? time of day? Who tells the story? Who are the characters?
   What is their conflict? How is it resolved?
2. What incidents or statements indicate that Silas is proud? shiftless
   or unreliable? Why did the conversation with Harold disturb him?
   What do lines 96–102 reveal about Silas' character?

3. What aspects of the characters of Mary and Warren are revealed in their reactions to Silas? Why does Warren object to keeping Silas? How and why does he change his attitude?
4. What do the definitions of "home" in lines 118–19 and 119–20 tell you about Warren and Mary, respectively? Is their relationship close and loving? bitterly argumentative? something else? Explain how one or the other of these definitions of "home" does or does not fulfill the meaning of "home" as you understand the word.
5. Is the poet sympathetic or unsympathetic to each of the characters? to Silas' plight?

Method

1. The meter of this poem is blank verse, or unrhymed iambic pentameter (see Glossary). It is a meter often used for drama, notably in Shakespeare's plays. Has Frost used this meter in a strict or rigid way—that is, does each line have exactly ten syllables in an unstressed-stressed pattern? Or has he loosened or varied the blank verse in order to create a conversational effect? Give examples from the poem to support your points. Do any lines seem awkward because Frost twisted normal speech to fit the meter? Explain.
2. The dialogue seems like a whispered conversation. What lines particularly suggest whispering? Why would whispering be appropriate, considering the situation?

Composition

In a composition, compare and contrast the character of Silas with that of Robinson's Bewick Finzer. (See page 10.)

Carl Sandburg
[1878–1967]

To Carl Sandburg, poetry was "the synthesis of hyacinths and biscuits," an art form in which sensitivity to beauty was combined with an appreciation of the commonplace. He was impatient with those who suggested that poetry was exclusive—for example, those who believed that only certain subjects were poetic or that only certain responses to a poem were valid. As he once wrote, "A poet explains what for him is poetry by what he presents to us in his poems. . . . We go to it [the poet's work], read it, look at it, perhaps go back to it many a time, and it is for each of us what we make of it."

Sandburg was born in Galesburg, Illinois, the son of Swedish immigrants. He had to leave school after the eighth grade and worked at a variety of jobs: delivering milk, bricklaying, dishwashing, and sign painting. After the Spanish-American War broke out in 1898, he enlisted in the Army, where he served both as a soldier and as a correspondent for the Galesburg *Evening Mail*.

His war experience made him decide to continue his education, and in 1899 he entered Lombard College in his home town. However, the semester before he was to get his degree, he left Lombard (which later granted him an honorary degree, as did many other colleges). He wanted to be a newspaper reporter, and for more than three decades he worked at various journalistic occupations—mostly in Chicago, where he settled in 1913 and where the poems that first brought him fame were published.

In the 1920's, when Sandburg began to give public readings of his poems, he often included in his programs American folk ballads that he would sing while accompanying himself on the guitar. His collection of folk ballads, *The American Songbag*, which was first published in 1927, went far toward popularizing the ballads of pioneer and frontier America.

Sandburg also showed his interest in the American past by writing a massive biography of Abraham Lincoln, in which he tried to show Lincoln as a boy and man who was sensitive to nature, to people, and to the needs and demands of his country. This biography, part of which won a Pulitzer prize, was both historically accurate and poetically evocative and is considered a classic of its kind.

Although Sandburg was an "all-around writer" (he wrote not only journalistic and literary prose, but also children's stories), he was most famous for his poetry. His poems reflect his personality—unaffected, rugged, full of common sense and warm humor. Their main subject was America, and the free verse he used indicated the vitality and variety of a free-moving, growing country.

Attempting to show what America was like, he revealed its rawness, ugliness, and brutality, as well as the beauty, idealism, and vigor that existed side by side with its seamier qualities. His outlook toward America and its people was, in general, sympathetic rather than critical. *The People, Yes* he proclaimed in the title of a book-length poem about his countrymen, and most of his poems exult rather than exhort.

Chicago

Hog Butcher for the World,
Toolmaker, Stacker of Wheat,
Player with Railroads and the Nation's Freight Handler;
Stormy, husky, brawling,
City of the Big Shoulders: 5

They tell me you are wicked and I believe them, for I have
    seen your painted women under the gas lamps luring the
    farm boys.
And they tell me you are crooked and I answer: Yes, it is true
    I have seen the gunman kill and go free to kill again.
And they tell me you are brutal and my reply is: On the faces
    of women and children I have seen the marks of wanton
    hunger.
And having answered so I turn once more to those who sneer
    at this my city, and I give them back the sneer and say to
    them:

Come and show me another city with lifted head singing so
    proud to be alive and coarse and strong and cunning.   10
Flinging magnetic curses amid the toil of piling job on job,
    here is a tall bold slugger set vivid against the little soft cities;
Fierce as a dog with tongue lapping for action, cunning as a
    savage pitted against the wilderness,
        Bareheaded,
        Shoveling,
        Wrecking,   15
        Planning,
        Building, breaking, rebuilding,
Under the smoke, dust all over his mouth, laughing with white
    teeth,
Under the terrible burden of destiny laughing as a young man
    laughs,
Laughing even as an ignorant fighter laughs who has never lost
    a battle,   20
Bragging and laughing that under his wrist is the pulse, and
    under his ribs the heart of the people,
            Laughing!
Laughing the stormy, husky, brawling laughter of Youth, half-
    naked, sweating, proud to be Hog Butcher, Toolmaker,
    Stacker of Wheat, Player with Railroads and Freight Han-
    dler to the Nation.

Meaning and Method

1. According to the speaker, why do people sneer at Chicago? Does
he consider their criticisms valid or justified? Why does he "give
them back the sneer" (line 9)? How does he feel about Chicago?
2. What are Chicago's virtues? Are they related to its vices, or do
they come from a very different aspect of the city?
3. Chicago is personified in the poem. As what is it personified? What
words or phrases carry through this personification? What does this
personification reveal about the speaker's impression of Chicago?
its mood? its destiny? Why does Chicago laugh?
4. What is the effect of the capitalized nouns and adjectives at the
beginning and end of the poem? For example, do they make you
think of a newspaper headline? a person shouting? something else?
    Although the first and last stanzas contain many repeated phrases,
is the tone of these stanzas the same?

5. The poet uses both exceptionally short (one-word) and exceptionally long lines. The short lines are used primarily for emphasis. What characteristics are the long lines intended to reflect or describe?

Composition

1. Write a free-verse poem or prose composition in which you attempt to describe your city or town. Try to convey an impression of what the city or town is like, and your attitude toward it, as Sandburg has done. Try to use personification and other figures of speech.

2. In a free-verse poem or prose composition, describe your impression of a city you have read about but have never seen, or a city you have visited for a short time only, or an ideal city, either on earth or on some other planet.

Grass

Pile the bodies high at Austerlitz and Waterloo.°
Shovel them under and let me work—
    I am the grass; I cover all.

And pile them high at Gettysburg
And pile them high at Ypres and Verdun.°   5
Shovel them under and let me work.
Two years, ten years, and passengers ask the conductor:
    What place is this?
    Where are we now?

    I am the grass.   10
    Let me work.

1. **Austerlitz and Waterloo:** major battlefields in the Napoleonic Wars.
5. **Ypres** (ē'pr') **and Verdun** (vər·dun'): major battlefields in the first World War.

Meaning and Method

1. How does the speaker show that war always leads to the same results? What are these results?

2. What is the tone of the poem? ironic? bitter? In your answer, comment on the attitudes of the grass and the passengers.
3. If the word "time" were substituted for "grass" whenever the latter is used, how would this affect the poem?

Composition

People often present their ideas by personifying an object. In a paragraph, personify a clock in your school, or at a football game, or at a railroad station. Or personify a tree in spring or autumn, or a sidewalk outside a hospital, a school, or the United Nations.

Cool Tombs

When Abraham Lincoln was shoveled into the tombs, he forgot the cooperheads° and the assassin . . . in the dust, in the cool tombs.

And Ulysses Grant lost all thought of con men and Wall Street, cash and collateral° turned ashes . . . in the dust, in the cool tombs.

Pocahontas' body, lovely as a poplar, sweet as a red haw in November or a pawpaw° in May, did she wonder? does she remember? . . . in the dust, in the cool tombs?

Take any streetful of people buying clothes and groceries, cheering a hero or throwing confetti and blowing tin horns . . . tell me if the lovers are losers . . . tell me if any get more than the lovers . . . in the dust . . . in the cool tombs.

1. **copperheads:** *here,* Northerners who sympathized with the Confederacy during the Civil War. A copperhead is a variety of venomous snake. 2. **collateral:** security for a loan. 3. **red haw . . . pawpaw:** wild fruits.

Meaning and Method

1. Why were the tombs a comfort to Lincoln? to Grant? Why could they not comfort Pocahontas? Why do you think the speaker repeated, "in the dust, in the cool tombs" at the end of every part?

"Cool Tombs" from *Cornhuskers* by Carl Sandburg, copyright 1918 by Holt, Rinehart and Winston, Inc., copyright 1946 by Carl Sandburg. Reprinted by permission of Holt, Rinehart and Winston, Inc.

2. Which of the following are closest to being losers: those who have held power in life? those who were beautiful? anyone who has loved and had love returned? Why do you think the speaker introduces "any streetful of people"—an anonymous mass—after concentrating on these famous historical characters? What is the theme of the poem?

3. Although there are only two perfect rhymes in this poem, Sandburg creates a musical effect by the use of *assonance*, the repetition of the same vowel sound usually between different consonants. "Cool" and "tomb," for example, both contain the same /oo/ sound. What vowel sound do "assassin," "Grant," "cash," and "collateral" have in common? Which words in the last line rhyme? Which words contain the same vowel sound as the rhyming words?

4. In stanza 3, the speaker uses figurative language to describe Pocahontas, whereas the stanzas about Lincoln and Grant do not contain figurative language. What does this suggest about the speaker's attitude toward Pocahontas? toward Lincoln and Grant?

Composition

Everyone has his own opinion about who the winners in life are. Your opinion depends on your values. Write a composition which begins "I think the winners in life are. . . ." Or choose one particular person, famous or not, who you feel is a winner. In both cases, explain the reasons for your attitudes.

Nocturne in a Deserted Brickyard

   Stuff of the moon
Runs on the lapping sand
Out to the longest shadows.
Under the curving willows,
And round the creep of the wave line,   5
Fluxions° of yellow and dusk on the waters
Make a wide dreaming pansy of an old pond in the night.

6. Fluxions: flowings, unceasing changes, motions.

Meaning and Method

1. What notion of beauty is Sandburg conveying by having a deserted brickyard as the setting? by the type of images he uses in his description?
2. The word "nocturne" has two meanings. It may refer to a night scene (the word is derived from the Latin *nocturnus,* which means "nightly"). Or it may refer to a musical composition that is romantic and often pensive in tone. Does Sandburg use the word in one or both of its meanings? Explain.
3. Why do you think Sandburg used *stuff* rather than *beams?* What words or phrases give an impression of the flowing quality of the moonlight? the movement of the water? Does the image of the "wide dreaming pansy" (line 7) seem a sudden flash of the imagination, or has it been prepared for previously?
4. What is the theme of the poem?

Composition

How close is this poem to Imagist poetry? Compare and contrast this poem with H. D.'s "Pear Tree" (page 39) or Ezra Pound's "In a Station of the Metro" (page 29).

The Harbor

Passing through huddled and ugly walls
By doorways where women
Looked from their hunger-deep eyes,
Haunted with shadows of hunger-hands,
Out from the huddled and ugly walls,   5
I came sudden, at the city's edge,
On a blue burst of lake,
Long lake waves breaking under the sun
On a spray-flung curve of shore;
And a fluttering storm of gulls,   10
Masses of great gray wings
And flying white bellies
Veering and wheeling free in the open.

Meaning and Method

1. What contrasting scenes are presented in the poem? What line provides a transition from one scene to the next? What words or phrases particularly convey the contrast? How does the mood of the poem change from one scene to the other?
2. The poet indicates the contrast both by images and the sounds of words. For example, in the first five lines, the heavy and dull /u/ vowel sound (as in "huddled") predominates. What words contain this sound? What is the predominant vowel sound in the last eight lines, and how does this change reflect the change of scene and mood? What are the predominant consonant sounds in the first five lines? How do they differ from those in the last eight lines?
3. What do you think the gulls symbolize? What do you think their presence is meant to show about city life? In your answer, comment on the presence of both the "huddled and ugly walls" and the gulls and the lake within the same city.

A Father Sees a Son Nearing Manhood

from THE PEOPLE, YES

A father sees a son nearing manhood.
What shall he tell that son?
"Life is hard; be steel; be a rock."
And this might stand him for the storms
and serve him for humdrum and monotony   5
and guide him amid sudden betrayals
and tighten him for slack moments.
"Life is a soft loam;° be gentle; go easy."
And this too might serve him.
Brutes have been gentled where lashes failed.   10
The growth of a frail flower in a path up
has sometimes shattered and split a rock.

8. loam: a type of soil.

A tough will counts. So does desire.
So does a rich soft wanting.
Without rich wanting nothing arrives.   15
Tell him too much money has killed men
and left them dead years before burial:
the quest of lucre beyond a few easy needs
has twisted good enough men
sometimes into dry thwarted worms.   20
Tell him time as a stuff can be wasted.
Tell him to be a fool every so often
and to have no shame over having been a fool
yet learning something out of every folly
hoping to repeat none of the cheap follies   25
thus arriving at intimate understanding
of a world numbering many fools.
Tell him to be alone often and get at himself
and above all tell himself no lies about himself
whatever the white lies and protective fronts   30
he may use amongst other people.
Tell him solitude is creative if he is strong
and the final decisions are made in silent rooms.
Tell him to be different from other people
if it comes natural and easy being different.   35
Let him have lazy days seeking his deeper motives.
Let him seek deep for where he is a born natural.
        Then he may understand Shakespeare
        and the Wright brothers, Pasteur, Pavlov,°
        Michael Faraday° and free imaginations   40
bringing changes into a world resenting change.
        He will be lonely enough
        to have time for the work
        he knows as his own.

39. Pavlov: Russian scientist (1849–1936) who showed that reflexes could be
conditioned. In his most famous experiment, he trained a dog to expect food
whenever a bell rang. He then showed that the ringing of the bell caused the
dog to salivate even when there was no food because the dog associated the bell
with food. **40. Michael Faraday:** British chemist and physicist (1791–1867)
who discovered the properties of electromagnetism.

Meaning and Method

1. How does the advice given in line 3 contradict that of line 8? Are the two contrasting statements truly contradictory or are both true in different ways?
2. What do you think a "rich soft wanting" (line 14) is? Does it have anything to do with money? Why or why not? What does the speaker mean by the paradox in lines 16 and 17?
3. Why should a man "be a fool every so often" (line 22)? Why does a man need solitude, in the speaker's opinion? Why will solitude help him to understand the men mentioned in lines 38–40? Does the speaker feel men should conform? be individualistic?
4. An *aphorism* (af'ə·riz'əm) is a brief statement of a principle that the speaker believes to be true, as, for example, a proverb. Choose several aphorisms from this poem and explain them in your own words.

Composition and Discussion

1. In a short composition, state some advice given by your parents, older brothers and sisters, or other adults, and explain why you agree or disagree with it.
2. Name some aphorisms you have heard and explain why you agree or disagree with them. Try wording some aphorisms of your own to explain your opinion and observations of contemporary living.

Vachel Lindsay
[1879–1931]

To Nicholas Vachel Lindsay, poetry was "the higher vaude-ville" because poems were meant to be recited or sung on stage for the enjoyment and enlightenment of the people. Lindsay's aim was to express the spirit of the American people, and he wanted to feel the people's response. His poems—many of which were written with stage directions calling for specific musical accompaniment—were actually performed dramatically by the poet in small towns and in cities across the United States.

In his late teens, Lindsay, who was born in Springfield, Illinois, studied to be a minister of the Disciples of Christ. He left after three years because he felt he had no religious vocation. He then studied art in Chicago and in New York but was unable to support himself with his work. Finally, he turned to poetry and spent four years—from 1908 through 1912—on walking tours, gathering bits and pieces of Americana for his writing. Appropriately enough, two of his books are entitled *Rhymes to Be Traded for Bread* (1912) and *A Handy Guide for Beggars* (1916).

In 1913 his poem "General William Booth Enters into Heaven" was published in the influential magazine *Poetry*, and Lindsay's originality and talent began to be recognized by the American literary world. He gave poetry recitals, and some of his poems were published. However, after five successful years Lindsay's rich poetic vein was more or less played out. Although he continued to write until 1929, the quality of his poems and the interest taken by people in them steadily declined. In 1931, Lindsay, discouraged by his failure, committed suicide.

Lindsay is best remembered for a small number of poems—poems in which he is an eloquent spokesman for the suffering "common man," poems in which he shows his deep devotion to the American dream of equality and his love for the American countryside. Most of these poems are emotional, but not senti-mental; their insights and images are as haunting and valid today as they were when Lindsay wrote them.

Abraham Lincoln Walks at Midnight

(*In Springfield, Illinois*)

It is portentous, and a thing of state
That here at midnight, in our little town
A mourning figure walks, and will not rest,
Near the old courthouse pacing up and down,

Or by his homestead, or in shadowed yards   5
He lingers where his children used to play,
Or through the market, on the well-worn stones
He stalks until the dawn-stars burn away.

A bronzed, lank man! His suit of ancient black,
A famous high top hat and plain worn shawl   10
Make him the quaint great figure that men love,
The prairie lawyer, master of us all.

He cannot sleep upon his hillside now.
He is among us—as in times before!
And we who toss and lie awake for long   15
Breathe deep, and start, to see him pass the door.

His head is bowed. He thinks on men and kings.
Yea, when the sick world cries, how can he sleep?
Too many peasants fight, they know not why,
Too many homesteads in black terror weep.   20

The sins of all the warlords burn his heart.
He sees the dreadnoughts° scouring every main.
He carries on his shawl-wrapped shoulders now
The bitterness, the folly, and the pain.

He cannot rest until a spirit-dawn   25
Shall come—the shining hope of Europe free:

22. **dreadnoughts** (dred′nôts′): heavily armed battleships used by the British in the first World War.

The league of sober folk, the workers' earth,
Bringing long peace to cornland, alp, and sea.

It breaks his heart that kings must murder still,
That all his hours of travail here for men   30
Seem yet in vain. And who will bring white peace
That he may sleep upon his hill again?

Meaning and Method

1. This poem was written in 1914, at the start of the first World War. Why did this war disturb Lincoln? In what ways is it like many previous wars? Support your answers with quotations from the text.
2. The ghost of Lincoln in this poem is a figure of great dignity. What words or phrases describing (a) his appearance, (b) his actions, and (c) his emotions contribute to this impression of dignity?
3. Lincoln has long been thought of as a spokesman for the "common people." Where in this poem does Lindsay indicate Lincoln's sympathy for "ordinary" men? his lack of sympathy for men in power?
4. The poet does not directly mention war until the fifth stanza. What words or phrases in the first four stanzas indicate that some great calamity has occurred? What words or phrases create a gloomy atmosphere? How does the image "white peace" (line 31) contrast with the dominant atmosphere of the poem?
5. How does the poet use (a) description, (b) verbs of action, and (c) other characters to make the ghost of Lincoln seem real?

Language: The Formation of Words

New words are frequently formed to describe innovations, ideas and inventions in transporation, communication, housing, science, and the social sciences. Sometimes these new words are formed in some way from existing words, thereby giving a clue to their meanings. For example, "dreadnought" is a combination of two words, "dread" and "nought." *Dread* means "fear"; *nought* means "nothing." A dreadnought, therefore, is an object that fears nothing—in this case, it is a large and heavily armed battleship.

Other relatively new words whose parts indicate their meanings are the following:

1. supersonic   3. genetics
2. automobile   4. microscope

The "clues" to the meanings of the preceding words, unlike "dreadnought," are found in the Greek or Latin words from which they are derived. Look up these words in a dictionary and be prepared to explain in class how close the meanings of these words are to their roots.

The Flower-Fed Buffaloes

The flower-fed buffaloes of the spring
In the days of long ago,
Ranged where the locomotives sing
And the prairie flowers lie low;
The tossing, blooming, perfumed grass   5
Is swept away by wheat,
Wheels and wheels and wheels spin by
In the spring that still is sweet.
But the flower-fed buffaloes of the spring
Left us long ago.   10
They gore no more, they bellow no more,
They trundle around the hills no more:
With the Blackfeet, lying low,
With the Pawnees, lying low.

Meaning and Method

1. What are the connotations of the phrase *flower-fed buffaloes of the spring?* How is the impression that is created by the phrase like or unlike your previous impressions of buffalo?
2. In lines 3 and 4 and 5 and 6, the speaker points out two specific changes that have occurred since the days when buffaloes roamed the prairies. What are these changes? What is his attitude toward them?
3. In what way are the buffaloes like the Pawnees and the Blackfeet? Do you think the poet regrets the fate of all three?
4. In lines 7 and 8, the poet creates the effect of the movement of the train by means of alliteration and repetition. Point out the words and sounds that are used to achieve this effect.
5. What is the tone of the poem? Is it happy? nostalgic? sentimental? something else?

"The Flower-Fed Buffaloes" from *Going to the Stars* by Vachel Lindsay. Reprinted by permission of Appleton-Century-Crofts, a division of Meredith Press.

Composition

In this poem, Lindsay uses the passing out of existence of a wild animal to indicate a far broader change. Are there any specific changes in your home town or city which also indicate broader changes? Write a short composition describing these changes, and telling what you think they indicate about the future.

The Leaden-eyed

Let not young souls be smothered out before
They do quaint deeds and fully flaunt their pride.
It is the world's one crime its babes grow dull,
Its poor are oxlike, limp, and leaden-eyed.

Not that they starve, but starve so dreamlessly;   5
Not that they sow, but that they seldom reap;
Not that they serve, but have no gods to serve;
Not that they die, but that they die like sheep.

Meaning and Method

1. What are the connotations of *leaden-eyed?* Which words in the first stanza contribute to the image of the term "leaden-eyed"? In the speaker's opinion, what causes people to become leaden-eyed?
2. Explain in your own words the speaker's objections in lines 5–8 to the lives of the "leaden-eyed." Is he primarily against physical wrongs? spiritual wrongs?
3. What techniques are used in lines 5–8 to emphasize the theme of the inescapable dullness of the lives of the "leaden-eyed"? Does alliteration also contribute to this effect? Why or why not? Give specific words or phrases to support your answers.

Composition and Discussion

1. Write your own prose statement of the central idea of the poem.
2. Be prepared to take part in a panel discussion on the subject, "Will the youth of today gain success and happiness by following the patterns accepted by society?"

The Santa-Fe Trail

(*A Humoresque*)

(I asked the old Negro: "What is that bird that sings so well?" He answered: "That is the Rachel-Jane." "Hasn't it another name—lark, or thrush, or the like?" "No. Jus' Rachel-Jane.")

I. In Which a Racing Auto Comes from the East

This is the order of the music of the morning:
First, from the far East comes but a crooning.
The crooning turns to a sunrise singing.
Hark to the *calm*-horn, *balm*-horn, *psalm*-horn.
Hark to the *faint*-horn, *quaint*-horn,
    saint-horn. . . .   5

To be sung delicately, to an improvised tune.

Hark to the *pace*-horn, *chase*-horn, *race*-horn.
And the holy veil of the dawn has gone.
Swiftly the brazen car comes on.
It burns in the East as the sunrise burns.
I see great flashes where the far trail turns.   10
Its eyes are lamps like the eyes of dragons.
It drinks gasoline from big red flagons.
Butting through the delicate mists of the
    morning,
It comes like lightning, goes past roaring.
It will hail all the windmills, taunting,
    ringing,   15
Dodge the cyclones,
Count the milestones,
On through the ranges of the prairie-dog
    tills—
Scooting past the cattle on the thousand
    hills. . . .

To be sung or read with great speed.

Ho for the *tear*-horn, *scare*-horn, *dare*-horn,   20
Ho for the *gay*-horn, *bark*-horn, *bay*-horn.
Ho for Kansas, land that restores us
When houses choke us, and great books
      bore us!
Sunrise Kansas, harvesters' Kansas,
A million men have found you before us.   25
A million men have found you before us.

To be read or
sung in a rolling
bass, with some
deliberation.

II. In Which Many Autos Pass Westward

I want live things in their pride to remain.
I will not kill one grasshopper vain
Though he eats a hole in my shirt like a door.
I let him out, give him one chance more.   30
Perhaps, while he gnaws my hat in his whim,
Grasshopper lyrics occur to him.

In an even,
deliberate,
narrative
manner.

I am a tramp by the long trail's border,
Given to squalor, rags, and disorder.
I nap and amble and yawn and look,   35
Write fool-thoughts in my grubby book,
Recite to the children, explore at my ease,
Work when I work, beg when I please,
Give crank-drawings that make folks stare
To the half-grown boys in the sunset glare,   40
And get me a place to sleep in the hay
At the end of a live-and-let-live day.

I find in the stubble of the new-cut weeds
A whisper and a feasting, all one needs:
The whisper of the strawberries, white
      and red,   45
Here where the new-cut weeds lie dead.

But I would not walk all alone till I die
Without some life-drunk horns going by.
Up round this apple-earth they come
Blasting the whispers of the morning dumb: 50

Cars in a plain realistic row.
And fair dreams fade
When the raw horns blow.

On each snapping pennant
A big black name: 55
The careering° city
Whence each car came.
They tour from Memphis, Atlanta,
    Savannah,
Tallahassee and Texarkana.   *Like a train-*
They tour from St. Louis, Columbus,   *caller in a*
    Manistee,   60 *Union Depot.*
They tour from Peoria, Davenport,
    Kankakee.
Cars from Concord, Niagara, Boston,
Cars from Topeka, Emporia, and Austin.
Cars from Chicago, Hannibal, Cairo.
Cars from Alton, Oswego, Toledo.   65
Cars from Buffalo, Kokomo, Delphi,
Cars from Lodi, Carmi, Loami.
Ho for Kansas, land that restores us
When houses choke us, and great books
    bore us!
While I watch the highroad   70
And look at the sky,
While I watch the clouds in amazing
    grandeur
Roll their legions without rain
Over the blistering Kansas plain—
While I sit by the milestone   75
And watch the sky,
The United States
Goes by.

Listen to the iron-horns, ripping, racking.   *To be given very*
Listen to the quack-horns, slack and clacking. 80 *harshly, with a*
Way down the road, trilling like a toad,   *snapping*
                                              explosiveness.

56. careering: moving swiftly, with a headlong motion.

Here comes the *dice*-horn, here comes the
    vice-horn,
Here comes the *snarl*-horn, *brawl*-horn,
    lewd-horn,
Followed by the *prude*-horn, bleak and
    squeaking:
(Some of them from Kansas, some of them
    from Kansas.)   85
Here comes the *hod*-horn, *plod*-horn,
    sod-horn,
Nevermore-to-*roam*-horn, *loam*-horn,
    home-horn.
(Some of them from Kansas, some of them
    from Kansas.)

> Far away the Rachel-Jane,
> Not defeated by the horns,   90
> Sings amid a hedge of thorns:
> "Love and life,
> Eternal youth—
> Sweet, sweet, sweet, sweet,
> Dew and glory,   95
> Love and truth,
> Sweet, sweet, sweet, sweet."

To be read or sung, well-nigh in a whisper.

WHILE SMOKE-BLACK FREIGHTS ON THE
    DOUBLE-TRACKED RAILROAD,
DRIVEN AS THOUGH BY THE FOUL FIEND'S
    OX-GOAD,
SCREAMING TO THE WEST COAST, SCREAMING
    TO THE EAST,   100
CARRY OFF A HARVEST, BRING BACK A FEAST,
AND HARVESTING MACHINERY AND HARNESS
    FOR THE BEAST,
THE HAND-CARS WHIZ, AND RATTLE ON THE
    RAILS,
THE SUNLIGHT FLASHES ON THE TIN
    DINNER-PAILS.

Louder and louder, faster and faster.

And then, in an instant, ye modern men,   105
Behold the procession once again,
The United States goes by!

In a rolling bass, with increasing deliberation.

Listen to the iron-horns, ripping, racking,
Listen to the *wise*-horn, desperate-to-*advise*
    horn,
Listen to the *fast*-horn, *kill*-horn,
    blast-horn. . . .   110
        Far away the Rachel-Jane
        Not defeated by the horns
        Sings amid a hedge of thorns:
        "Love and life,
        Eternal youth,   115
        Sweet, sweet, sweet, sweet,
        Dew and glory,
        Love and truth.
        Sweet, sweet, sweet, sweet."
The mufflers open on a score of cars   120
With wonderful thunder,
Crack, crack, crack,
Crack-crack, crack-crack,
Crack, crack, crack,
Listen to the gold-horn . . .   125
Old-horn . . .
Cold-horn . . .
And all of the tunes, till the night comes
    down
On haystack, and anthill, and wind-bitten
    town.
Then far in the west, as in the beginning,   130
Dim in the distance, sweet in retreating,
Hark to the faint-horn, quaint-horn,
    saint-horn,
Hark to the calm-horn, balm-horn,
    psalm-horn. . . .

They are hunting the goals that they
    understand:
San Francisco and the brown sea-sand.   135
My goal is the mystery the beggars win.
I am caught in the web the night winds spin.
The edge of the wheat-ridge speaks to me.

With a snapping explosiveness.

To be sung or read well-nigh in a whisper.

To be brawled in the beginning with a snapping explosiveness, ending in a languorous chant.

To be sung to exactly the same whispered tune as the first five lines.

This section beginning sonorously, ending in a languorous whisper.

I talk with the leaves of the mulberry tree.
And now I hear, as I sit all alone   140
In the dusk, by another big Santa-Fe stone,
The souls of the tall corn gathering round
And the gay little souls of the grass in
    the ground.
Listen to the tale the cottonwood tells.
Listen to the windmills, singing o'er the
    wells.   145
Listen to the whistling flutes without price
Of myriad prophets out of paradise.
Hearken to the wonder
That the night-air carries. . . .
Listen . . . to . . . the . . . whisper . . .   150
Of . . . the . . . prairie . . . fairies
    Singing o'er the fairy plain:
    "Sweet, sweet, sweet, sweet.
    Love and glory,
    Stars and rain,   155
    Sweet, sweet, sweet, sweet. . . ."

To the same whispered tune as the Rachel-Jane song—but very slowly.

Meaning and Method

1. What is the mood established in the opening lines? How does the entry of a car break "the holy veil of dawn" (line 7)? Which of the sounds in lines 4–6 refer to the sounds of a car horn, and how do these sounds contrast with other sounds in the same lines?

2. Which words or phrases in the description in lines 9–19 indicate that, in the speaker's view, the car is a sort of monster? Which words or phrases indicate the speed and noise of the car?

3. What does the fact that the speaker will not kill "one grasshopper vain" (line 28) show about his attitude toward life? In your answer, comment on lines 27–32. What is humorous about line 32? How does the speaker's confession that he is a "tramp" (line 33) indicate the contrast between his attitude toward life and that of the drivers of cars? Why, in your opinion, does he nevertheless want to hear their "life-drunk horns going by" (line 48)?

4. The Santa Fe Trail was a trade route, from 1821 to 1880, between Independence, Missouri, and Santa Fe, New Mexico. What is the speaker's attitude toward "progress" with cars and railroads (see lines 82–84, 86 and 87, and 98–104)? How do these lines contrast

with the song of the Rachel-Jane (lines 89–97)? The song of the Rachel-Jane (lines 89–97) and the horn sounds of lines 82–84 and 86 and 87 symbolize two different ways of life and sets of values. What are these? For which set of values does the speaker have more sympathy?

5. In lines 134–43, the speaker explicitly contrasts his attitude toward life with that of the car drivers. Which attitude is more materialistic? How do you know? In what other ways are their attitudes different?

6. Lindsay called his poem "A Humoresque"—that is, a playful, lively musical piece. In what ways is it playful or humorous? In what ways is it musical? In your answer, comment on the poet's use of onomatopoeia, alliteration, internal rhyme, and the repetition of sounds.

Language: Oral Interpretation of Poetry

Read a passage from the poem aloud, following the stage directions. Then read another, or perhaps the same one, ignoring the stage directions. Which sounds better? Why? How much variety of sound is there in the poem? In what way is this unlike other poems you have read?

Composition

This poem is about a certain type of development in America, but it implies more than it acutally states. Write a composition about an aspect of progress in the United States. Express your opinion by implication rather than directly.

Wallace Stevens
[1879–1955]

For the last thirty-nine years of his life, Wallace Stevens—a poet so subtle, so aware of the delicate nuances of words and sounds that he was called a "poet's poet"—worked in executive positions for an insurance company in Hartford, Connecticut. But Stevens did not consider his success at two seemingly unlike vocations strange. "Money is a kind of poetry," he once wrote, and the careful attention to details that made him a successful businessman contributed greatly to making him a successful poet.

In a way, Stevens's life was an acting out of one of his favorite themes: there is a "resemblance between things" in nature, and this resemblance gives a basic rhythm and ordered harmony to a world that seems disjointed. The job of the poet, Stevens felt, was to bind "parts of reality" together, to show the unifying relationships that exist. One might say that Stevens in his life illustrated the basic "resemblance" that bound two such superficially different "parts of reality" as an insurance executive and a poet.

Stevens was also an art collector, and in his poetry he often seemed to be an impressionistic painter. In fact, the title of one of his collections of poetry, *The Man with the Blue Guitar* (1937), was from a painting by Picasso. Like the nineteenth-century impressionistic painters, he evoked scenes and moods, using words as they used daubs of color to achieve a sense of luminosity and darkness, of shades of color, of the way that the slightest shift of light can profoundly change a scene.

Stevens was born in Reading, Pennsylvania, and attended Harvard University and the New York Law School. He received his law degree in 1903 and practiced law in New York for more than a decade before moving to Hartford. His first collection of poems, *Harmonium*, was published in 1923. The book was not a popular success, and he waited for twelve years before collecting his second volume, *Ideas and Order*.

During the rest of his life, Stevens received many honors for poetry, including a Pulitzer prize in 1955 for his *Collected Poems*. Despite their apparently simple surfaces, his poems are difficult. Those who have learned to overcome the obstacles of Stevens's poems often experience a strange excitement—caused in part by what the critic M. L. Rosenthal called Stevens's "joyous verbal geometrics," and in part by the curious intensity of his detached approach to life.

Study of Two Pears

I

Opusculum paedagogum.°
The pears are not viols,
Nudes or bottles.
They resemble nothing else.

II

They are yellow forms   5
Composed of curves
Bulging toward the base.
They are touched red.

III

They are not flat surfaces
Having curved outlines.   10
They are round
Tapering toward the top.

IV

In the way they are modeled
There are bits of blue.
A hard dry leaf hangs   15
From the stem.

V

The yellow glistens.
It glistens with various yellows,

1. Opusculum paedagogum: *Latin*, a little work that teaches.

Citrons, oranges and greens
Flowering over the skin.   20

VI

The shadows of the pears
Are blobs on the green cloth.
The pears are not seen
As the observer wills.

Meaning and Method

1. Stevens is describing the way pears look. Does he want you to notice form? color? texture? smell? taste?
2. Does the poet want to teach the reader to look carefully at an object and see it precisely as it is? Or does he want to teach the reader to transform it imaginatively into something it resembles?

   If the poem is read as a commentary on the use of figurative language in poetry, would you say that the poet approves of figurative language? disapproves of it? neither? Consider lines 2–4, 9 and 10, and 23 and 24.
3. Why is "blobs" (line 22) a precise word in context?
4. It has been suggested that the fifth stanza was inspired by a still life by Paul Cézanne (1839–1906), a French impressionist painter. In fact, Stevens may very well be describing a painting of pears rather than pears themselves. What words reflect the language of painting?
5. Stevens's purpose in this poem was to teach, so he began with a scholarly Latin phrase. Is the poem impersonal and factual like a scientific dissertation, or does it have emotional overtones? What is the mood or tone of the poem?

Language: Words from Latin

Stevens begins his poem with two Latin words. Even if these words had not been footnoted, you might have guessed their general meaning by thinking of their resemblances to English words. *Opusculum,* for example, recalls our word *opus,* which is "a literary or musical work." *Paedagogum* is similar to the word *pedagogue,* which means "an educator."

Many words in English came either directly from Latin or indirectly through languages such as French and Italian, which were derived from Latin.

Check your dictionary to see which of the following words in Stevens's poem were derived directly or indirectly from Latin:

1. bottle	**3.** form	**5.** pear	**7.** shadow	**9.** viol
2. curve	**4.** nude	**6.** round	**8.** various	**10.** yellow

Nomad Exquisite

As the immense dew of Florida
Brings forth
The big-finned palm
And green vine angering for life,

As the immense dew of Florida   5
Brings forth hymn and hymn
From the beholder,
Beholding all these green sides
And gold sides of green sides,

And blessed mornings,   10
Meet° for the eye of the young alligator,
And lightning colors
So, in me, come flinging
Forms, flames, and the flakes of flames.

11. Meet: fitting.

Meaning and Method

1. What are the denotations and connotations of *nomad?* of *exquisite?* In what way is the observer in this poem a "nomad exquisite"?
2. What words or phrases indicate the tropical lushness of the scenery? What is unusual about the description of plants in lines 3 and 4?
3. How does the beholder respond emotionally to nature in this poem? What do the words "hymn" and "blessed" suggest about the effect of the scenery on the beholder? How is the speaker's reaction similar to the beholder's?

4. What do you think is meant by "lightning colors" (line 12)? How is the tropical climate reflected in the imagery in line 14?
5. Could lines 13 and 14 be interpreted to mean (a) that the observer, imaginatively inspired by the scene, responds by writing poetry? (b) that reality sparks imagination? (c) that a poet looks at reality imaginatively and then shapes it into form? (d) all of these? (e) something else?
6. The repetition of words and of sounds in this poem adds to the effect of twining tropical lushness. For example, the /f/ and /ôr/ sounds in "Florida" are repeated in "forth" (lines 2 and 6). What other words repeat one or both of these sounds? What sounds are repeated in lines 13 and 14?

Domination of Black

At night, by the fire,
The colors of the bushes
And of the fallen leaves,
Repeating themselves,
Turned in the room,   5
Like the leaves themselves
Turning in the wind.
Yes: but the color of the heavy hemlocks
Came striding.
And I remembered the cry of the peacocks.   10

The colors of their tails
Were like the leaves themselves
Turning in the wind,
In the twilight wind.
They swept over the room,   15
Just as they flew from the boughs of the hemlocks
Down to the ground.
I heard them cry—the peacocks.
Was it a cry against the twilight

Or against the leaves themselves   20
Turning in the wind,
Turning as the flames
Turned in the fire,
Turning as the tails of the peacocks
Turned in the loud fire,   25
Loud as the hemlocks
Full of the cry of the peacocks?
Or was it a cry against the hemlocks?

Out of the window,
I saw how the planets gathered   30
Like the leaves themselves
Turning in the wind.
I saw how the night came,
Came striding like the color of the heavy hemlocks
I felt afraid.   35
And I remembered the cry of the peacocks.

Meaning

1. What is the scene Stevens is describing? At what time of day and time of year does the poem take place? How would the time of day affect the color of the hemlocks? What are the connotations of "the color of the *heavy* hemlocks / Came *striding*" (lines 8 and 9)?

2. As you read the poem, it becomes clear that the fire, the hemlocks, the leaves, and the peacocks are all symbolic. Fire, which suggests heat, light, and warmth, probably represents life. What might dead leaves symbolize? Considering the fact that one variety of hemlock is the poison hemlock, and that the darkness of the hemlock is emphasized, explain what the hemlock might symbolize. Do lines 8 and 9 indicate that "the color of the hemlocks" overcomes the color of the fire? If so, what might this implication mean symbolically?

3. Peacocks not only suggest beautiful colors but also superficial pride. Their cry is a piercing sound and is regarded as a bad omen.

   How might the peacocks and their cry symbolize human beings or the human condition? In your answer, comment on the three possibilities for the cry given in lines 19, 20–27, and 28, and on the symbolic meanings of "twilight," "leaves," and "hemlock."

4. Of what do you think the speaker is "afraid" in line 35? Is he afraid of death? of the constant change of things that characterizes reality?

Method

1. What elements in the poem or in the description contribute to the atmosphere of mystery? Why might the poet have wanted to create this atmosphere?
2. How does the mood of the first seven lines contrast with and serve to intensify the mood established by the rest of the poem?
3. What words emphasize the resemblance and the movement of the fire, the word, the peacocks, the hemlocks, the plants? Does this emphasis symbolize the constant change in life? its inevitable movement toward death? both? neither? How does the use of free verse also emphasize this movement?

Composition and Discussion

Wallace Stevens once wrote of this poem, "I am sorry that a poem of this sort has to contain any ideas at all, because its sole purpose is to fill the mind with the images and sounds that it contains. . . . You are supposed to get heavens full of the colors and full of sounds and you are supposed to feel as you would if you actually got all this." *

What do you think of his statement? Should some poems be read for their images and sounds only? Can understanding and appreciation be separated? Is a poet's meaning essential to an understanding and interpretation of a poem, or may interpretations vary from reader to reader?

Be prepared to take part in an open class discussion of these questions or to write a composition defending or refuting Mr. Stevens's statement.

The Anecdote of the Jar

I placed a jar in Tennessee,
And round it was, upon a hill.
It made the slovenly wilderness
Surround that hill.

*Letters of Wallace Stevens, selected and edited by Holly Stevens, (New York: Knopf, 1966), page 251.

The wilderness rose up to it,   5
And sprawled around, no longer wild.
The jar was round upon the ground
And tall and of a port in air.°

It took dominion everywhere.
The jar was gray and bare.   10
It did not give of bird or bush,
Like nothing else in Tennessee.

8. of . . . air: *here,* of a military bearing in appearance or demeanor. *Port* also has connotations of *harbor,* a place of safety.

Meaning and Method

1. What is the effect of the jar on its surroundings? What are the jar's limitations?
2. What characteristics of the jar are mentioned in the first two stanzas? What are the connotations of these characteristics? Are they primarily positive or negative in context? What characteristics of the jar are mentioned in line 10? Are these characteristics primarily positive or negative, especially in context?
3. Does the jar symbolize art? human order? something else? Does the hill symbolize the wilderness or unordered nature? In your answer, consider the fact that a man places the jar on the hill.
4. Except in lines 8–10, the poem is unrhymed. Considering the meaning of lines 8–10, explain why the poet might have introduced rhyming words at this point.

Composition and Discussion

1. Stevens once said, "The ordinary is always what one makes it." In a composition, explain what you think he meant and give one or more examples to support your points.
2. Prepare to take part in a discussion of symbolism. Among the topics you can include in the discussion are the following: the influence of symbols in our daily lives; symbols taken from folklore, mythology, or the Bible; the rejection by people today of many traditional symbols; the creation of new symbols; the function of symbolism in literature, especially in poetry.

The Ordinary Women

Then from their poverty they rose,
From dry catarrhs,° and to guitars
They flitted
Through the palace walls.

They flung monotony behind,   5
Turned from their want, and, nonchalant,
They crowded
The nocturnal halls.

The lacquered loges° huddled there
Mumbled zay-zay and a-zay, a-zay.   10
The moonlight
Fubbed° the girandoles.°

And the cold dresses that they wore,
In the vapid haze of the window-bays,
Were tranquil   15
As they leaned and looked

From the window-sills at the alphabets,
At beta b and gamma g,°
To study
The canting° curlicues   20

Of heaven and of the heavenly script.
And there they read of marriage-bed.
Ti-lill-o!
And they read right long.

2. **catarrhs** (kə·tärz′): inflammations of the mucous membranes, as in influenza. 9. **loges:** upper sections or boxes in a theater. 12. **Fubbed:** archaic form of *fobbed*, cheated or deceived, introduced by fraud or deceit. **girandoles:** *here*, branched candlesticks or chandeliers. 18. **beta b and gamma g:** *beta* and *gamma* are Greek letters. 20. **canting:** tilting. *Cant* also means hypocritical moral or religious talk, or affected piety in speech.

"The Ordinary Women," copyright 1923 and renewed 1951 by Wallace Stevens, from *Harmonium* by Wallace Stevens. Reprinted by permission of Alfred A. Knopf, Inc.

The gaunt guitarists on the strings   25
Rumbled a-day and a-day, a-day.
The moonlight
Rose on the beachy° floors.

How explicit the coiffures became,
The diamond point, the sapphire point,   30
The sequins
Of the civil° fans!

Insinuations of desire,
Puissant° speech, alike in each,
Cried quittance   35
To the wickless° halls.

Then from their poverty they rose,
From dry guitars, and to catarrhs
They flitted
Through the palace walls.   40

---

28. beachy: pebbly or sandy. **32. civil:** *here*, polite, observing the proper social amenities. **34. Puissant** (pyo͞o′ə·sənt): powerful **36. wickless:** A wick is a candle's twisted fibers to which one puts the match. Wickless is "without a wick."

Meaning and Method

1. What are the lives of the ordinary women like? (See lines 1 and 2.) Why do the women go to the palace? How do the lives of the women while in the palace contrast with their ordinary lives?

   Note that the women went from catarrhs to guitars. How do these things symbolize contrasting ways of life?

2. What words or phrases indicate that life in the palace is artificial? that it is rich only superficially? In your answer, comment on the meaning of lines 11 and 12 and line 36.

3. How is the last stanza different from the first? What does this change show about the reaction of the ordinary women to what they saw?

4. Do you think that the poet feels that the ordinary women failed to comprehend this life so different from their own because they were "ordinary" and limited? that they intuitively understood the sterility of this life? both? something else?

5. The poet uses many words that are exotic or esoteric, that is, ordinarily understood by only a few. Which words are exotic or
esoteric? Why do you think he uses these words?

Composition

Many people go to the movies—particularly those made in Hollywood—to escape from the dreary reality of their daily lives. How might
Hollywood movies encourage escapism? Do you think this escapism is
basically a good or a bad thing?

In a short composition, discuss the reasons for your opinions about
the function of movies. Try to use examples of movies you have seen
or heard about to support your points.

The Emperor of Ice-Cream

Call the roller of big cigars,
The muscular one, and bid him whip
In kitchen cups concupiscent° curds.°
Let the wenches dawdle in such dress
As they are used to wear, and let the boys   5
Bring flowers in last month's newspapers.
Let be be the finale of seem.
The only emperor is the emperor of ice-cream.

Take from the dresser of deal,°
Lacking the three glass knobs, that sheet   10
On which she embroidered fantails° once
And spread it so as to cover her face.
If her horny° feet protrude, they come
To show how cold she is, and dumb.
Let the lamp affix its beam.   15
The only emperor is the emperor of ice-cream.

---

3. **concupiscent:** desirous, highly desirable. **curds:** coagulated portions of milk;
here, ice cream. 9. **deal:** pine or fir. 11. **fantails:** pigeons characterized by fan-
like tail feathers. 13. **horny:** hard, calloused.

Meaning and Method

1. What is the mood created by the first three lines? Is it mysterious? frightening? tranquil? peaceful? something else? What are the connotations of *concupiscent*? How does the repetition of the /k/ sound in lines 1–3 contribute to this mood?

2. What scene does the poem describe? What images suggest shabbiness? How do the connotations of *emperor* contrast with the scene described in the poem?

3. Does *ice cream* suggest permanence or impermanence? In the context of the poem, does it convey favorable or unfavorable connotations? Does it connote something desirable? something cheap? Does ice cream symbolize death? Does it symbolize, as Stevens once said, "an absolute good"?

4. In his poetry, Stevens often praised the ability of the artistic imagination to transform reality into something beautiful. How does the theme of this poem contrast with the previous statement? Explain what the word "seem" (line 7) means. Why is "be"—that is, reality—the "finale of seem"? How does death provide the final reality to life? Which lines suggest the inability of artistic imagination to transform death into something beautiful? What might the lamp (line 15) symbolize?

Elinor Wylie
[1885–1928]

The literary career of Elinor [Hoyt] Wylie was limited almost entirely to the last seven years of her life. As a young girl growing up in Philadelphia and Washington society, she had considered writing as a profession. But it was not until after she was divorced from her second husband, Horace Wylie, that she began to write extensively. Her third husband, William Rose Benét, a poet himself, introduced her to the literary life of New York City and encouraged her to write.

Her collection of poems, *Nets to Catch the Wind* (1921), impressed critics, who praised her technical brilliance and her ability to capture subtle moods. Her subsequent volumes—*Black Armour* (1923), *Trivial Breath* (1928), *Angels and Earthly Creatures* (1929)—won even higher praise. Mrs. Wylie also wrote four novels—*Jennifer Lorn* (1923), *The Venetian Glass Nephew* (1925), *The Orphan Angel* (1926), and *Mr. Hodge and Mr. Hazard* (1928).

According to the poet Louise Bogan, Mrs. Wylie's poetry is marked by her "ability to fuse thought and passion into the most admirable and complex forms." Moreover, she displays the "craftman's concern for phrasing and for the particular qualities of words." Her vivid images and her use of sound patterns to convey moods and feelings make her poems exciting yet delicate.

Wild Peaches

I

When the world turns completely upside down
You say we'll emigrate to the Eastern Shore°
Aboard a river boat from Baltimore;

2. **Eastern Shore:** a section of Maryland bordering on Chesapeake Bay.

We'll live among wild peach trees, miles from town,
You'll wear a coonskin cap, and I a gown   5
Homespun, dyed butternut's dark gold color.
Lost, like your lotus-eating ancestor,
We'll swim in milk and honey till we drown.

The winter will be short, the summer long,
The autumn amber-hued, sunny and hot,   10
Tasting of cider and of scuppernong;°
All seasons sweet, but autumn best of all.
The squirrels in their silver fur will fall
Like falling leaves, like fruit, before your shot.

II

The autumn frosts will lie upon the grass   15
Like bloom on grapes of purple-brown and gold.
The misted early mornings will be cold;
The little puddles will be roofed with glass.
The sun, which burns from copper into brass,
Melts these at noon, and makes the boys unfold   20
Their knitted mufflers; full as they can hold,
Fat pockets dribble chestnuts as they pass.

Peaches grow wild, and pigs can live in clover;
A barrel of salted herrings lasts a year;
The spring begins before the winter's over.   25
By February you may find the skins
Of garter snakes and water moccasins
Dwindled and harsh, dead-white and cloudy-clear.

III

When April pours the colors of a shell
Upon the hills, when every little creek   30
Is shot with silver from the Chesapeake
In shoals new-minted by the ocean swell,
When strawberries go begging, and the sleek

11. scuppernong: a type of grape cultivated in the southern United States.

Blue plums lie open to the blackbird's beak,
We shall live well—we shall live very well.   35

The months between the cherries and the peaches
Are brimming cornucopias° which spill
Fruits red and purple, somber-bloomed and black;
Then, down rich fields and frosty river beaches
We'll trample bright persimmons, while you kill   40
Bronze partridge, speckled quail, and canvasback.°

IV

Down to the Puritan marrow of my bones
There's something in this richness that I hate.
I love the look, austere, immaculate,
Of landscapes drawn in pearly monotones.   45
There's something in my very blood that owns
Bare hills, cold silver on a sky of slate,
A thread of water, churned to milky spate°
Streaming through slanted pastures fenced with stones.

I love those skies, thin blue or snowy gray,   50
Those fields sparse-planted, rendering meager sheaves;
That spring, briefer than apple-blossom's breath,
Summer, so much too beautiful to stay,
Swift autumn, like a bonfire of leaves,
And sleepy winter, like the sleep of death.   55

37. cornucopias: horns of plenty. 41. canvasback: a type of sea duck. 48. spate: an overflow, possibly caused by a sudden, violent storm.

Meaning and Method

1. What do you think of when you hear the phrase "wild peaches"? Why might the speaker and the "you" want to "live among wild peach trees, miles from town"? Does the speaker think a life like this is possible? From the first section, can you guess the relationship between the speaker and the "you"?
2. "Lotus-eating ancestor" (line 7) is an allusion to a section in the *Odyssey* in which some of Ulysses' sailors go ashore, eat a plant called the lotus, and are enveloped by a dreamlike feeling of such

pleasure that they do not want to return to the ship. In what ways is the world pictured in the first and second sections a dream world of pleasure? What are its major characteristics? What does the speaker mean by line 8?

3. Which images or metaphors appealing to the senses in the first three parts emphasize the lushness of nature? Which images or metaphors in the last part in particular contrast with those in previous parts. In what general ways do the two descriptions contrast?

4. How does the speaker's idea of time and beauty in the fourth section contrast with the ideas previously expressed? Which of the speaker's approaches is more intense—that in the first three sections or that in the last? Explain.

5. After reading the last part, reread the first. Do any of the early lines of the poem foreshadow the feelings expressed in lines 42 and 43? Do you think the world pictured in the first three parts is primarily the speaker's idea or that of the "you"? Why? Is there a conflict of personalities suggested in the poem? If so, where?

6. Does the speaker completely reject the sensuous life presented in the first sections, or is she attracted to it? both? Does she derive any sensuous pleasure from the landscape and weather described in the last section?

7. Mrs. Wylie conveys an impression of the lushness of the landscape described in the first three sections by constantly repeating the slow, heavy /u/ sound as in *lush*. Find several examples of the use of this technique. What other sounds are repeated in order to emphasize the slow-moving, rich life she is describing?

Language: Symbols from Mythology

"Wild Peaches" contains a reference to the mythological *cornucopia* (line 37). The *cornucopia* is called the horn of plenty because it is always full of food and drink. It was named after the horn of the goat Amalthea, that suckled the infant Zeus.

Check each of the following words in an unabridged dictionary. What does each word symbolize? What is the origin of the symbolism?

1. owl   3. laurel wreath
2. caduceus   4. olive branch
        5. winged foot

Composition

A utopia (yoo·tō'pē·ə) is an imaginary place in which life is ideal or perfect. Write a composition describing your idea of a utopia. You may concentrate on a specific utopia—a utopian school, course, home, or store—or you may write about a more general utopia, such as a utopian town, city, or country.

Let No Charitable Hope

Now let no charitable hope
Confuse my mind with images
Of eagle and of antelope:
I am in nature none of these.

I was, being human, born alone;   5
I am, being woman, hard beset;
I live by squeezing from a stone
The little nourishment I get.

In masks outrageous and austere
The years go by in single file;   10
But none has merited my fear,
And none has quite escaped my smile.

Meaning and Method

1. Because of the use of the word *Now* in line 1, one interpretation of the setting of this poem is that the speaker is responding to someone who has praised her. With line 3 as your guide, try to guess what the praise was. Why does she call the praise a "charitable hope"? Why does she reject it? In your answer, comment on the connotations of *eagle* and of *antelope*.
2. How does her own picture of herself contrast with the images of *eagle* and of *antelope*? Which lines indicate that she makes an effort to get whatever good she can from a hard, barren world?
3. What is the speaker's concept of time and life? How does she react to each year and its passing? Do you think she is proud of herself as she is, or does she mock herself?

Madman's Song

Better to see your cheek grown hollow,
Better to see your temple worn,
Than to forget to follow, follow,
After the sound of a silver horn.

Better to bind your brow with willow   5
And follow, follow until you die,
Than to sleep with your head on a golden pillow,
Nor lift it up when the hunt goes by.

Better to see your cheek grown sallow
And your hair grown gray, so soon, so soon,   10
Than to forget to hallo, hallo,
After the milk-white hounds of the moon.

Meaning and Method

1. The silver horn is the horn that is actually sounded in a hunt. How is the poet using the horn symbolically?
2. Does the speaker feel that it is important to join the "hunt" for its own sake? to reach a specific goal? to follow an ideal?
3. How does the contrast between the "sound of a silver horn" (line 4) and a "golden pillow" (line 7) indicate the difference between the two types of life that one might choose? Is the type of life extolled in this poem one that is commonly extolled by people in our society? How does the title of the poem indicate the poet's answer to that question?

Robinson Jeffers
[1887-1962]

For nearly fifty years, Robinson Jeffers and his wife lived in Carmel, California, in a stone house that he had built with his own hands. The house, standing on a cliff overlooking the Pacific, was surrounded by a small forest, which allowed Jeffers to lead a hermit-like existence.

In this setting (and partly because of it) he composed poems extolling primitive nature. He particularly admired those things that endure without thought, such as rocks and trees, and those savage animals and birds, such as eagles and hawks, which constantly struggle for power and life itself. Civilization, on the other hand, seemed to him weak, propped up by illusions. Man, he felt, was a doomed race, and his disappearance would leave the world better off. Like the English poet Thomas Hardy, whose pessimism Jeffers shared, he saw nature as indifferent to man's fate. Man is caught in a struggle for existence; he will die and be forgotten, yet life will go on. In spite of this, man must face life with dignity and integrity.

John Robinson Jeffers, the son of a teacher of biblical languages, was born in Pittsburgh, Pennsylvania. He was educated in private schools in Pittsburgh, in Switzerland, and in Germany, and received a thorough education in Greek and Latin classics as well as in modern languages and literatures. A precocious student, he enrolled at the University of Pittsburgh at the age of fifteen, and at the age of eighteen, received a B.A. degree from Occidental College in California.

For the next several years, Jeffers searched vainly for an occupation. After receiving an M.A. in literature from the University of Southern California, he enrolled in the medical school there but left after three years without a degree. He then spent a year studying forestry at the University of Washington.

No occupation other than that of a writer seemed to appeal to him. In 1912, his first book of poetry, *Flagons and Apples,* was published, and in the same year he received a modest legacy that enabled him to settle in Carmel and spend the rest of his life observing nature and writing. His second book, *Talmar and Other*

Poems (1924), was highly praised and gave him recognition as an important new poet.

As might be expected from his philosophy of life, his poems are notable for giving an impression of power—a power shown in bold images and themes, and in the use of long, compact lines. His poems range from short but intense lyrics to long, dramatic tragic narratives, usually about contemporary life. He was also very much influenced by his study of Greek classics, and he wrote three "reconstructions" of classical Greek tragedies—*Medea* (1946), *Hippolytus* (1954), and *The Cretan Woman* (1954)—emphasizing the violence inherent in the stories.

Boats in a Fog

Sports and gallantries, the stage, the arts, the antics of
    dancers,
The exuberant voices of music,
Have charm for children but lack nobility; it is bitter
    earnestness
That makes beauty; the mind
Knows, grown adult.
                A sudden fog-drift muffled the ocean,   5
A throbbing of engines moved in it,
At length, a stone's throw out, between the rocks and the
    vapor,
One by one moved shadows
Out of the mystery, shadows, fishing-boats, trailing each
    other,
Following the cliff for guidance,   10
Holding a difficult path between the peril of the sea-fog
And the foam on the shore granite.
One by one, trailing their leader, six crept by me,
Out of the vapor and into it,
The throb of their engines subdued by the fog, patient and
    cautious,   15

Coasting all round the peninsula
Back to the buoys in Monterey harbor.° A flight of pelicans
Is nothing lovelier to look at;
The flight of the planets is nothing nobler; all the arts lose
    virtue
Against the essential reality   20
Of creatures going about their business among the equally
Earnest elements of nature.

17. **Monterey harbor:** a port in California. Frequent fogs and shoals of rocks make this a dangerous area for boats.

Meaning and Method

1. Why does the speaker feel that "sports and gallantries, the stage," art, ballet, and music lack nobility. According to the speaker, what makes something beautiful? How do the fishing boats fit the definition specifying what creates beauty?
2. Jeffers once wrote, "Nature is always the norm in relation to which man is measured." Do the persons in the boats measure up well or poorly against nature's norm?
3. What words or phrases indicate the slowness of the boats? the presence of fog?
4. In what ways does the use of free verse reflect the scene described?
5. State the speaker's philosophy of life as it appears in this poem.

Hurt Hawks

I

The broken pillar of the wing jags from the clotted shoulder,
The wing trails like a banner in defeat,
No more to use the sky forever but live with famine
And pain a few days: cat nor coyote
Will shorten the week of waiting for death, there is game
    without talons.   5
He stands under the oak-bush and waits
The lame feet of salvation; at night he remembers freedom

And flies in a dream, the dawns ruin it.
He is strong and pain is worse to the strong, incapacity is
    worse.
The curs of the day come and torment him   10
At distance, no one but death the redeemer will humble that
    head,
The intrepid readiness, the terrible eyes.
The wild God of the world is sometimes merciful to those
That ask mercy, not often to the arrogant.
You do not know him, you communal people, or you have
    forgotten him;   15
Intemperate and savage, the hawk remembers him;
Beautiful and wild, the hawks, and men that are dying,
    remember him.

II

I'd sooner, except the penalties, kill a man than a hawk;
    but the great redtail
Had nothing left but unable misery
From the bone too shattered for mending, the wing that
    trailed under his talons when he moved.   20
We had fed him six weeks, I gave him freedom,
He wandered over the foreland hill and returned in the
    evening, asking for death,
Not like a beggar, still eyed with the old
Implacable arrogance. I gave him the lead gift in the twilight.
    What fell was relaxed,
Owl-downy, soft feminine feathers; but what   25
Soared: the fierce rush: the night-herons by the flooded river
    cried fear at its rising
Before it was quite unsheathed from reality.

Meaning and Method

1. What do the connotations of the metaphor *broken pillar of the
   wing* (line 1) and of the simile *like a banner in defeat* (line 2)
   indicate about the hawk's nature? about the speaker's point of view?
2. What are the characteristics of the hawk? Does his injury change
   these qualities? Do other creatures change their attitude toward
   him? How do you know that the hawk is not afraid of death?

3. How does the speaker's attitude toward the hawk contrast with his attitude toward people? What is the tone of the phrase "you communal people"? What do the hawks and dying men know about God?
4. Why did the speaker feed the hawk? What is the "lead gift" (line 24) he finally gave to the hawk? What words in lines 25–27 indicate that even in death the hawk retained its violent, murderous nature?
5. What is the speaker's attitude toward wild nature? toward civilization?
6. What does the hawk symbolize?

Marianne Moore

Before the Brooklyn Dodgers were transformed into the Los Angeles Dodgers, they probably had no greater fan than an erudite poet who lived in Brooklyn and wore gay, elaborate hats. In verse as well as in person, Marianne Moore, the poet, cheered the Dodgers. "A neat bunt, please; a cloud breaker, a drive . . . ," she once implored them in a poem written during a World Series.

Miss Moore's enthusiasm for the Dodgers is one of the pieces in a puzzling personality that seems composed of parts that do not fit neatly together. For most of her life, she has been a city dweller, but she has written some very observant and imaginative poems about plants and animals. (In one poem, she described an elephant as "black earth preceded by a tendril"; in another, she called a basilisk a "nervous naked sword on little feet.")

Her poems are experimental and complex in form, yet her philosophy of life is based on conventional and basically simple values. She admires such virtues as fortitude, self-reliance, and endurance, and believes, as she once said, "that the unselfish behavior of individual to individual is the basis of world peace." Although her work is deeply rooted in other people's writings, the individuality of her poems is their most striking characteristic. She builds many of her poems around quotations from surprisingly varied sources, such as Leo Tolstoy's diary, the regulations of the Department of the Interior, and advertisements found in newspapers.

Marianne Moore was born in St. Louis, Missouri, in 1887 and educated at a private school in Carlisle, Pennsylvania. She attended Bryn Mawr College, and after graduation returned to Carlisle to study at the Carlisle Commercial School. From 1911 through 1915, she taught commercial subjects at the Indian School in Carlisle.

In the 1920's after she had moved to New York, she worked as a librarian at the New York Public Library, and then spent several years as the editor of *Dial*, one of the most influential and forward-looking literary magazines of the period. In 1921, her first book of verse, *Poems*, was published without her knowledge by the poet H. D. (see page 39) and the novelist Winifred Bryher, and in 1924, her next volume, *Observations*, appeared.

Miss Moore's poems have had a special attraction for other

poets, who admire her technical mastery, vivid and original images, and subtlety of thought and expression. The value of her verse was acknowledged in 1951 when her *Collected Poems* was awarded the Pulitzer prize for poetry. But the general reader often finds some of the extremely compact poems difficult and obscure.

Poetry

I, too, dislike it: there are things that are important beyond all
      this fiddle.
  Reading it, however, with a perfect contempt for it, one
      discovers in
  it, after all, a place for the genuine.
     Hands that can grasp, eyes
     that can dilate,° hair that can rise   5
       if it must, these things are important not because a

high-sounding interpretation can be put upon them but
      because they are
  useful. When they become so derivative as to become
      unintelligible,
  the same thing may be said for all of us, that we
     do not admire what   10
     we cannot understand: the bat
      holding on upside down or in quest of something to

eat, elephants pushing, a wild horse taking a roll, a tireless
      wolf under
  a tree, the immovable critic twitching his skin like a horse
      that feels a flea, the base-
  ball fan, the statistician—   15
     nor is it valid
      to discriminate against "business documents and

5. **dilate:** widen or expand.

schoolbooks";° all of these phenomena are important. One
      must make a distinction
   however: when dragged into prominence by half poets, the
      result is not poetry,
nor till the poets among us can be   20
    "literalists of
   the imagination"°—above
      insolence and triviality and can present

for inspection, imaginary gardens with real toads in them,
      shall we have
   it. In the meantime, if you demand on the one hand   25
   the raw material of poetry in
    all its rawness and
    that which is on the other hand
      genuine, then you are interested in poetry.

17–18. business . . . schoolbooks: quoted, according to Miss Moore, from Leo
Tolstoy's diary. See *The Diaries of Leo Tolstoy*, translated from the Russian by
C. J. Hogarth and A. Srinis (New York: Dutton, 1917), page 94: "Where the
boundary between prose and poetry lies, I shall never be able to understand.
The question is raised in manuals of style, yet the answer to it lies beyond me.
Poetry is verse: prose is not verse. Or else poetry is everything with the exception of business documents and schoolbooks." 21–22. literalists of the imagination: quoted, according to Miss Moore, from an essay by William Butler Yeats,
"William Blake and the Imagination" in *Ideas of Good and Evil* (A. H. Bullen,
1903), page 182: "The limitation of his view was from the very intensity of his
vision; he was a too literal realist of imagination as others are of nature."

Meaning and Method

1. What reason does the poet give in line 1 for "disliking" poetry?
   What saving grace of poetry does she find in line 3?
2. In lines 4–8, the poet states that human responses such as hands
   grasping and eyes dilating are "useful," and she indicates that
   "genuine" poetry can cause these responses. Before she discusses
   genuine poetry, however, she turns to poetry to which we cannot
   respond—"unintelligible" poetry. What reason does she give in
   line 8 for poetry being "unintelligible"?
3. The Russian novelist Leo Tolstoy (1828–1910) once wrote in his
   diary that "poetry is everything with the exception of business
   documents and schoolbooks." Does Miss Moore quote part of this

statement in lines 17 and 18 because she agrees with it? What does she consider the proper subjects for poetry?

4. A "literalist" is a person who sticks closely to the denotative meanings of words in a statement and does not permit his imagination to wander. What do you think the poet means by the paradox "literalists of the imagination" (lines 21 and 22)?

5. What do you think is meant by the statement that poets should present "imaginary gardens with real toads in them" (line 24)? Would the statement have the same meaning if "real birds" were substituted for "real toads"? Why or why not?

6. Attempt to paraphrase Miss Moore's idea of poetry. For example, what does she think are the proper subjects for poetry? Is there any subject not proper? If so, why? Does she seem to think that poetry should have an immediate, direct effect on the reader?

Languages: The Formation of Plurals

The words "hands" (line 4) and "phenomena" (line 18) illustrate two of the various ways in which plurals can be formed. The plural form of most nouns in English is made by adding *s* or *es* to the end of the singular form, as in *hand, hands; potato, potatoes*. For nouns ending in -*y* preceded by a consonant the plural is formed by changing the *y* to *i* and adding *es*, as in *beauty, beauties; ivory, ivories;* and *city, cities*.

However, English has kept the foreign plural form of many words that have been borrowed from other languages—as in *phenomenon, phenomena* from the Greek; and as in *alumnus, alumni* from the Latin. And still other plurals are simply older forms from our own language.

Check your dictionary for the plurals of the following words. Which of these words came from Old English? Which came from other languages?

1. alumna	4. child	7. mouse
2. axis	5. criterion	8. oasis
3. cherub	6. knife	9. ox

Composition

Using as your topic sentence *The poet must present imaginary gardens with real toads*, defend Miss Moore's definition of the function of a poet. Explain what this statement means and give some examples to illustrate your explanation. Then, in your paper, analyze at least three poems written by other poets that you feel illustrate Miss Moore's definition.

What Are Years?

What is our innocence,
what is our guilt? All are
      naked, none is safe. And whence°
is courage: the unanswered question,
the resolute doubt—   5
dumbly calling, deafly listening—that
in misfortune, even death,
      encourages others
      and in its defeat, stirs

      the soul to be strong? He   10
sees deep and is glad, who
      accedes° to mortality
and in his imprisonment, rises
upon himself as
the sea in a chasm,° struggling to be   15
free and unable to be,
      in its surrendering
      finds its continuing.

      So he who strongly feels,
behaves. The very bird,   20
      grown taller as he sings, steels
his form straight up. Though he is captive,
his mighty singing
says, satisfaction is a lowly
thing, how pure a thing is joy.   25
      This is mortality,
      this is eternity.

3. **whence:** from what place or source. 12. **accedes:** agrees to, yields to. 15. **chasm:** deep gorge.

Meaning and Method

1. According to the poet in lines 1–3, does it matter whether we as individuals are innocent or guilty? If *naked* is interpreted as meaning "vulnerable" or "defenseless," and *innocence* and *guilt* as "goodness" and "evilness," how could you explain the word *safe* (line 3)?

2. *Oxymoron*, a figure of rhetoric, is a combination of contradictory, paradoxical, or incongruous words, as in "cruel kindness," and "bitter sweet."

   In line 5, the speaker uses an oxymoron to define courage as "the resolute doubt," and in line 6, the speaker uses two other paradoxes: "dumbly calling" and "deafly listening." What is the speaker saying about courage by means of these oxymora?

3. In the second stanza, the speaker sees the courageous man as one who "accedes to mortality"—that is, accepts the fact that he is going to die. However, the acceptance is not passive, as is seen in the comparison to "the sea in a chasm" (line 15). What are the characteristics of "the sea in a chasm" and of the courageous man? Does either simply accede to fate? What is the paradox in lines 17 and 18, and how does it grow out of the previous extended comparison?

4. In the third stanza, the speaker compares the courageous man to a caged bird that sings. What major quality does this type of man have? Why does singing help the bird? What would be the counterpart of singing in a man's life?

5. Why are the following italicized words particularly appropriate in the context of the poem: "*steels* / his form *straight up*" (lines 21 and 22)?

6. The poem as a whole is an answer to the title, "What Are Years?" Do you think that the answer could be paraphrased as follows: "Years are the setting and boundaries of our lives. If we recognize these boundaries and yet spiritually fight against their confinement, we can attain immortality or eternity"? In what way is "satisfaction" (line 24) a product of "mortality," while "joy" (line 25) is a product of "eternity"?

Composition and Discussion

Write a composition or have a class discussion in which you give your definition of courage. Explain what your definition includes and what it excludes. Illustrate the importance of courage in life by referring to a specific incident or incidents or to a specific person or persons.

Silence

My father used to say,
"Superior people never make long visits,
have to be shown Longfellow's grave
or the glass flowers at Harvard.
Self-reliant like the cat—   5
that takes its prey to privacy,
the mouse's limp tail hanging like a shoelace from it's
    mouth—
they sometimes enjoy solitude,
and can be robbed of speech
by speech which has delighted them.   10
The deepest feeling always shows itself in silence;
not in silence, but restraint."
Nor was he insincere in saying, "Make my house your inn."
Inns are not residences.

Meaning and Method

1. According to the father in this poem, which of the following
   are characteristics of "superior people": (a) self-reliance; (b) silence;
   (c) restraint; (d) concern for and responsiveness to other people;
   (e) something else?
2. Explain the last two lines. How does the thought expressed in these
   lines follow from the theory of "superior people" expressed by the
   father in the first twelve lines, especially in line 2?

Composition

To what places in your town or city would you take a visitor who
had only one day to spend with you? Why would you choose these
places? Are there places you would deliberately avoid? If so, why? Do
you think a town or city is best shown by taking your visitors to specific
places, or by letting them wander at will? Include your answers to these
questions in a composition combining description and explanation.

To a Steam Roller

The illustration
is nothing to you without the application.
    You lack half wit. You crush all the particles down
        into close conformity, and then walk back and forth
           on them.

Sparkling chips of rock   5
are crushed down to the level of the parent block.
    Were not "impersonal judgment in aesthetic
        matters, a metaphysical° impossibility," you

might fairly achieve
it. As for butterflies, I can hardly conceive
    of one's attending upon you, but to question
        the congruence° of the complement° is vain, if it exists.   10

8. **metaphysical:** concerning the ultimate nature of reality. 10. **congruence:** agreement. **complement:** that which must be added to complete a whole.

Meaning and Method

1. What is the job of a steam roller? How does the steam roller in performing its task come close to making an "impersonal judgment"?
2. Does the speaker seem to prefer the "chips of rock" or the "parent block"? How do the connotations of *close conformity* (line 4), *sparkling* (line 5), and *crushed down to the level of* (line 6) suggest which the speaker prefers?
3. How do the characteristics of butterflies contrast with those of a steam roller?
4. In the poem, Miss Moore personifies the steam roller. What type of person does the steam roller represent? In your answer explain lines 1 and 2. Which seems to symbolize the goals and values of modern society—the steam roller or the butterflies?
5. Analyze the syllabic structure of each line of the poem. Is the poem written in free verse?

Critics and Connoisseurs*

There is a great amount of poetry in unconscious
    fastidiousness. Certain Ming°
        products, imperial floor-coverings of coach-
wheel yellow, are well enough in their way but I have seen
                something
    that I like better—a   5
        mere childish attempt to make an imperfectly ballasted°
                animal stand up,
      similar determination to make a pup
        eat his meat from the plate.

I remember a swan under the willows in Oxford,
    with flamingo-colored, maple-   10
        leaflike feet. It reconnoitred like a battle-
ship. Disbelief and conscious fastidiousness were the staple
        ingredients in its
        disinclination to move. Finally its hardihood was
            not proof against its
            proclivity° to more fully appraise such bits   15
            of food as the stream

bore counter to it; it made away with what I gave it
    to eat. I have seen this swan and
    I have seen you; I have seen amibition without
understanding in a variety of forms. Happening to stand   20
      by an ant hill, I have
        seen a fastidious ant carrying a stick north, south, east,
            west, till it turned on
        itself, struck out from the flower-bed into the lawn,
        and returned to the point

---

* **Connoisseurs** (kŏn′ə·sûrz′): persons with specialized knowledge in a subject;
those competent to judge what is choice or rare. **2. Ming:** a Chinese dynasty
(1368–1644) noted for art objects (particularly porcelain) of extremely high
quality and delicacy. **6. ballasted:** steadied. **15. proclivity:** natural tendency.

from which it had started. Then abandoning the stick as   25
  useless and overtaxing its
      jaws with a particle of whitewash—pill-like but
heavy, it again went through the same course of procedure.
        What is
    there in being able   30
      to say that one has dominated the stream in an attitude
            of self-defense;
      in proving that one has had the experience
        of carrying a stick?

Meaning and Method

1. The word *fastidiousness* may be defined as "extreme delicacy or re-
finement, or difficulty in pleasing in matters of taste." Why would
the Ming products *not* be examples of "unconscious / fastidiousness" (lines 1 and 2)? Why are the child's actions in lines 5–8
considered examples of unconscious fastidiousness? What is the
attitude of the speaker toward the Ming products? toward the
child's actions?
2. In lines 9–18, the speaker describes a swan. What are its characteristics? Is the speaker's attitude toward it wholly positive or wholly
negative? neither?
3. Why is the ant an example of "ambition without understanding"
(lines 19 and 20)? Is the speaker's attitude toward the ant wholly
positive or wholly negative? neither?
4. Why might the swan be considered a symbol of the connoisseurs?
Why might the ant be said to represent critics? How can the
figurative meanings of "stick" (line 22) and "whitewash" (line 27)
be connected with critics?
5. What do the questions in lines 29–33 tell you about the speaker's
attitude toward both the connoisseur and the critic? Which words
or images recall the swan? Which recall the ant?
6. What concrete images does the poet use to make her abstract
points?

Composition and Discussion

1. Write a character sketch describing a fastidious person—for example, a person who will eat only certain foods or buy only certain
styles or colors of clothes. Choose a setting (such as a cafeteria)
that would emphasize the person's fastidiousness. You can make your
description humorous or serious.

2. Some critics and connoisseurs engage in criticism and arts in the same way that an ant carries a stick, that is, for its own sake. Should a person do something simply to be able to say that one has done it? Or should a person's actions be guided by some overall plan that gives one a purpose in doing something? Discuss whether or not many people have a plan, a guiding principle in their lives. Should they have?

3. From reading these poems by Marianne Moore, draw some general conclusions about her poetic techniques and themes. What characteristics, such as diction, imagery, tone, mark her style? How are her themes related to moral and ethical problems? What subjects seem to interest her? Test the validity of your generalizations by reading other poems by Miss Moore.

John Crowe Ransom

John Crowe Ransom was born in Pulaski, Tennessee, in 1888. He attended Vanderbilt University in Nashville, Tennessee, and was a Rhodes Scholar at Oxford University. After a year in England, he returned home and became a member of the English faculty at Vanderbilt. In 1922, he and several other young writers, including Allen Tate and Robert Penn Warren, began the short-lived but extremely influential literary magazine, *The Fugitive*. The purpose of the journal was to encourage a renaissance of southern literature, particularly in poetry.

During the 1930's Ransom's interest shifted from poetry to criticism, both social and literary. He wrote essays defending the agrarian way of life as superior to that produced by modern industry and science. He left Vanderbilt in 1937 to become a professor of English at Kenyon College in Ohio. At Kenyon, he founded *The Kenyon Review* and used its pages to present his philosophy and his literary criticism. Criticism and teaching, Ransom believed, should emphasize an intensive analysis of literary texts rather than a study of their historical backgrounds. This type of criticism became widely known as the New Criticism.

As a poet, Ransom is limited in theme and tone: his best poems are about death and the effects of the passing of time. His tone is usually a blend of irony and mocking wit.

Bells for John Whiteside's Daughter

There was such speed in her little body,
And such lightness in her footfall,
It is no wonder her brown study
Astonishes us all.

Her wars were bruited° in our high window.　　　　5
We looked among orchard trees and beyond

5. **bruited:** talked about.

Where she took arms against her shadow,
Or harried unto the pond

The lazy geese, like a snow cloud
Dripping their snow on the green grass,   10
Tricking and stopping, sleepy and proud,
Who cried in goose, Alas,

For the tireless heart within the little
Lady with rod that made them rise
From their noon apple-dreams and scuttle   15
Goose-fashion under the skies!

But now go the bells, and we are ready;
In one house we are sternly stopped
To say we are vexed at her brown study,
Lying so primly propped.   20

Meaning and Method

1. Which words or phrases tell you that the speaker lives in a rural area, spends some time at home, and is a neighbor of John White-side?

   What do the words *bruited, harried* and *took arms* connote about the speaker's attitude toward the girl and her activities?

2. A *brown study* usually denotes a state of absent-mindedness or reverie. How is the little girl's "brown study" different from the usual ones? What happened to her? (Consider the title and the last line.) Why is everyone so astonished at what happened?

3. What words or phrases in lines 5–16 give an impression that the girl lived in a fairy-tale world? Why might her world seem like a fairy tale to the speaker now?

4. Why is the word "vexed" (line 19) an *understatement?* (An understatement is a remark that is deliberately restrained, often to point up the significance of its contents or the situation discussed.) Are there any other understatements in the poem? Considering the situation, what might the poet have wished to avoid by using under-statements?

5. What is the mood of the poem? Why is the tone or situation ironic? Consider line 7 and line 13. What could the word "shadow" symbolize?

6. In the poem, Ransom uses *slant rhyme;* that is, approximate or near rhyme. Slant rhyme is based on assonance or consonance. For example, "body" (line 1) and "study" (line 3) are slant rhymes.

Find other examples of slant rhymes in the poem. Point out examples of true rhyme and explain how they differ from slant rhyme.

How does the use of slant rhyme create a jarring effect, which reinforces the tone of the poem?

Language: Words with French Origins

French was extensively spoken in England after the French-speaking Normans conquered England in 1066. In the century after the conquest, a flood of words from French drastically altered the spoken and written language of England. Old English, or Anglo-Saxon (450–1150) gradually developed into Middle English (1150–1500), a stage during which many words were derived either from Old French (800–1300) or from Middle French (1300–1500). In the modern English period, which like modern French began in the sixteenth century, French additions to the English language have continued.

For example, the word "bruited" in line 5 comes from the French word *bruit*, which means "noise." As you can see, the modern English spelling and meaning are extremely close to the spelling and meaning of the modern French word. Other words and expressions that have entered our language from French are the following:

1. avant-garde	**6.** gourmet	**11.** resignation
2. couturier	**7.** hatchet	**12.** routine
3. critique	**8.** liberty	**13.** sobriety
4. elegant	**9.** margarine	**14.** unique
5. environs	**10.** palette	**15.** vignette

Look up the origin of these words in a dictionary. How close is each of these words in spelling and meaning to the original French?

Janet Waking

Beautifully Janet slept
Till it was deeply morning. She woke then
And thought about her dainty-feathered hen,
To see how it had kept.

"Janet Waking," copyright 1927 by Alfred A. Knopf, Inc. and renewed 1955 by John Crowe Ransom, from *Selected Poems* by John Crowe Ransom. Reprinted by permission of Alfred A. Knopf, Inc.

One kiss she gave her mother,   5
Only a small one gave she to her daddy
Who would have kissed each curl of his shining baby;
No kiss at all for her brother.

"Old Chucky, Old Chucky!" she cried,
Running on little pink feet upon the grass   10
To Chucky's house, and listening. But alas,
Her Chucky had died.

It was a transmogrifying° bee
Came droning down on Chucky's old bald head
And sat and put the poison. It scarcely bled,   15
But how exceedingly

And purply did the knot
Swell with the venom and communicate
Its rigor! Now the poor comb stood up straight
But Chucky did not.   20

So there was Janet
Kneeling on the wet grass, crying her brown hen
(Translated far beyond the daughters of men)
To rise and walk upon it.

And weeping fast as she had breath   25
Janet implored us, "Wake her from her sleep!"
And would not be instructed in how deep
Was the forgetful kingdom of death.

13. **transmogrifying:** transforming, changing or altering, often with grotesque
or humorous effect.

Meaning and Method

1. What details create an impression of Janet's love for her hen? What
   is the speaker's attitude toward Janet? toward the hen? For example, is the speaker sympathetic? detached? ironic? amused? more
   than one of these? In your answer, comment on the use of the
   word "transmogrifying" (line 13).
2. What do you think the speaker means in line 22 when he says that
   the hen was "Translated far beyond the daughters of men"?

3. Why does Janet use the word *sleep* in line 26 rather than *death*? Why is death's kingdom "forgetful"? (Consider such meanings of the word as "neglectful," "oblivious," "heedless.") How may Janet's waking be interpreted literally as well as figuratively?
4. What are the connotations of the name *Chucky*? Why are lines 13 and 14 humorously ironic?
5. Does the speaker think the hen's death is important? Is the child's reaction to it important?

Piazza* Piece

—I am a gentleman in a dustcoat trying
To make you hear. Your ears are soft and small
And listen to an old man not at all,
They want the young men's whispering and sighing.
But see the roses on your trellis dying   5
And hear the spectral° singing of the moon;
For I must have my lovely lady soon,
I am a gentleman in a dustcoat trying.

—I am a lady young in beauty waiting
Until my truelove comes, and then we kiss.   10
But what gray man among the vines is this
Whose words are dry and faint as in a dream?
Back from my trellis, Sir, before I scream!
I am a lady young in beauty waiting.

* **Piazza** (pē·az′ə): an open area or public square in a town or city, especially in Italy. In American usage, the word means a veranda or porch. 6. **spectral**: like a specter or ghost, ghostly.

Meaning and Method

1. From line 3, we learn that the first speaker is an old man. He is looking at the lady through a trellis covered with roses. What do lines 5 and 6 say about beauty and youth?
2. Is there a difference between "a lady young in beauty" and a "beautiful young lady"? Is it possible that she may not be so young

in years but think herself so? Why does she not hear the man (lines 2–4)?

3. Which words and phrases support the contention that the man symbolizes old age or death? What is ironic about line 9 being repeated as line 14?

4. What do you think is the theme of the poem?

5. Ransom uses the sonnet form but in a novel way. What is the purpose of the repetition of line 1 in line 8 and line 9 in line 14?

Composition and Discussion

Discuss Ransom's treatment of death in the three poems you have just studied. What is the theme of each poem? How does his treatment of death differ in each poem?

Claude McKay
[1890–1948]

Jamaica, America, Russia, and Morocco successively inspired Claude McKay's creative instincts. His first important collection of poems, *Songs of Jamaica* (1912), commemorated his love for his native land. The year this book appeared McKay left the island to come to America to study agriculture. He intended to return home to teach scientific farming, but after two years at Kansas State, he abandoned agriculture for literature. He left school and worked at a series of jobs in order to support himself while writing poetry.

In 1921, McKay became an editor for both *The Liberator* and *The Masses*, two radical, socialistic publications. A year later, his most important volume of poetry, *Harlem Shadows*, was published. In the same year, McKay, a Communist sympathizer, visited Russia, where he was received as a hero. However, the repressive actions of the Russian government left him disenchanted with the Communist system. His stay in Russia caused him to become physically ill, and he traveled through Europe and Africa in an attempt to regain his health. He lived for a number of years in southern France and in Morocco before returning to the United States in 1928.

McKay then turned from poetry to prose. His novel, *Home to Harlem*, a national best seller in 1928, was followed by two others, *Banjo* (1929) and *Banana Bottom* (1933), as well as by a collection of stories, *Gingertown* (1932). Many of his later writings were religious essays and pamphlets, inspired by his interest in and conversion to Catholicism. During the last few years of his life, McKay was seriously ill and did little writing. As a result his reputation declined and he died in poverty.

Flame-Heart

So much I have forgotten in ten years,
So much in ten brief years! I have forgot
What time the purple apples come to juice,
And what month brings the shy forget-me-not.

"Flame-Heart" from *Selected Poems of Claude McKay*. Reprinted by permission of Twayne Publishers, Inc.

I have forgot the special, startling season   5
Of the pimento's flowering and fruiting;
What time of year the ground doves brown the fields
And fill the noonday with their curious fluting.
I have forgotten much, but still remember
The poinsettia's red, blood-red, in warm December.   10

I still recall the honey-fever grass,
But cannot recollect the high days when
We rooted them out of the ping-wing path
To stop the mad bees in the rabbit pen.
I often try to think in what sweet month   15
The languid painted ladies used to dapple°
The yellow byroad mazing° from the main,
Sweet with the golden threads of the rose-apple.
I have forgotten—strange—but quite remember
The poinsettia's red, blood-red, in warm December.   20

What weeks, what months, what time of the mild year
We cheated school to have our fling at tops?
What days our wine-thrilled bodies pulsed with joy
Feasting upon blackberries in the copse?°
Oh, some I know! I have embalmed the days,   25
Even the sacred moments when we played,
All innocent of passion, uncorrupt,
At noon and evening in the flame-heart's shade.
We were so happy, happy, I remember,
Beneath the poinsettia's red in warm December.   30

16. dapple: spot, mark with color. 17. mazing: forming an intricate pattern.
24. copse: thicket.

Meaning and Method

1. The poem describes McKay's love for his native Jamaica. What was life on the island like? Give examples of his use of images of sight, smell, and taste to re-create Jamaican life?
2. How do the first two and last two lines of the poem suggest that the poet's life had changed, had become less enjoyable since he left home? What does the poinsettia symbolize?

If We Must Die

If we must die, let it not be like hogs
Hunted and penned in an inglorious spot,
While round us bark the mad and hungry dogs,
Making their mock at our accursed lot.
If we must die, O let us nobly die,   5
So that our precious blood may not be shed
In vain; then even the monsters we defy
Shall be constrained to honor us though dead!
O kinsmen! We must meet the common foe!
Though far outnumbered let us show us brave,   10
And for their thousand blows deal one deathblow!
What though before us lies the open grave?
Like men we'll face the murderous, cowardly pack,
Pressed to the wall, dying, but fighting back!

Meaning and Method

1. "If We Must Die" was written as a reaction against the race riots
   that occurred in America during 1919.

   What is the theme of the poem? Is McKay saying that Negroes
   should turn to violence? that they should defend themselves against
   the oppressors?

2. During the second World War, the Prime Minister of England,
   Winston Churchill, read this sonnet before the House of Commons.
   How was the situation in England during the war similar to that of
   Negroes in America in 1919?

Composition and Discussion

Discuss whether or not violence is ever a permissible method of
effecting social change. Can violence be an affirmative force, or is it
always destructive? Does violence by one side lead to violence by the
other? Is nonviolent civil disobedience a more effective strategy to
bring about desired reforms? Can political action achieve the same results as civil disobedience or violent upheaval?

"If We Must Die" from *Selected Poems of Claude McKay*. Reprinted by permission of
Twayne Publishers, Inc.

America

Although she feeds me bread of bitterness,
And sinks into my throat her tiger's tooth,
Stealing my breath of life, I will confess
I love this cultured hell that tests my youth!
Her vigor flows like tides into my blood,   5
Giving me strength erect against her hate.
Her bigness sweeps my being like a flood.
Yet as a rebel fronts° a king in state,
I stand within her walls with not a shred
Of terror, malice, not a word of jeer.   10
Darkly I gaze into the days ahead,
And see her might and granite wonders there,
Beneath the touch of Time's unerring hand,
Like priceless treasures sinking in the sand.

8. fronts: faces.

Meaning and Method

1. What is McKay's attitude toward America? What characteristics of the country does he like? What negative characteristics are suggested by lines 1 and 2?
2. What will be the effect of "Time's unerring hand" upon America?

Composition

Historians frequently point out that most empires or powerful nations are destroyed by moral decay from within rather than by external conquest. For example, the Roman Empire decayed from within long before it was invaded by the barbarians.

Discuss the theory that if the United States declines as a world power, it will be because of internal, not external causes. Are domestic problems such as racism, poverty, and pollution greater threats to the country than is, say, communism?

"America" from *Selected Poems of Claude McKay*. Reprinted by permission of Twayne Publishers, Inc.

Edna St. Vincent Millay
[1892–1950]

Few modern poets have enjoyed the distinction of receiving both popular and critical acclaim. Edna St. Vincent Millay is one of the few. Her dual success began with her first published poem, "Renascence," and has continued long after her death. The critic Babette Deutsch perhaps best summarized Miss Millay's appeal to readers when she wrote that the poet's "ecstasy over the sensuous pleasures of meadow and seaboard, the romantic irony, the light and lovely melodies that enchanted Miss Millay's contemporaries, have exercised a spell over successive generations of girls and boys."

Miss Millay was born in Rockland, Maine, and grew up there and in nearby Camden. She began writing poetry in her childhood, a practice she continued throughout her years at Barnard and Vassar colleges. Her first collection of verse, *Renascence and Other Poems*, appeared in 1917, the year she was graduated from Vassar.

For the next few years, Miss Millay lived in Greenwich Village, writing poems, short stories, and satiric sketches for magazines. She also wrote several verse dramas and acted with the Provincetown Players. Her writings at this time expressed her rebellion against the stuffy conventionality of contemporary life and her disillusionment with the postwar society.

In 1923, she married Eugen Boissevain and moved to a farm in New York State. In the same year, Miss Millay won the Pulitzer prize for her book *The Harp-Weaver and Other Poems*. In subsequent collections, her poems analyzed loneliness, sorrow, and lost love. The later poems also reflected her growing interest in political and social events both here and in Europe.

Renascence

All I could see from where I stood
Was three long mountains and a wood;
I turned and looked another way,
And saw three islands in a bay.
So with my eyes I traced the line   5
Of the horizon, thin and fine,
Straight around till I was come
Back to where I'd started from;
And all I saw from where I stood
Was three long mountains and a wood.   10

Over these things I could not see;
These were the things that bounded me.
And I could touch them with my hand,
Almost, I thought, from where I stand!
And all at once things seemed so small   15
My breath came short, and scarce at all.
But, sure, the sky is big, I said;
Miles and miles above my head.
So here upon my back I'll lie
And look my fill into the sky.   20
And so I looked, and after all,
The sky was not so very tall.
The sky, I said, must somewhere stop . . .
And—sure enough!—I see the top!
The sky, I thought, is not so grand;   25
I 'most could touch it with my hand!
And, reaching up my hand to try,
I screamed, to feel it touch the sky.

I screamed, and—lo!—Infinity
Came down and settled over me;   30
Forced back my scream into my chest;
Bent back my arm upon my breast;

And, pressing of the Undefined
The definition on my mind,
Held up before my eyes a glass   35
Through which my shrinking sight did pass
Until it seemed I must behold
Immensity made manifold;
Whispered to me a word whose sound
Deafened the air for worlds around,   40
And brought unmuffled to my ears
The gossiping of friendly spheres,
The creaking of the tented sky,
The ticking of Eternity.

I saw and heard, and knew at last   45
The How and Why of all things, past,
And present, and forevermore.
The universe, cleft° to the core,
Lay open to my probing sense
That, sickening, I would fain pluck thence   50
But could not—nay! but needs must suck
At the great wound, and could not pluck
My lips away till I had drawn
All venom out.—Ah, fearful pawn!
For my omniscience° paid I toll   55
In infinite remorse of soul.
All sin was of my sinning, all
Atoning mine, and mine the gall
Of all regret. Mine was the weight
Of every brooded wrong, the hate   60
That stood behind each envious thrust,
Mine every greed, mine every lust.

And all the while for every grief,
Each suffering, I craved relief
With individual desire;   65
Craved all in vain! And felt fierce fire
About a thousand people crawl;
Perished with each—then mourned for all!

48. **cleft:** divided, split. 55. **omniscience:** infinite knowledge.

A man was starving in Capri;
He moved his eyes and looked at me;   70
I felt his gaze, I heard his moan,
And knew his hunger as my own.
I saw at sea a great fog bank
Between two ships that struck and sank;
A thousand screams the heavens smote;   75
And every scream tore through my throat;
No hurt I did not feel, no death
That was not mine; mine each last breath
That, crying, met an answering cry
From the compassion that was I.   80
All suffering mine, and mine its rod;
Mine, pity like the pity of God.

Ah, awful weight! Infinity
Pressed down upon the finite Me!
My anguished spirit, like a bird,   85
Beating against my lips I heard;
Yet lay the weight so close about
There was no room for it without.°
And so beneath the weight lay I
And suffered death, but could not die.   90
Long had I lain thus, craving death,
When quietly the earth beneath
Gave way, and inch by inch, so great
At last had grown the crushing weight,
Into the earth I sank till I   95
Full six feet under ground did lie,
And sank no more—there is no weight
Can follow here, however great.
From off my breast I felt it roll,
And as it went my tortured soul   100
Burst forth and fled in such a gust
That all about me swirled the dust.

Deep in the earth I rested now.
Cool is its hand upon the brow

88. without: outside.

And soft its breast beneath the head   105
Of one who is so gladly dead.
And all at once, and over all,
The pitying rain began to fall.
I lay and heard each pattering hoof
Upon my lowly, thatchèd roof.   110
And seemed to love the sound far more
Than ever I had done before.
For rain it hath a friendly sound
To one who's six feet under ground;
And scarce the friendly voice or face,   115
A grave is such a quiet place.

The rain, I said, is kind to come
And speak to me in my new home.
I would I were alive again
To kiss the fingers of the rain,   120
To drink into my eyes the shine
Of every slanting silver line,
To catch the freshened, fragrant breeze
From drenched and dripping apple trees.
For soon the shower will be done,   125
And then the broad face of the sun
Will laugh above the rain-soaked earth
Until the world with answering mirth
Shakes joyously, and each round drop
Rolls, twinkling, from its grass-blade top.   130
How can I bear it, buried here,
While overhead the sky grows clear
And blue again after the storm?
O, multi-colored, multi-form,
Belovèd beauty over me,   135
That I shall never, never see
Again! Spring silver, autumn gold,
That I shall never more behold!—
Sleeping your myriad magics through,
Close-sepulchered away from you!   140
O God, I cried, give me new birth,
And put me back upon the earth!

Upset each cloud's gigantic gourd
And let the heavy rain, down-poured
In one big torrent, set me free,   145
Washing my grave away from me!

I ceased; and through the breathless hush
That answered me, the far-off rush
Of herald wings came whispering
Like music down the vibrant string   150
Of my ascending prayer, and—crash!
Before the wild wind's whistling lash
The startled storm-clouds reared on high
And plunged in terror down the sky!
And the big rain in one black wave   155
Fell from the sky and struck my grave.

I know not how such things can be;
I only know there came to me
A fragrance such as never clings
To aught save happy living things;   160
A sound as of some joyous elf
Singing sweet songs to please himself,
And, through and over everything,
A sense of glad awakening.
The grass, a-tiptoe at my ear,   165
Whispering to me I could hear;
I felt the rain's cool fingertips
Brushed tenderly across my lips,
Laid gently on my sealèd sight,
And all at once the heavy night   170
Fell from my eyes and I could see!—
A drenched and dripping apple tree,
A last long line of silver rain,
A sky grown clear and blue again.
And as I looked a quickening gust   175
Of wind blew up to me and thrust
Into my face a miracle
Of orchard-breath, and with the smell—

I know not how such things can be!—
I breathed my soul back into me.   180

Ah! Up then from the ground sprang I
And hailed the earth with such a cry
As is not heard save from a man
Who has been dead, and lives again.
About the trees my arms I wound;   185
Like one gone mad I hugged the ground;
I raised my quivering arms on high;
I laughed and laughed into the sky,
Till at my throat a strangling sob
Caught fiercely, and a great heart-throb   190
Sent instant tears into my eyes:
O God, I cried, no dark disguise
Can e'er hereafter hide from me
Thy radiant identity!
Thou canst not move across the grass   195
But my quick eyes will see Thee pass,
Nor speak, however silently,
But my hushed voice will answer Thee.
I know the path that tells Thy way
Through the cool eve of every day;   200
God, I can push the grass apart
And lay my finger on Thy heart!

The world stands out on either side
No wider than the heart is wide;
Above the world is stretched the sky—   205
No higher than the soul is high.
The heart can push the sea and land
Farther away on either hand;
The soul can split the sky in two,
And let the face of God shine through.   210
But East and West will pinch the heart
That cannot keep them pushed apart;
And he whose soul is flat—the sky
Will cave in on him by and by.

Meaning and Method

1. At the beginning of the poem, the speaker is standing, looking around. Is the view limited? unlimited? Does what she sees make her feel happy? sad? dissatisfied? Does she feel confined, or does she feel free?

2. Because the sky seems "big" (line 17) and less confining, she decided to lie on her back and look at it (lines 19 and 20). Why was she disappointed by the sky? Lines 28 and 29 are obviously meant to be interpreted figuratively. What, then, does the sky symbolize?

3. Did the vision of Infinity make the speaker feel freer? happier? neither? What did Infinity reveal to the speaker in lines 29–44? in lines 45–49? Of what problems is the "great wound" (line 52) a symbol, and what happened to the speaker after she had unwillingly but compulsively sucked at the wound?

4. Why did the speaker want to die in line 91? Why did she change her mind when she envisioned herself buried and hearing the "pitying rain" (line 108) begin to fall? What did she miss about life?

5. In lines 145 and 146, the speaker asks God to "set me free/ Washing my grave away from me!" To what natural experiences were her senses awakened in lines 159–80? What evidence is there that she appreciated the world more after her awakening than she did before?

6. Compare and contrast the ideas and mood in the last twelve lines with those in the first twenty-eight lines. Why is the speaker freer at the end? What revelation has she received?

7. The title of the poem, "Renascence," means "rebirth" or "reawakening." Is this rebirth primarily physical or spiritual? both?

8. What words and phrases in lines 29–40 and lines 83–90 give a sense of the heaviness and violence of Infinity? Do you think that the poet wanted to show that a vision of Infinity is too much for a mortal to bear? Explain.

9. What images in lines 119–38 particularly appeal to the senses? Why are these images appropriate, considering the speaker's thoughts and ideas in this section? Why are the images in lines 159–80 more detailed than those in lines 1–28?

10. What words or phrases convey the speaker's suffering in lines 69–82? escape from torment in lines 103–06? ecstasy in lines 181–91? What do the sharp changes of mood show about the character of the speaker?

Composition and Discussion

1. Write a description of a place that makes you feel confined, or a place that makes you feel free. In your description use sensory words to make the reader see, hear, smell, touch, or taste what you are describing.

2. The theme of "Renascence" is that although man must live in an imperfect world, the infinite is within the reach of all, and what one attains depends on what is in one's soul and heart. Discuss whether or not you agree with this philosophy. Give reasons to support your position.

Euclid Alone Has Looked on Beauty Bare

Euclid° alone has looked on Beauty bare.°
Let all who prate of Beauty hold their peace,
And lay them prone upon the earth and cease
To ponder on themselves, the while they stare
At nothing, intricately drawn nowhere   5
In shapes of shifting lineage; let geese
Gabble and hiss, but heroes seek release
From dusty bondage into luminous air.
O blinding hour, O holy, terrible day,
When first the shaft° into his vision shone   10
Of light anatomized! Euclid alone
Has looked on Beauty bare. Fortunate they
Who, though once only and then but far away,
Have heard her massive sandal set on stone.

1. Euclid: A Greek mathematician who lived in the third century B.C. He set forth the basic principles of plane geometry. **bare:** in its purest form. **10. shaft:** ray of light or understanding.

Meaning and Method

1. What type of people do you think might "prate of Beauty" (line 2)? Do you think that these people would ordinarily think of geometry as beautiful? In the speaker's opinion, are these people

"Euclid Alone Has Looked on Beauty Bare" from *Collected Poems* by Edna St. Vincent Millay, copyright 1912, 1923, 1928, 1940, 1951, 1955 by Edna St. Vincent Millay and Norma Millay Ellis. Published by Harper & Row, and reprinted by permission of Norma Millay Ellis.

admirable? selfish? superficial? strongly individual? What are the connotations of *prate?* Would the effect be different if the speaker had said *talk* about beauty?

2. What advice does the speaker give in lines 4–6 to those "who prate of Beauty"? How can they stare "At nothing"? Is she telling them to think in abstract terms?

3. What evidence is there for the interpretation that "light" in line 11 symbolizes insight or a moment of truth or revelation? Consider the connotations of *blinding, holy,* and *terrible* (line 9), which the speaker uses to describe this experience.

4. To whom is the speaker referring when she says, "let geese / Gabble and hiss" (lines 6 and 7)? What is meant by "but heroes seek release / From dusty bondage into luminous air" (lines 7 and 8)?

5. The "her" in line 14 refers to Beauty, which the poet has personified. What is meant by "massive sandal set on stone"? Does it mean form imposing itself on formlessness? Does the poem stress the beauty of mathematics as compared to the beauty of material objects? Is the beauty of abstract forms superior to that of concrete ones? Discuss.

6. Considering the speaker's admiration for geometry, why is the use of the sonnet form appropriate?

I Shall Go Back Again to the Bleak Shore

I shall go back again to the bleak shore
And build a little shanty on the sand,
In such a way that the extremest band
Of brittle seaweed will escape my door
But by a yard or two; and nevermore   5
Shall I return to take you by the hand;
I shall be gone to what I understand,
And happier than I ever was before.
The love that stood a moment in your eyes,
The words that lay a moment on your tongue,   10
Are one with all that in a moment dies,

A little under-said and over-sung.
But I shall find the sullen rocks and skies
Unchanged from what they were when I was young.

Meaning and Method

1. Why does the speaker want to return to "the bleak shore" (line 1) with its "sullen rocks and skies" (line 13)? What does she imply in line 7 about her awareness or knowledge of the "you" in the poem?
2. What is meant by line 12? How does "over-sung" contrast with "sullen" (line 13)?
3. Compare line 14 with lines 9–11. What contrast does the speaker want to make?
4. In what sense could the speaker be talking about a return to a former emotional state rather than a return to a physical place? Is this kind of return possible? Why would such a return be bleak?

Dirge Without Music

I am not resigned to the shutting away of loving hearts in the
    hard ground.
So it is, and so it will be, for so it has been, time out of mind:
Into the darkness they go, the wise and the lovely. Crowned
With lilies and with laurel they go; but I am not resigned.

Lovers and thinkers, into the earth with you.   5
Be one with the dull, the indiscriminate dust.
A fragment of what you felt, of what you knew,
A formula, a phrase remains—but the best is lost.

The answers quick and keen, the honest look, the laughter,
    the love—
They are gone. They are gone to feed the roses. Elegant and
    curled   10

Is the blossom. Fragrant is the blossom. I know. But I do
    not approve.
More precious was the light in your eyes than all the roses
    in the world.

Down, down into the darkness of the grave
Gently they go, the beautiful, the tender, the kind;
Quietly they go, the intelligent, the witty, the brave.   15
I know. But I do not approve. And I am not resigned.

Meaning and Method

1. A *dirge* is a song of mourning. Considering the poet's attitude toward death in this poem, explain why she calls it a "Dirge Without
   Music."
2. Does the speaker think that anything left behind can compensate
   for the loss of a person? What does she consider the essence of a
   living person? Why does she list types of people in lines 3, 5, 14,
   and 15? What does death do to all of them?
3. Why does the poet feel that it is no consolation that the bodies
   of the dead "feed the roses"—that is, create or enhance beauty in
   nature?
4. Would you say that the mood of the poem is one of violent protest?
   controlled protest? something else?
5. Are the rhyme scheme and the rhythm the same throughout the
   poem, or do they change?

Composition

1. The poet Louise Bogan wrote that Miss Millay at times "fell
victim to sentimentality and the dangers of self-pity and self-regard."
In a composition, analyze the poems included in this book to see
whether or not you agree with Miss Bogan's contention.

2. Analyze Miss Millay's images and choice of words. Are her images
clear and well-defined? Are her words vague or concrete? Compare and
contrast her images with those of one of the Imagist poets, such as
Amy Lowell.

Archibald MacLeish

In 1923, Archibald MacLeish suddenly abandoned his promising law career to sail to France with his wife and children in order to become a writer. For years he had been preparing himself for both careers: two collections of his poems were published while he was studying law at Harvard. It was perhaps inevitable that one day he would be forced to choose which career he most desired.

During his five years in Europe, MacLeish wrote four books of verse, which were notable for their lyric power and for an increasing mastery of poetic technique. His early collections show the influence of Ezra Pound (see page 26) and T. S. Eliot, but by the time he returned to the United States, MacLeish had developed an individual style. His stylistic independence is clearly seen in his Pulitzer prize winning verse narrative, *Conquistador* (1932). The poem, inspired by a trip to Mexico in 1929 during which he traveled the path originally traced by the explorer Cortés, narrates a fictional account of the Spanish conquest of the Aztecs.

In the 1930's, MacLeish worked on the editorial staff of *Fortune* Magazine. His articles for *Fortune* and the poems he wrote during this period reflect his newly developed social conscience and his knowledge of living conditions in the United States. As the second World War approached, his poetry and his verse radio plays became variations on a single political theme: the American people must recognize and resist the dangers of Fascism.

MacLeish was appointed to his first federal government post in 1939 when President Franklin D. Roosevelt named him Librarian of Congress. Although the position itself was scholarly rather than political, MacLeish soon became one of the President's trusted advisers. In 1941, while the war devastated Europe, Roosevelt appointed MacLeish (who remained Librarian of Congress) to the post of director of the Office of Facts and Figures, and in 1942 he became Assistant Director of the Office of War Information. From 1944 through 1945, he was an Assistant Secretary of State.

His career of public service and influence continued through 1946, when he became the chairman of the American delegation to UNESCO in Paris. Public service, however, did not provide him sufficient time to write. In 1949 he left it finally to accept an appointment as Boylston Professor of Rhetoric and Oratory at Harvard University, a less time-consuming position.

Throughout his literary career, MacLeish has won various honors. Among them were the two Pulitzer prizes he received in the 1950's—in poetry for his *Collected Poems: 1917–1952* (1952) and in drama for his verse play *J. B.* (1958), a modernized version of the biblical story of Job.

Ars Poetica *

A poem should be palpable° and mute
As a globed fruit,

Dumb
As old medallions to the thumb,

Silent as the sleeve-worn stone   5
Of casement ledges where the moss has grown—

A poem should be wordless
As the flight of birds.

*

A poem should be motionless in time
As the moon climbs,   10

Leaving, as the moon releases
Twig by twig the night-entangled trees,

Leaving, as the moon behind the winter leaves,
Memory by memory the mind—

* **Ars Poetica:** *Latin,* "The Art of Poetry," from the epistle on poetry by the Roman poet Horace (65–8 B.C.). **1. palpable:** capable of being touched or felt.

A poem should be motionless in time   15
As the moon climbs.

*

A poem should be equal to:
Not true.

For all the history of grief
An empty doorway and a maple leaf.   20

For love
The leaning grasses and two lights above the sea—

A poem should not mean
But be.

Meaning and Method

1. A poem is "palpable" (line 1) if it contains concrete images. What images in lines 1–8 satisfy this definition? What connotations do the adjectives *globed* (line 2), *old* (line 4), and *sleeve-worn* (line 5) contribute to the images of which they are a part?

2. Besides being palpable, a poem should be "mute," "dumb," "silent," and "wordless." How can a poem—a collection of words—be wordless or dumb? How could MacLeish's paradoxical definitions be a comment on the connotative nature of the words that make up a poem?

3. A poem is like the moon because it seems to remain unchanged while creating various effects over a span of time. How does the moon "release" the "night-entangled trees" (line 12)? How might a poem "release" its readers in a similar way? In what way does a poem leave like "the moon behind the winter leaves, / Memory by memory the mind" (lines 13 and 14)?

4. A poem should be imaginative and symbolic rather than factual or literal. According to this, should a poem be experienced rather than analyzed? Should a poem re-create reality, or should it make a statement about reality? Does this definition of a poem apply to all poetry—narrative and dramatic poetry, for example? Or does it apply to lyric poems, especially Imagist. Give reasons for your answers.

The End of the World

Quite unexpectedly as Vasserot
The armless ambidextrian° was lighting
A match between his great and second toe
And Ralph the lion was engaged in biting
The neck of Madame Sossman while the drum   5
Pointed, and Teeny was about to cough
In waltz-time swinging Jocko by the thumb—
Quite unexpectedly the top blew off:

And there, there overhead, there, there, hung over
Those thousands of white faces, those dazed eyes,   10
There in the starless dark the poise, the hover,
There with vast wings across the canceled skies,
There in the sudden blackness the black pall
Of nothing, nothing, nothing—nothing at all.

2. **ambidextrian:** one who is able to use both hands equally well.

Meaning and Method

1. What type of performance is described in lines 1–8? Assuming that the performance is symbolic of the world we live in, explain the poet's attitude toward present-day civilization.
2. How does the poet describe the spectators? Are the spectators admirable? contemptible? What does the poet think that the end of the world will reveal?
3. What words or phrases in the sestet of this sonnet give the impression that something is about to happen? What words shatter this illusion?
4. Is the tone of this poem satiric? ironic? both? something else?

"The End of the World" from *Collected Poems: 1917–1952* by Archibald MacLeish, copyright 1952 by Archibald MacLeish. Reprinted by permission of the publisher, Houghton Mifflin Company.

E. E. Cummings
[1894–1962]

"So far as I am concerned, poetry and every art was and is and forever will be strictly and distinctly a question of individuality," said Edward Estlin Cummings in one of a series of "nonlectures" given at Harvard in 1952. "Individuality" accurately summarizes Cummings's own philosophy of life. In his poems he praises the immense value of a single, vital, loving human being and satirizes the people and the products of a "machinemade" civilization. His literary style mirrors his offbeat approach to life: words are often curiously divided; capital letters spring up in the middle of words, and lower-case letters begin names or sentences; punctuation is absent or is used as if it joined words together rather than separated them.

Cummings was born and grew up in Cambridge, Massachusetts, where his father was a well-known minister and teacher. (The poem "my father moved through dooms of love" is a tribute to his father.) Cummings said that as a child he learned to fear all "collectivities," that is, all groups, because they destroy one's individuality.

In 1917, a year after he earned his M.A. from Harvard, he enlisted in a volunteer ambulance corps and went to France. Because of a censor's mistake, he was imprisoned in a French camp for writing treasonable letters. His detention for three months provided the material for his popular war novel, *The Enormous Room* (1922). When America entered the war, he enlisted in the U.S. Army but was stationed in this country. After the war, Cummings returned to France to study painting and to write. Eventually, he settled in New York.

His first book of poetry, *Tulips and Chimneys* (1923), received mixed reactions. The strange typography startled and confused some readers and excited others. Cummings's lyric talent was generally recognized, but the controversy over his style often prevented proper attention from being paid to the poems themselves.

Eventually, familiarity with Cummings's poems brought an understanding that his seemingly eccentric typography was based on design rather than whim. Sensitive readers saw that his innova-

147

tions not only made the eye respond more fully than it did to conventional poetry, but they guided the ear as well by indicating the timing, accentuation, and even the pitch of the poems. Nevertheless, his technique has remained more or less controversial. The critic Allen Tate complained that "he replaces the old poetic conventions with equally limited conventions of his own." Others feel that by involving the reader in the poem Cummings enhances the lyric power of his poetry.

ecco the ugliest sub

```
e
cco° the uglies
t

s
ub                                              5
sub

urba
n skyline on earth between whose d
owdy

hou                                            10
se
s

l
ooms an eggyellow smear of wintry sunse
t                                              15
```

1–2. ecco: *Italian,* here is; originally from the Latin *ecce,* behold.

Meaning and Method

1. The prefix *sub* generally means "under," "beneath," or "below." Why do you think the poet prefixed the word "suburban" with "sub"? (If the words had not been divided, the first eight lines

would be: Ecco the ugliest subsuburban . . . .) What is the effect
of the repetition of the /u/ sounds?

2. The poet's purpose is to paint a scene. What is the effect of using
"eggyellow smear" to describe the sunset? What comment is the
poet making about this suburb and its effect on nature?

3. What is the effect of the typographical arrangement? Does it add
to or distract from the effectiveness of the poem?

Composition and Discussion

1. Cummings criticized many aspects of modern life. For example,
in his book *EIMI* (Greek for "I am"), Cummings wrote that "The
'modern man' equals a defenseless literate bombarded with slogans
mottoes pictures and whatever else will tend to unmake him; i.e., make
him need something unnecessary." What "slogans mottoes pictures"
was Cummings referring to? Do they make man "need something unnecessary"? Is man defenseless against these things? Do these things
"unmake" him?

In a discussion, explain why you think Cummings's statement is a
fair or an unfair analysis of "modern man."

2. Write a thoughtful sentence and arrange it typographically. The
sentence can summarize your opinion of modern art, textbooks, a river,
or a topic of your own choice. It should contain an image that captures
your emotional response to your subject.

my father moved through dooms of love

> my father moved through dooms of love
> through sames of am through haves of give,
> singing each morning out of each night
> my father moved through depths of height
>
> this motionless forgetful where   5
> turned at his glance to shining here;
> that if (so timid air is firm)
> under his eyes would stir and squirm

newly as from unburied which
floats the first who,his april touch   10
drove sleeping selves to swarm their fates
woke dreamers to their ghostly roots

and should some why completely weep
my father's fingers brought her sleep:
vainly no smallest voice might cry   15
for he could feel the mountains grow.

Lifting the valleys of the sea
my father moved through griefs of joy;
praising a forehead called the moon
singing desire into begin   20

joy was his song and joy so pure
a heart of star by him could steer
and pure so now and now so yes
the wrists of twilight would rejoice

keen as midsummer's keen beyond   25
conceiving mind of sun will stand,
so strictly(over utmost him
so hugely)stood my father's dream

his flesh was flesh his blood was blood:
no hungry man but wished him food;   30
no cripple wouldn't creep one mile
uphill to only see him smile.

Scorning the pomp of must and shall
my father moved through dooms of feel;
his anger was as right as rain   35
his pity was as green as grain

septembering arms of year extend
less humbly wealth to foe and friend
than he to foolish and to wise
offered immeasurable is   40

proudly and(by octobering flame
beckoned)as earth will downward climb,
so naked for immortal work
his shoulders marched against the dark

his sorrow was as true as bread: 45
no liar looked him in the head;
if every friend became his foe
he'd laugh and build a world with snow.

My father moved through theys of we,
singing each new leaf out of each tree   50
(and every child was sure that spring
danced when she heard my father sing)

then let men kill which cannot share,
let blood and flesh be mud and mire,
scheming imagine,passion willed,   55
freedom a drug that's bought and sold

giving to steal and cruel kind,
a heart to fear,to doubt a mind
to differ a disease of same,
conform the pinnacle of am   60

though dull were all we taste as bright,
bitter all utterly things sweet,
maggoty° minus and dumb death
all we inherit,all bequeath

and nothing quite so least as truth   65
—i say though hate were why men breathe—
because my father lived his soul
love is the whole and more than all

63. maggoty: infested with maggots, which feed on decaying and dead matter.

Meaning and Method

1. An *elegy* is a poem in praise of a dead person. What do the following lines or groups of lines tell you about the poet's father?
   (a) singing each morning out of each night
       my father moved through depths of height (lines 3 and 4)
   (b)   his april touch
       drove sleeping selves to swarm their fates
       woke dreamers to their ghostly roots (lines 10–12).
   (c) joy was his song and joy so pure
       a heart of star by him could steer (lines 21 and 22).
   (d) his anger was as right as rain
       his pity was as green as grain (lines 35 and 36).
   (e) My father moved through theys of we (line 49).
2. What was the reaction of other people to the poet's father?
3. In what ways is the world as described in lines 53–66 unlike the world of the poet's father? If the word "conform" (line 60) is read as an infinitive, what do you think the poet means by this line?
4. What attitudes and actions of the poet's father show that the last line states the theme of the poem?
5. Cummings frequently used a word as a part of speech other than that which it usually is. For example, the words "sames," "am," "haves," and "give" (line 2) are used as nouns, as are "where" in "forgetful where" (line 5) and "here" in "shining here" (line 6). One result of this is that words seem to become living things in this poem. For example, "if" squirms under the poet's father's eyes in lines 7 and 8; "why" weeps in line 13. These words seem to be things because they are symbols of attitudes and people. What or whom do "if" and "why" symbolize in the context of the poem? What is referred to by "the pomp of must and shall" in line 33? What other words or phrases in this poem seem to symbolize people or attitudes?
6. The life cycle of the poet's father is reflected in the references to the seasons of the year, as in "april" (line 10) and "midsummer" (line 25). What are the other references to the seasons? What characteristics or qualities of the poet's father are reflected by each season?
7. The word "doom" originally meant a statute, an ordinance, a judgment, a sentence. How, then, would you interpret the title and the first line? In your answer, discuss the meaning of lines 33 and 34 and 53–68.

what if a much of a which of a wind

what if a much of a which of a wind
gives the truth to summer's lie;
bloodies with dizzying leaves the sun
and yanks immortal stars awry?
Blow king to beggar and queen to seem   5
(blow friend to fiend:blow space to time)
—when skies are hanged and oceans drowned,
the single secret will still be man

what if a keen of a lean wind flays
screaming hills with sleet and snow: 10
strangles valleys by ropes of thing
and stifles forests in white ago?
Blow hope to terror;blow seeing to blind
(blow pity to envy and soul to mind)
—whose hearts are mountains,roots are trees,   15
it's they shall cry hello to the spring

what if a dawn of a doom of a dream
bites this universe in two,
peels forever out of his grave
and sprinkles nowhere with me and you?   20
Blow soon to never and never to twice
(blow life to isn't:blow death to was)
—all nothing's only our hugest home;
the most who die,the more we live

Meaning and Method

1. Each stanza of this poem consists of a four-line question and a
   four-line answer. In general the questions ask, What if the world
   were destroyed? What kind of catastrophe is the poet referring to
   in each of these stanzas? How does the tone of the answers differ
   from that of the questions? For example, is one fearful whereas the
   other is joyful?

2. What do you think is meant by the following lines or phrases in the context of the poem?
   (a) gives the truth to summer's lie (line 2).
   (b) Blow king to beggar (line 5).
   (c) stifles forests in white ago (line 12).
   (d) —whose hearts are mountains,roots are trees (line 15).
   (e) —all nothing's only our hugest home (line 23).
3. In your opinion, what is the theme of the poem? What similarity regarding theme is found in the last couplet of each stanza? How would you explain the paradoxical statement "the most who die, the more we live" (line 24)?
4. Cummings uses sound effects and specific verbs to give the impression of wind and its destructive effects. What words in the first stanza emphasize the /w/ and /i/ sounds in the word "wind"? What words in the second stanza use the /s/ sound to convey the constant and rough movement of the wind? What specific verbs are used in each of the three stanzas to convey precisely the destructive actions of the wind or of the more abstract "doom of a dream" (line 17)?

somewhere i have never traveled

somewhere i have never traveled,gladly beyond
any experience,your eyes have their silence:
in your most frail gesture are things which enclose me,
or which i cannot touch because they are too near

your slightest look easily will unclose me   5
though i have closed myself as fingers,
you open always petal by petal myself as Spring opens
(touching skilfully,mysteriously)her first rose

or if your wish be to close me,i and
my life will shut very beautifully,suddenly,   10
as when the heart of this flower imagines
the snow carefully everywhere descending;

nothing which we are to perceive in this world equals
the power of your intense fragility:whose texture
compels me with the colour of its countries,   15
rendering° death and forever with each breathing

(i do not know what it is about you that closes
and opens;only something in me understands
the voice of your eyes is deeper than all roses)
nobody,not even the rain,has such small hands   20

16. **rendering:** giving, as in a judgment or because it is due to the other party.

Meaning and Method

1. The speaker describes two contrasting effects his love has on him. What words in lines 3 and 5 and in lines 17 and 18 summarize these contrasting effects? From the speaker's point of view, are both of these effects good?

   How does the speaker relate these effects to the world of nature? In your answer, explain the metaphors used in lines 7 and 12.
2. The words *power* (line 14), *compels* (line 15), and *rendering* (line 16) connote an exceptionally strong force. Where else in the poem do you get the impression of the beloved's strong influence over the speaker?
3. Assume that the punctuation at the end of the third stanza is intended to indicate the beloved's coldness—the closing of the flower in the snow. What, then, does the lack of punctuation at the end of the other stanzas suggest?

anyone lived in a pretty how town

anyone lived in a pretty how town
(with up so floating many bells down)
spring summer autumn winter
he sang his didn't he danced his did.

Women and men(both little and small)   5
cared for anyone not at all

they sowed their isn't they reaped their same
sun moon stars rain

children guessed(but only a few
and down they forgot as up they grew   10
autumn winter spring summer)
that noone loved him more by more

when by now and tree by leaf
she laughed his joy she cried his grief
bird by snow and stir by still   15
anyone's any was all to her

someones married their everyones
laughed their cryings and did their dance
(sleep wake hope and then)they
said their nevers they slept their dream   20

stars rain sun moon
(and only the snow can begin to explain
how children are apt to forget to remember
with up so floating many bells down)

one day anyone died i guess   25
(and noone stooped to kiss his face)
busy folk buried them side by side
little by little and was by was

all by all and deep by deep
and more by more they dream their sleep   30
noone and anyone earth by april
wish by spirit and if by yes.

Women and men(both dong and ding)
summer autumn winter spring
reaped their sowing and went their came   35
sun moon stars rain

Meaning and Method

1. "Anyone" (line 1) and "noone" (line 12) are used as proper names. What are the connotations of these names? Do the names suggest that these two people are important? ordinary? How did "anyone" approach life? with gloom? with joy? How was "anyone's" approach to life different from that of the "women and men" described in the second stanza? Do the words "little and small" refer only to the physical size of these people? What is the attitude of these women and men toward "anyone"? Are they selfish? loving?

2. "Didn't" and "did" (line 4) and "isn't" and "same" (line 7) are used as nouns. How do the verbs in these lines emphasize the difference between the lives of "anyone" and the lives of the "women and men"?

3. "Anyone" was loved by "noone." Did they have a warm, loving relationship? a cold, formal one?

4. What are the connotations of *someones* and *everyones* (line 17)? Do these names suggest that the people are important? ordinary? Why are these names plural whereas "anyone" and "noone" are singular?

5. How do lines 25–32 suggest that for "anyone" and "noone" death is not a separation but a further joining together? Why is the phrase "they dream their sleep" in the present tense? The phrase "they slept their dream" is used to describe the life of the "someones" and "everyones" (line 20). Why is it in the past tense? What does it suggest about their life?

6. The poet presents a contrast between children and adults in the poem. What did some children once know or guess about anyone and noone that the women and men did not know? Does the fact that they forgot *as up they grew* (line 10) indicate that as adults they lost touch with natural emotion? In your answer, comment on the poet's treatment of ordinary adults, and try to explain why there is no mention of the children in the last stanza (they had previously been mentioned in the third and sixth stanzas).

7. Cummings uses two refrains in the poem: the first—that of the seasons of the year—begins in line 3; the second—that of the weather—begins in line 8. Why does Cummings use these refrains throughout the poem?

8. The beginning of this poem is reminiscent of the beginnings of fairy stories ("Once upon a time, there lived in a faraway kingdom . . .") This fantasy effect is further enhanced by the arrange-

ment of words and the rhythm, which makes the bells seem dreamlike and the life of the town move with an unearthly lightness and leisurely pace. Read the poem aloud, trying to convey this "floating" effect by means of your pace and emphasis.

9. This poem has been interpreted not only as a love story but also as a tale of lost childhood. In this interpretation, anyone and noone grow into the someones and everyones; that is, children become adults. Analyze the poem according to this interpretation. Are the women and men the adults in the world of children? What is the death referred to in lines 25–32? Can the poem be interpreted both as a love story and as a fable of lost childhood?

Composition

Write a critical evaluation of Cummings as a poet. Consider the form and content of his poems. For example, what is gained and/or what is lost by Cummings's use of verbs as nouns, by his unusual punctuation, by his arrangement of lines? Are his subjects or topics unusual? Are his themes different from those of more "standard" poets?

Stephen Vincent Benét
[1898–1943]

America provided both the subjects and inspiration for most of the poems and stories of Stephen Vincent Benét. A reader of his works often gets the feeling that everything about America fascinated him: its folklore and history, its landscape and place names, and even the problems of living in its industrial cities. His work also reflects an attempt to write in the folk tradition of American literature: he used vernacular American speech, idioms, and rhythms, and often imitated American folk ballads and tall tales. As he says in "American Names,"

> I have fallen in love with American names,
> The sharp names that never get fat,
> The snakeskin-titles of mining-claims,
> The plumed war-bonnet of Medicine Hat,
> Tucson and Deadwood and Lost Mule Flat.*

Benét was born in Bethlehem, Pennsylvania, the son of an Army officer. The family enjoyed and had a talent for literature; Stephen's brother, William Rose, and his sister, Laura, also became writers. Stephen's ability was recognized quite early. By the time he was seventeen, he had won prizes for his early works and had written a book of dramatic monologues, *Five Men and Pompey* (1915). In the same year as his book appeared, he entered Yale University, where he wrote for and edited the *Yale Literary Magazine*. He remained at Yale in order to do graduate work, submitting a volume of poetry, *Heavens and Earth* (1920), as his master's thesis.

Although his early poetry imitated the works of traditional English poets, Benét soon turned to native historical themes. By 1928, he had produced a Civil War epic, *John Brown's Body*. This long narrative was immediately successful and is now regarded as a minor America classic. Benét also wrote short stories, many of which are based on American folklore. His most famous story, "The

Devil and Daniel Webster," unites American history with its folk legends.

At the time of his death, 1943, he was working on another verse epic, *Western Star,* in which he tried to recreate the impulses that caused people to go westward from Europe to America, and then to America's west coast. The first part of this apparently multivolumed work was published posthumously and was awarded the Pulitzer prize.

In addition to writing poetry and short stories, Benét wrote novels and radio scripts—the latter undertaken in the 1930's "to help mobilize the emotions of this country for war." His death in the middle of the second World War was partly the result of over-work caused by his writing radio and literary propaganda for the United States.

Both before and after his death, critics have been hard put to judge Benét's work. One called him "a poet of almost the first rank." Others dismissed him completely as "merely a popular poet." Despite the critics, his work continues to be read and to excite readers by its vigor.

Jake Diefer Leaves
His Native Pennsylvania
from JOHN BROWN'S BODY

Jake Diefer, the barrel-chested Pennsylvanian,
Hand like a ham and arms that could wrestle a bull,
A roast of a man, all solid meat and good fat,
A slow-thought-chewing Clydesdale horse of a man,
Roused out of his wife's arms. The dawn outside   5
Was ruddy as his big cheeks. He yawned and stretched
Gigantically, hawking° and clearing his throat.

7. **hawking:** coughing up phlegm.

His wife, hair tousled around her like tousled corn,
Stared at him with sleep-blind eyes.
                              "Jake, it ain't come morning,
Already yet?"
                      He nodded and started to dress.   10
She burrowed deeper into the bed for a minute
And then threw off the covers.
                              They didn't say much
Then, or at breakfast. Eating was something serious.
But he looked around the big kitchen once or twice
In a puzzled way, as if trying hard to remember it.   15
She, too, when she was busy with the first batch
Of pancakes, burned one or two, because she was staring
At the SALT on the salt box, for no particular reason.
The boy ate with them and didn't say a word,
Being too sleepy.
                      Afterward, when the team   20
Was hitched up and waiting, with the boy on the seat,
Holding the reins till Jake was ready to take them,
Jake didn't take them at once.
                              The sun was up now,
The spilt-milk-mist of first morning lay on the farm,
Jake looked at it all with those same mildly puzzled eyes,   25
The red barn, the fat rich fields just done with the winter,
Just beginning the work of another year.
The boy would have to do the rest of the planting.
He blew on his hands and stared at his wife dumbly.
He cleared his throat.   "Well, good-by, Minnie," he said,   30
"Don't you hire any feller for harvest without you write me,
And if any more of those lightning rodders come around,
We don't want no more dum lightning rods."
                              He tried
To think if there was anything else, but there wasn't.
She suddenly threw her big, red arms around his neck,   35
He kissed her with clumsy force.
                      Then he got on the wagon
And clucked to the horses as she started to cry.

Meaning and Method

1. How does Benét's description of commonplace details increase the poignancy of Diefer's departure?
2. Give examples of figurative language that is used to characterize Diefer. What do Diefer's comments (lines 30–33) reveal about his character?

The Shrine of Gettysburg

from JOHN BROWN'S BODY

You took a carriage to that battlefield.
Now, I suppose, you take a motor bus,
But then, it was a carriage—and you ate
Fried chicken out of wrappings of waxed paper,
While the slow guide buzzed on about the war   5
And the enormous, curdled summer clouds
Piled up like giant cream puffs in the blue.
The carriage smelled of axle grease and leather
And the old horse nodded a sleepy head
Adorned with a straw hat. His ears stuck through it.   10
It was the middle of hay fever summer
And it was hot. And you could stand and look
All the way down from Cemetery Ridge,
Much as it was, except for monuments
And startling groups of monumental men   15
Bursting in bronze and marble from the ground,
And all the curious names upon the gravestones. . . .
So peaceable it was, so calm and hot,
So tidy and great-skied.
                    No men had fought
There but enormous, monumental men   20
Who bled neat streams of uncorrupting bronze,
Even at the Round Tops, even by Pickett's boulder,

"The Shrine of Gettysburg" from *John Brown's Body* from *Selected Works of Stephen Vincent Benét*, published by Holt, Rinehart and Winston, Inc. Copyright, 1927, 1928, by Stephen Vincent Benét; copyright renewed 1955 by Rosemary Carr Benét. Reprinted by permission of Brandt & Brandt.

Where the bronze, open book could still be read
By visitors and sparrows and the wind:
And the wind came, the wind moved in the grass,   25
Saying . . . while the long light . . . and all so calm . . .
       "Pickett came
      And the South came
      And the end came,
      And the grass comes,   30
      And the wind blows
      On the bronze book
      On the bronze men
      On the grown grass,
      And the wind says   35
      'Long ago
      Long
      Ago.' "
Then it was time to buy a paperweight
With flags upon it in decalcomania°   40
And hope you wouldn't break it, driving home.

40. decalcomania (di·kal′kə·mä′nē·ə) : a design or print that is transferred from specially prepared paper to porcelain, glass, or other material.

Meaning and Method

1. What does the word "monumental" (lines 15 and 20) mean? What do lines 19–21 mean? Is Benét praising the men who fought at Gettysburg? Or is he saying that people idealize the past and the war and in doing so forget that real men died in the battle?
2. Explain why the tone of the last three lines is ironic. What do these lines imply about the people who are visiting the shrine at Gettysburg? How are these implications supported by the first seven lines of the selection?

Composition

Find out how the town, city, street, area, county, or state in which you live got its name. Write a short composition explaining the origins of the name.

Hart Crane

[1899–1932]

The poems of Hart Crane are both extremely original and extremely obscure. In part, Crane's poems are difficult because of his belief that the logic of suggestion was "much more direct and creative" than the logic of reason. As a result, his poems are unified by the principle that one idea suggests another. The reader, in order to understand the meaning of the work, must make a series of mental leaps with the poet. Crane tried to express complex ideas and connotations of words in brief metaphors, set in lines in which the syntax is often twisted. But in spite of the difficulties created by his style, Crane's poems are noteworthy for their extraordinary lyric power.

Harold Hart Crane was born in Garretsville, Ohio, and grew up in Dayton and Cleveland. His parents were separated shortly after settling in Cleveland. His father was determined to make his only son into a businessman, to "drive the poetry nonsense" away. The attempt, which continued periodically until Crane was twenty-one, further alienated him from his father. The turmoil of early life left permanent scars on his personality; he was possessed by a sense of guilt and a tendency toward self-destruction.

After Crane's final break with his father in 1920, he settled in New York, determined to be a poet. His first volume of poems, *White Buildings* (1926), marked him as a major new talent. His poetry reveals many of the conflicts that dominated his life, as well as his attempts to overcome these conflicts and give unity to his existence. His shorter lyrics portray a man's quest for enduring love and absolute beauty. In his epic poem, *The Bridge* (1930), he tried to create an almost mystical interpretation of the past, present, and future of America. The bridge—the Brooklyn Bridge—symbolized modern industrial creativity. He intended the poem to be "an epic of modern consciousness" and a glorification of the United States and modern progress. Although the poem contains many sections of lyric power, it is only partly successful because, in Crane's words, it "rises out of the past that so overwhelms the present with its worth and vision that I'm at a loss to explain my delusion that there exist any real links between that past and a future worthy of it."

Despite his attempts to resolve the conflicts that tormented him, his private life revealed the self-destructive tendencies that in the end would destroy him. He succumbed more and more to sensual excesses, including alcoholism. Eventually, these excesses conquered him. At the age of thirty-two, while returning to the United States from Mexico, where he had spent a year on a Guggenheim Foundation Fellowship, Crane jumped from the ship into the Gulf of Mexico and drowned.

Van Winkle

from THE BRIDGE

[Streets spread past store and factory—sped by sunlight and her smile . . .]

Macadam,° gun-gray as the tunny's° belt,
Leaps from Far Rockaway° to Golden Gate:
Listen! The miles a hurdy-gurdy° grinds—
Down gold arpeggios° mile on mile unwinds.   5

Times earlier, when you hurried off to school,
—It is the same hour though a later day—
You walked with Pizarro in a copybook,
And Cortés rode up, reining tautly in—
Firmly as the coffee grips the taste—and away!   10

There was Priscilla's° cheek close in the wind,
And Captain Smith, all beard and certainty,

2. **Macadam** (mə·kad′əm): small stones spread to make a pavement or road, often with tar or asphalt as a binder. **tunny:** tuna. 3. **Far Rockaway:** a part of New York City located on the south shore of Long Island. 4. **hurdy-gurdy:** a mechanized instrument run by turning a handle, such as that played by an organ grinder. 5. **arpeggios** (är·pej′ē·ōz): the notes of a chord of music played rapidly in succession rather than simultaneously. 11. **Priscilla:** Priscilla Mullins, courted by John Alden for Miles Standish in Longfellow's *The Courtship of Miles Standish*.

And Rip Van Winkle, bowing by the way—
"Is this Sleepy Hollow, friend—?" And he—

[Like memory, she is time's truant, shall take you by the
    hand . . .]   15

And Rip forgot the office hours,
                and he forgot the pay;
Van Winkle sweeps a tenement
              way down on Avenue A—

The grind-organ says . . . Remember, remember   20
The cinder pile at the end of the backyard
Where we stoned the family of young
Garter snakes under . . . And the monoplanes
We launched—with paper wings and twisted
Rubber bands . . . Recall—recall   25
                       the rapid tongues
That flittered from under the ash heap day
After day whenever your stick discovered
Some sunning inch of unsuspecting fiber—
It flashed back at your thrust, as clean as fire.   30

And Rip was slowly made aware
      that he, Van Winkle, was not here
nor there. He woke and swore he'd seen Broadway
    a Catskill° daisy chain in May—

So memory, that strikes a rhyme out of a box   35
Or splits a random smell of flowers through glass—
Is it the whip stripped from the lilac tree
One day in spring my father took me,
Or is it the Sabbatical, unconscious smile
My mother almost brought me once from church   40
And once only, as I recall—?

34. Catskill: the mountain range in New York State where Rip Van Winkle
lived.

It flickered through the snow screen, blindly
It forsook her at the doorway, it was gone
Before I had left the window. It
Did not return with the kiss in the hall.   45

Macadam, gun-gray as the tunny's belt,
Leaps from Far Rockaway to Golden Gate, . . .
Keep hold of that nickel for car-change, Rip—
Have you got your *Times*—?
And hurry along, Van Winkle—it's getting late!   50

Meaning and Method

1. What words or phrases in the first five lines give the impression of
   the speed and activity at which the streets advance—that is, at
   which America has been built and continues to grow? Why are the
   arpeggios "gold"?
2. The speaker is apparently walking through the streets of Brooklyn
   on his way to work in the morning (the "bridge" is the Brooklyn
   Bridge). The time of day makes him think of the days when he
   went to school, where he learned about the early history of the
   New World, and of Rip Van Winkle, who, in Washington Irving's
   story, fell asleep for twenty years and woke to find a completely
   different world (see lines 6–14).
       Were these characters vivid to the schoolboy, or were they irrele-
   vant and dull to him?
3. Why is line 36 ironic? What attitude of his father's does the
   speaker remember? What does the change in his mother's smile,
   described in lines 39–45, show about her attitude toward the boy?
4. Why, in your opinion, does the poet entitle the poem "Van
   Winkle"? Why does Van Winkle not fit into modern society?
5. Crane wrote that the central theme of *The Bridge* is to show "the
   continuous and living evidence of the past in the inmost vital substance of the present." How does "Van Winkle" illustrate this
   theme? Why is memory "time's truant"?

Language: Words from Proper Names

Some words in English have been derived from proper names. For
example, the word *macadam* (line 2) comes from the name of a Scottish
engineer, John L. McAdam (1756–1836).

Look up the origin and the meaning of the following words:

1. bobby	**4.** derrick	**7.** lynch law	**10.** silhouette
2. boycott	**5.** guy	**8.** martinet	**11.** timothy
3. davenport	**6.** hansom	**9.** shrapnel	**12.** volt

Royal Palm

Green rustlings, more than regal charities
Drift coolly from the tower of whispered light.
Amid the noontide's blazed asperities°
I watched the sun's most gracious anchorite°

Climb up as by communings, year on year   5
Uneaten of the earth or aught earth holds,
And the gray trunk, that's elephantine, rear
Its frondings° sighing in aetherial° folds.

Forever fruitless, and beyond that yield
Of sweat the jungle presses with hot love   10
And tendril till our deathward breath is sealed—
It grazes the horizons, launched above

Mortality—ascending emerald-bright,
A fountain at salute, a crown in view—
Unshackled, casual of its azured height   15
As though it soared suchwise through heaven too.

3. asperities (as·per′ə·tēz): harshness. **4. anchorite:** hermit; a person who has withdrawn from the world, usually for religious reasons. **8. frondings:** A frond is a large leaf of tropical plants. **aetherial:** also spelled ethereal, light or airy.

Meaning and Method

1. The speaker has presented a picture of the palm tree as being unaffected by its surroundings. What words or phrases indicate that it is untouched by the harsh heat and light of a tropical noon?
2. What does the jungle symbolize in the poem? What does the palm tree symbolize? Which does the speaker admire more?

Langston Hughes
[1902–1967]

In *The New Negro* (1925), the scholar Alain Locke hailed the coming of age of Negro authors. Locke was referring to a group of young writers, such as Langston Hughes, Claude McKay, Jean Toomer, and others, who made up what today is called the Negro, or Harlem, Renaissance. Through the poetry of Claude McKay and Countee Cullen, through the folk stories of Zora Neale Hurston, through the fiction of Eric Walrond and Jean Toomer, the vitality and the diversity of life within the black experience were described to the world. The authors who made up the movement wrote in various forms and in widely different styles; the bond that held them together was their intention "to express our individual dark-skinned voices without fear or shame." The man who wrote those words, Langston Hughes, more than anyone else encompassed the broad range of interests that made up the movement.

Hughes was born in Joplin, Missouri, and was educated in various places in the Midwest. When he was twelve, his parents separated, and his father moved to Mexico, where Hughes would visit him in the summers between school terms. His trips to Mexico whetted his interest in travel, and after a year at Columbia University and a year of odd jobs in New York City, he signed up to work on a freighter that went to Africa and to Holland. In 1924, he lived in Paris, supporting himself by working as a waiter, a cook, and a doorman. He also traveled through Italy before he came back to the United States—with twenty-five cents in his pockets.

Shortly after his return to America, Hughes took a job as a bus boy in a Washington, D.C., hotel. While working there, he recognized the poet Vachel Lindsay (see page 75), and one night left some poems beside his plate. After reading the poems, Lindsay in turn recognized Hughes's ability and proceeded to read the young man's poems at a poetry recital he was giving in the hotel's auditorium. The encouragement provided for him by Lindsay spurred Hughes on to continue writing and submitting his poems to magazine and book publishers, and in 1926 the first of his many books of verse, *The Weary Blues*, was published.

Although Langston Hughes's subsequent fame was won mostly as a poet, he was also successful in a variety of other literary enterprises. He wrote short stories, children's books, several Broadway plays, and movie scripts. In the 1930's, he was the executive director of the Harlem Suitcase Theater, which he called "the only Negro Workers' Theater" in New York. He was also an influential journalist, using in his columns a fictional character he called Jesse B. Semple, and nicknamed "Simple," to present the opinions and advice of an imaginary Negro laborer on political affairs and daily behavior. Many of the "Simple" stories appeared in Hughes's three prose collections: *Simple Speaks His Mind* (1950), *Simple Takes a Wife* (1953), and *Simple Stakes a Claim*.

Simple, like many of the other speakers in Hughes's verse and prose, "spoke" the Negro dialect. Yet neither the dialect nor his emphasis on the problems of Negroes prevented Hughes's work from being successfully translated into a number of languages—including Chinese, Dutch, Russian, Yiddish, and Czech, as well as French, Spanish, and German. Hughes's work can be effectively translated because it deals with emotions—particularly with those of joy and sorrow—which the simple or dialect words of any language can communicate. As the poet and anthologist Arna Bontemps commented, the works of Hughes "are for readers who will judge them with their hearts as well as their heads. By that standard, he has always measured well. He still does."

The following selections—"Harlem," "Good Morning," and "Island"—are from *Lenox Avenue Mural*.

Harlem

What happens to a dream deferred?
    Does it dry up
    like a raisin in the sun?
    Or fester like a sore—
    And then run?   5
Does it stink like rotten meat?

Or crust and sugar over—
like a syrupy sweet?

Maybe it just sags
like a heavy load.   10

Or does it explode?

Good Morning

Good morning, daddy!
I was born here, he said,
watched Harlem grow
until colored folks spread
from river to river   5
across the middle Manhattan
out of Penn Station
dark tenth of a nation,
planes from Puerto Rico,
and holds of boats, chico,°   10
up from Cuba Haiti Jamaica,
in busses marked New York
from Georgia Florida Louisiana
to Harlem Brooklyn the Bronx
but most of all to Harlem   15
dusky sash across Manhattan
I've seen them come dark
    wondering
    wide-eyed
    dreaming   20
out of Penn Station—
but the trains are late.
The gates open—
but there're bars
at each gate.   25

10. chico (chē′kō): *Spanish,* boy.

What happens
to a dream deferred?
Daddy, ain't you heard?

Island

Between two rivers
North of the park,
Like darker rivers
The streets are dark.

Black and white,   5
Gold and brown—
Chocolate-custard
Pie of a town.

Dream within a dream
Our dream deferred.   10

Good morning, daddy!

Ain't you heard?

Meaning and Method

1. *To defer* is to delay or put off. Why is—or was—Harlem a place of dreams "deferred" ("Harlem," line 1)? In your own words, explain the possible reactions seen as a result of deferring a dream.
2. Lines 17–25 of "Good Morning" can be interpreted both literally and symbolically. Explain the symbolic meaning of "late" trains and "open" gates with bars.
3. Is the tone of the poem—or of each of its three parts—bitter? resigned? sarcastic? ironic? What other adjectives might suitably describe the tone?
4. In the last line of both "Good Morning" and "Island," the speaker uses the word "ain't," which is usually not found in "literary" writing. Why did the poet use this word? What other words or phrases in the poem are normally not found in "literary" writing?
5. The last part of the poem is entitled "Island." How can the word

"island" refer literally to Manhattan as an island and also to Harlem
as an island?
6. What is the *dream* Hughes mentions throughout the poem? Is it the
   American dream of economic success? What is the Negro's "dream
   within a dream"?
7. Why did Hughes omit punctuation in lines 3–8 and 12–20 of "Good
   Morning"? What does it suggest about the black migration to New
   York?

Peace

We passed their graves:
The dead men there,
Winners or losers,
Did not care.

In the dark   5
They could not see
Who had gained
The victory.

Meaning and Method

1. Does the title "Peace" refer to the results of the victory? to the condition of the dead? to both?
2. What is the theme of the poem?

Harlem Sweeties

Have you dug the spill
Of Sugar Hill?°
Cast your glims°

2. Sugar Hill: a fashionable section of Harlem during the 1920's. 3. glims:
eyes.

On this sepia° thrill:
Brown sugar lassie,   5
Caramel treat,
Honey-gold baby
Sweet enough to eat.
Peach-skinned girlie,
Coffee and cream,   10
Chocolate darling
Out of a dream.
Walnut tinted
Or cocoa brown,
Pomegranate-lipped   15
Pride of the town.
Rich cream-colored
To plum-tinted black,
Feminine sweetness
In Harlem's no lack.   20
Glow of the quince
To blush of the rose.
Persimmon bronze
To cinnamon toes.
Blackberry cordial,°   25
Virginia Dare wine—
All those sweet colors
Flavor Harlem of mine!
Walnut or cocoa,
Let me repeat: 30
Caramel, brown sugar,
A chocolate treat.
Molasses taffy,
Coffee and cream,
Licorice, clove, cinnamon   35
To a honey-brown dream.
Ginger, wine-gold,
Persimmon, blackberry,
All through the spectrum
Harlem girls vary—   40

---

4. sepia (sē′pē•ɔ): reddish brown. 25. cordial: a liqueur; an after-dinner drink.

So if you want to know beauty's
Rainbow-sweet thrill,
Stroll down luscious,
Delicious, *fine* Sugar Hill.

Meaning and Method

1. How does the poet use images of sight and taste to praise the beauty of Negro women? Why is the setting of the poem, Sugar Hill, effective?
2. How does the poem suggest the diversity that exists in a black community?

Where? When? Which?

When the cold comes
With a bitter fragrance
Like rusty iron and mint,
And the wind blows
Fresh and sharp as integration   5
With an edge like gentle apartheid,°
And it is winter,
And the cousins of the too thin suits
Ride on bitless horses
Tethered by something worse than pride,   10
Which areaway, or bar,
Or station waiting room will not say,
Horse and horseman, outside!
With old and not too gentle
Colorless apartheid?   15

6. apartheid (ə·pärt′hīt): a policy of strict segregation of races practiced in the Union of South Africa.

Meaning and Method

1. What comment on integration does the poet make in lines 5 and 6 when he talks of a wind "Fresh and sharp as integration / With an edge like gentle apartheid"?

2. Is "colorless apartheid" (line 15) a condition of life in the United States or some other country? Or does it refer to death? In your answer, comment on the connotations of the phrase *bitless horses* (line 9). If "colorless apartheid" refers to death, explain who or what is being separated. What, then, does the poem say about the equality of all races?

Composition

Write a composition detailing some of the provisions of the system of apartheid. Why was it instituted? What effect do you think it will have finally?

Kenneth Fearing

[1902–1961]

The setting for most of the poems of Kenneth Fearing is the modern American city. He believed that city life caused conformity because it forced people to fit into stereotyped patterns. The outcome of this conformity was that man lost his vitality; modern man became a ghost walking aimlessly through a nightmare he could not control.

Fearing satirized the conventions and the life style of city dwellers. His poems contain words and phrases taken from local slang, newspaper headlines, and advertising. He uses this flat, non-poetic language in order to re-create the stifled, shallow lives of the people he portrays. In *Afternoon of a Pawnbroker* (1943) and *Stranger at Coney Island* (1948), he presents a bitter, almost despairing view of some aspects of twentieth-century America.

Fearing knew intimately the settings and characters he wrote about. He was born in Oak Park, Illinois, a well-to-do suburb of Chicago. The young man rebelled against the enclosed, upper-middle-class life his father, a successful lawyer, provided. And so after graduating from the University of Wisconsin in 1924, Fearing drifted through a series of jobs: he was a reporter, mill-hand, salesman, clerk, and teacher. He moved to New York City, where he worked as a free-lance writer and novelist. He died in 1961 from a chest tumor.

American Rhapsody (4)

First you bite your fingernails. And then you comb your hair
    again. And then you wait. And wait.
(They say, you know, that first you lie. And then you steal,
    they say. And then, they say, you kill.)

"American Rhapsody (4)" by Kenneth Fearing, originally appeared in *The New Yorker*. Reprinted by permission of the Estate of Kenneth F. Fearing, Ira Keonig, Executor.

Then the doorbell rings. Then Peg drops in. And Bill. And
    Jane. And Doc.
And first you talk, and smoke, and hear the news and have a
    drink. Then you walk down the stairs.
And you dine, then, and go to a show after that, perhaps, and
    after that a night spot, and after that come home again, and
    climb the stairs again, and again go to bed.   5

But first Peg argues, and Doc replies. First you dance the
    same dance and you drink the same drink you always drank
    before.
And the piano builds a roof of notes above the world.

And the trumpet weaves a dome of music through space. And
    the drum makes a ceiling over space and time and night.
And then the table-wit. And then the check. Then home again
    to bed.
But first, the stairs.   10

And do you now, baby, as you climb the stairs, do you still
    feel as you felt back there?
Do you feel again as you felt this morning? And the night
    before? And then the night before that?

(They say, you know, that first you hear voices. And then
    you have visions, they say. Then, they say, you kick and
    scream and rave.)

Or do you feel: What is one more night in a lifetime of nights?
What is one more death, or friendship, or divorce out of two,
    or three? Or four? Or five?   15
One more face among so many, many faces, one more life
    among so many million lives?

But first, baby, as you climb and count the stairs (and they
    total the same) did you, sometime or somewhere, have a
    different idea?
Is this, baby, what you were born to feel, and do, and be?

Meaning and Method

1. Is the "you" a woman or a man? Does it matter? Does the "you" lead a varied, interesting life? a repetitious, dull life? Is the "you's" life basically satisfying? dissatisfying? How do you know?
2. The sentences in parentheses in lines 2 and 13 deal with the lives of two types of people outside the normal bounds of society—criminals and madmen. Are these parenthetical statements meant to contrast with the actual life of the "you"? to show the characteristics that the "you" may be suppressing? both? neither?
3. What is the speaker's attitude toward the "you"? Do you think he considers himself superior? Is he concerned? ironic? saddened?
4. Among the definitions of the word *rhapsody* are the following: (a) a series of disconnected and often extravagant statements, gathered or composed in a state of excitement; rapt or rapturous statements; (b) a musical composition of irregular form, suggesting that it was improvised; (c) a miscellaneous collection; a medley.

   Which of these meanings do you think the poet took into account when he entitled the poem "American Rhapsody (4)"? Is the title used ironically or satirically? In your answer, comment on what the poem reveals about the poet's attitude toward American life.

Composition and Discussion

Discuss whether or not you agree with Fearing's implication that boredom is typical of American life. Does television contribute to or help prevent boredom? How can one avoid becoming bored? avoid falling into a "rut"?

Countee Cullen
[1903–1946]

"Good poetry," Countee Cullen held, "is a lofty thought beautifully expressed." Cullen's books of poetry, beginning with *Color* (1925), illustrate his belief. The poems in *Color* reflect his lyric talent, his romantic temperament, and his skill at working in traditional forms such as the sonnet. They also mark his complete poetic development.

Although his later volumes—*Copper Sun, The Ballad of the Brown Girl,* and *The Black Christ and Other Poems*—contain many fine poems, they do not show any stylistic advancement or the deepening intellectual complexity that are generally expected from young writers. He had little interest in the technical experimentation found in his contemporaries.

Like most important black writers in the 1920's Cullen was associated with the Negro Renaissance. He had grown up in Harlem, and after gaining degrees from New York University and Harvard, he became an editor of *Opportunity: Journal of Negro Life,* a magazine that published works by young black authors. However, Cullen soon drifted away from the movement and eventually from writing poetry; he wrote little poetry in the last decade and a half of his life. During this period, he taught English and French in a New York City public school.

In the 1930's and 1940's, his interests shifted to other literary forms. In 1932, his novel about Harlem life, *One Way to Heaven,* was published. He also wrote a volume of children's stories, *The Lost Zoo,* and collaborated with Arna Bontemps on a Broadway musical, *St. Louis Woman* (1946). Although Cullen has been praised for his work in these other literary fields, his reputation rests primarily on the poems published in the 1920's.

Uncle Jim

"White folks is white," says Uncle Jim;
"A platitude,"° I sneer;
And then I tell him so is milk,
And the froth upon his beer.

His heart walled up with bitterness,   5
He smokes his pungent pipe,
And nods at me as if to say,
"Young fool, you'll soon be ripe!"

I have a friend who eats his heart
Away with grief of mine,   10
Who drinks my joy as tipplers drain
Deep goblets filled with wine.

I wonder why here at his side,
Face-in-the-grass with him,
My mind should stray the Grecian urn°   15
To muse on Uncle Jim.

2. **platitude:** a commonplace statement; an obvious truism. **15. Grecian urn:** probably a reference to John Keats's poem, "Ode on a Grecian Urn." The Grecian urn is sometimes considered a symbol of beauty.

Meaning and Method

1. What does the use of the word "platitude" tell you about the "I" of the poem? Would Uncle Jim have used this word? Why or why not? What other details of the poem reinforce or enlarge the characteristics of the speaker?
2. The speaker and Uncle Jim are black; is the speaker's friend (line 9) black or white? How do you know? How close is their relation?
3. What contrasting attitudes toward white people are shown by the speaker and Uncle Jim? Why do you think Uncle Jim's "heart walled up with bitterness" (line 5)? What is implied by the phrase "White folks is white" (line 1)? What is suggested about black-white relations by Uncle Jim's statement, "Young fool, you'll soon be ripe!"?

Composition and Discussion

In a composition or in a discussion, mention ways in which education helps to remove or decrease prejudice. How does it weaken the stereotypes that one race has toward another?

From the Dark Tower

We shall not always plant while others reap
The golden increment° of bursting fruit,
Not always countenance, abject° and mute,
That lesser men should hold their brothers cheap;
Not everlastingly while others sleep   5
Shall we beguile their limbs with mellow flute,
Not always bend to some more subtle brute;
We were not made eternally to weep.

The night whose sable breast relieves the stark,
White stars is no less lovely being dark,   10
And there are buds that cannot bloom at all
In light, but crumple, piteous, and fall;
So in the dark we hide the heart that bleeds,
And wait, and tend our agonizing seeds.

2. **increment:** increase. 3. **abject:** groveling, low.

Meaning and Method

1. What are the connotations of *dark tower*? Consider each word—*dark* and *tower*—separately. How does the title relate to the subject of the poem? to the attitude of the speaker?
2. What is the main thought of the speaker in the octave of this sonnet? What attitude or idea is emphasized by the repetition of "not" in lines 1–8? What is the main thought of the speaker in the sestet of this sonnet? How is this thought related to that of the octave?
3. What words or phrases in the poem extend the metaphor of planting in line 1?

"From the Dark Tower," copyright 1927 by Harper & Brothers; renewed 1955 by Ida M. Cullen, from *On These I Stand* by Countee Cullen. Reprinted by permission of Harper & Row, Publishers.

Richard Eberhart

"I tend to philosophize about everything, to conclude nothing," Richard Eberhart once wrote. And as might be expected, his poetry reflects this approach to life. But although his writing tends to be intellectual and abstract, it also contains strong emotional responses to life. His verse shows his recognition of and sympathy with man's desire to find meaning in an existence constricted both by one's personal failings and by death.

Eberhart's intellectual approach to life and to poetry is not surprising for a person of his varied and extensive educational background. He was born in Austin, Minnesota, in 1904, and studied at the University of Minnesota and received his B.A. from Dartmouth College. After spending some time as a deck hand on tramp steamers, he went to Cambridge University in England for further study, receiving a second B.A. in 1929. He returned to America and spent a year tutoring the son of the King of Siam (now Thailand). He also studied at Harvard before going back to England to obtain his M.A. from Cambridge.

From 1933 through 1942, Eberhart taught at a private preparatory school in Massachusetts, but with the advent of the second World War, resigned to enter the U.S. Navy, where he rose to the rank of lieutenant commander. Although he became an executive in a wax manufacturing company after the war, his academic interests remained strong. In the 1950's he resigned his full-time business position (remaining on the board of directors) to return to teaching. He has since taught at various schools, including Princeton and Dartmouth and the universities of Washington, Connecticut, and Massachusetts.

The Groundhog

In June, amid the golden fields,
I saw a groundhog lying dead.
Dead lay he; my sense shook,
And mind outshot our naked frailty.
There lowly in the vigorous summer   5
His form began its senseless change,
And made my senses waver dim
Seeing nature ferocious in him.
Inspecting close his maggots'° might
And seething cauldron of his being,   10
Half with loathing, half with a strange love,
I poked him with an angry stick.
The fever arose, became a flame
And Vigor circumscribed° the skies,
Immense energy in the sun,   15
And through my frame a sunless trembling.
My stick had done nor good nor harm.
Then stood I silent in the day
Watching the object, as before;
And kept my reverence for knowledge   20
Trying for control, to be still,
To quell the passion of the blood;
Until I had bent down on my knees
Praying for joy in the sight of decay.
And so I left; and I returned   25
In Autumn strict of eye, to see
The sap gone out of the groundhog,
But the bony sodden hulk remained.
But the year had lost its meaning,
And in intellectual chains   30
I lost both love and loathing,
Mured up° in the wall of wisdom.

---

9. **maggots:** the larvae of insects, especially those living on decaying matter.
14. **circumscribed:** encompassed or confined within certain bounds. 32. **Mured up:** walled in, imprisoned.

"The Groundhog" from *Collected Poems 1930–1960* by Richard Eberhart, © 1960 by Richard Eberhart. Reprinted by permission of Oxford University Press, Inc. and Chatto and Windus Ltd.

Another summer took the fields again
Massive and burning, full of life,
But when I chanced upon the spot   35
There was only a little hair left,
And bones bleaching in the sunlight
Beautiful as architecture;
I watched them like a geometer,°
And cut a walking stick from a birch.   40
It has been three years, now.
There is no sign of the groundhog.
I stood there in the whirling summer,
My hand capped a withered heart,
And thought of China and of Greece,   45
Of Alexander° in his tent;
Of Montaigne° in his tower,
Of Saint Theresa° in her wild lament.

39. **geometer:** one who studies geometry, the branch of mathematics that treats abstract form. 46. **Alexander:** Alexander the Great (356–323 B.C.), the conqueror of the Persian Empire. 47. **Montaigne** (mon·tän′): Michel de Montaigne (1533–1592), a French philosopher and essayist. He had a tower library in which he thought and wrote. 48. **Saint Theresa:** Saint Theresa of Avila (1515–1582), a Spanish nun who was a mystic and writer.

Meaning and Method

1. Why did the sight of the dead groundhog upset the poet? How did the setting and the time of year intensify his reaction?
2. Why does the poet in line 9 describe the maggots—which, individually, are tiny insects—as having "might" and strength? What does the poet mean by saying he poked the dead animal with "an angry stick"? Why was he angry?
3. What evidence is there in lines 1–24 that the poet was disgusted by death and feels that death is senseless but all-powerful? Why does he pray "for joy at the sight of decay"?
4. In lines 25–32, the poet describes his return to the same spot in autumn. What change had taken place in the groundhog? Did the poet react to the dead animal intellectually or emotionally? Does he feel his reaction was an appropriate response to death?
5. In lines 33–40, the poet describes his third visit—a chance one—to the place at which he had seen the dead groundhog. What change had occurred since his last visit? How did his attitude contrast with that of his first visit? What does he mean when he says he was "like

a geometer"? Does geometry suggest an intellectual or an emotional
awareness of death? What is the significance of the *walking stick*
as contrasted with the *angry stick* (line 12)?

6. Three years later the poet returned, and there was no sign of the
groundhog. Why did this cause the poet to think of the lost civiliza-
tions of China and Greece? What different approaches to life are
suggested by (a) Alexander, (b) Montaigne, and (c) Saint Theresa?
Does any approach to life overcome death? Does the poet finally
accept the fact of death?

The Horse Chestnut Tree

Boys in sporadic° but tenacious° droves
Come with sticks, as certainly as Autumn,
To assault the great horse chestnut tree.

There is a law governs their lawlessness.
Desire is in them for a shining amulet°   5
And the best are those that are highest up.

They will not pick them easily from the ground.
With shrill arms they fling to the higher branches,
To hurry the work of nature for their pleasure.

I have seen them trooping down the street   10
Their pockets stuffed with chestnuts shucked,° unshucked.
It is only evening keeps them from their wish.

Sometimes I run out in a kind of rage
To chase the boys away; I catch an arm,
Maybe, and laugh to think of being the lawgiver.   15

1. **sporadic** (spô·rad′ik): occasional. **tenacious:** stubborn, tough, holding
strongly. 5. **amulet** (am′yə·lit): a charm worn to protect the wearer against
evil, accident, and other misfortunes. 11. **shucked:** with the shell or husk
removed.

"The Horse Chestnut Tree" from *Collected Poems 1930–1960* by Richard Eberhart,
© 1960 by Richard Eberhart. Reprinted by permission of Oxford University Press, Inc.
and Chatto and Windus Ltd.

I was once such a young sprout myself
And fingered in my pocket the prize and trophy.
But still I moralize upon the day

And see that we, outlaws on God's property,
Fling out imagination beyond the skies,   20
Wishing a tangible° good from the unknown.

And likewise death will drive us from the scene
With the great flowering world unbroken yet,
Which we held in idea, a little handful.

21. **tangible:** able to be touched; of definite shape; real.

Meaning and Method

1. In lines 1–9, the speaker tells how groups of boys fling sticks up
   to the higher branches of a horse chestnut tree in order to knock
   down the chestnuts at the top. Why do they want the chestnuts?
   Why will they "not pick them easily from the ground" (line 7)?
2. Which words or phrases in the first three lines emphasize the idea
   of lawlessness mentioned in line 4?
3. Line 4 reads, "There is a law governs their lawlessness." Does the
   speaker feel that they are somehow obeying a natural law? How does
   line 2 enforce the idea that the boys are following inevitable laws of
   nature?
4. What is the speaker's reaction to the boys in lines 13–15? Can you
   tell what causes his reaction? Why does he become a "lawgiver" and
   why does he "laugh to think of being the lawgiver"?
5. In lines 19–24, the speaker draws an analogy between the actions
   of the boys and himself and the place of man on earth in relation
   to God. How does man spiritually imitate the boys throwing sticks
   at the horse chestnut tree? Does man, like the boys, try for something at the very top? What is implied about man's place in the
   universe by the phrase "outlaws on God's property"?
6. What will chase man away from the "spiritual" horse chestnut tree,
   as the speaker has chased the boys from the real one? Will man's
   assaults on life have any more effect than the boys' assaults on the
   tree? What do the ideas we gather from life by "flinging our imagination beyond the skies" have in common with the chestnuts the
   boys gather. From this analogy, state the theme of the poem.

If I Could Only Live at the Pitch
That Is Near Madness

If I could only live at the pitch° that is near madness
When everything is as it was in my childhood
Violent, vivid, and of infinite possibility:
That the sun and the moon broke over my head.

Then I cast time out of the trees and fields,   5
Then I stood immaculate in the Ego;°
Then I eyed the world with all delight,
Reality was the perfection of my sight.

And time had big handles on the hands,
Fields and trees a way of being themselves.   10
I saw battalions of the race of mankind
Standing stolid, demanding a moral answer.

I gave the moral answer and I died
And into a realm of complexity came
Where nothing is possible but necessity   15
And the truth wailing there like a red babe.

1. **pitch:** in music, a standard for establishing a tone. The pitch near madness is the place on a scale ranging from normalcy to madness. 6. **Ego:** the thinking, feeling self; *here*, the concern with the responses of the self alone, rather than of society.

Meaning and Method

1. Madness is a state in which a person lives partly in a fantasy world where sensory impressions are often more acute than they usually are. How, according to the speaker, is childhood like madness? What do you think he means when he says he wants to live at the pitch "near madness" (line 1)? What is meant by line 4?
2. What does line 6 indicate about how a child regards the world? According to lines 5 and 6, is a child bound by time? or by other people?

"If I Could Only Live at the Pitch That Is Near Madness" from *Collected Poems 1930–1960* by Richard Eberhart, © 1960 by Richard Eberhart. Reprinted by permission of Oxford University Press, Inc. and Chatto and Windus Ltd.

3. The speaker indicates that "battalions of the race of mankind" (line 11) demanded that he grow up, take responsibility and give "a moral answer" (line 12). What is his reaction to this demand?
4. The adult world is a "realm of complexity" (line 14). How do the possibilities of this world (line 15) contrast with those of the world of the child (line 3)? Which is more limited? Why? Does line 16 suggest that truth is found in the adult world, or that it is ignored there?
5. What is the theme of this poem?

Composition

In a composition, examine the theory that, as adults, people lose the idealism they had as children. Are adults more practical than children? Is this good or bad? Does the loss of idealism lead to the "generation gap"?

Phyllis McGinley

When Phyllis McGinley's first book, *On the Contrary* (1934), appeared, a reviewer for *The New York Times* said that she "has instinctively grasped the fact that light verse, so called, must also suggest that modicum of truth which saves the poem from buffoonery." The most prevalent element in Miss McGinley's work is humor, sometimes sparkling and gay, sometimes tender, sometimes sly, but usually good-natured. Her topics are drawn from her family and her life in a suburban community, but the situations and the people described in her poems appeal to a range of readers not limited to those in suburbia. Her appeal is universal because each of her readers can see in her poems elements of himself, of his friends and neighbors, and of situations that have occurred in his life.

Phyllis McGinley was born in Oregon in 1905 and grew up in Colorado and Utah. She attended the universities of Utah and California and taught for a year before she came to New York City. While in New York, she worked as an advertising copywriter and as a teacher. In 1937, she married Charles Hayden, a telephone company executive, and settled down in Larchmont, New York. Since then, she has been given numerous honorary degrees and has been awarded the Pulitzer prize for her book *Times Three* (1960).

Love Letter to a Factory

(Composed upon reading in *The New York Times* that each employee of General Brass & Machine Works, Inc., will receive a day off with pay for his birthday.)

> Hoist high the glass!
> Ah! Let us drink
> To General Brass
> And Machine Works, Inc.,
> Where every hand   5

Who earns his pay
Can sleep till noon on his natal day.°

From tropic blaze
   To arctic bound'ry,
Who will not praise   10
   This noble foundry,
Which crowns its workers
Of either sex
Each a Regina or a Rex?°

For what's the best   15
   Of benefits worth
Compared to a rest
   On the day of one's birth?
What is overtime?
What's a bonus?   20
Here is a gift without an onus°—
The only holiday ever designed
To be enjoyed with a peaceful mind.

Humanity strains
   Its Christmas powers,   25
Assembling trains
   In the little hours.
The Fourth's unsafe
For a car to get out.
Memorial Day, it's always wet out.   30
Labor Day's hot, the New Year's infirm,
Washington's feast invites the germ,
While the turkey hid in Thanksgiving's straw
Is having to dine with one's brothers-in-law,
But a man's a king   35
Who sits and rocks
While the rest of the world is punching clocks.

---

7. natal day: birthday; *natal* means "dating from birth, or pertaining to one's birth," from the Latin *nasci,* "to be born." **14. Regina ... Rex:** *Latin* for queen and king, respectively. **21. onus:** burden or responsibility.

So shout it to Lewis,
    Cry it to Quill°—
A job to do is   40
    Before them still.
Away with pensions!
    Let's all set sights
Toward big conventions
    On Birthday Rights.   45
Tell Hoosier, Alaskan,
    Cape Codder, Mohican:
What General Brass can
    Do, A.T.&T. can,
Detroit can, Milan can,   50
    And Steel can and Silk can,
American Can can
    And Carnation Milk can,

Till, idling legal,
    His personal morn,   55
Every man's regal
    And glad he was born.

38, 39. Lewis . . . Quill: John L. Lewis (1880–1969) and Michael Quill (1905–1966), who were heads of the United Mine Workers (UMW) and the New York City Transport Workers Union (TWU), respectively.

Meaning and Method

1. According to lines 24–37, why is a day off on one's birthday better than on any other legal holiday?
2. Why is "turkey" (line 33) a *pun*—here, the humorous use of two different but more or less incongruous meanings of the same word? What is the meaning of the word "turkey" in the context of line 33?
3. Explain the humor in the various uses of the word "can" in lines 48–53?
4. Is the poem simply a humorous poem, or is the poet also satirizing the idea. For example, does she really think the company is "noble" (line 4)? Is she being satirical as well as funny in lines 38–45?

Love Letter to an Institution

Of all museums,
I've a pet museum,
And it's not the Morgan°
Or the Met Museum,
Or the Frick Museum,   5
Which steals the heart,
Or a trick museum
Like the Modern Art.°
I must confess
It's a queer museum,   10
A more or less
Done-by-ear museum,
But it suits my nature
As knife suits fork:
The Museum of the City of New York.   15

A bit like an auction,
A bit like a fair,
Everything is cozy that's collected there.
Everything is cheerful as a Currier & Ives:°
Capes made for gentlemen,   20
Caps for their wives;
Lamps lit at dark
By Great-Grandmama;
Central Park
In a diorama°   25

3. Morgan: the Morgan Library in New York City. The library has exhibits of
graphics, prints, and rare books. **4, 5, 8. Met Museum . . . Frick Museum
. . . Modern Art:** The Metropolitan Museum of Art, the Frick Museum, and
the Museum of Modern Art are museums in New York City that exhibit paint-
ings, sculptures, and other art objects. **19. Currier & Ives:** a print made by the
firm of Nathaniel Currier and James Merritt Ives, nineteenth-century lithog-
raphers who depicted scenes from American life. **25. diorama:** a three-dimen-
sional exhibit in which modeled figures and objects are set in a naturalistic fore-
ground blended into a painted background.

(Where boys are sledding
And their runners curl);
A brownstone° wedding
With a flower girl;
Doll-house parlors with carpet on the floor;   30
Patriotic posters from the first World War;
A solitary spur
That belonged to Aaron Burr;
And a small-scale model
Of a ten-cent store.   35

There for the dawdler,
Yesterday is spread—
Toys that a toddler
Carried once to bed;
Hoopskirts, horsescars,°   40
Flags aplenty;
Somebody's dance dress, circa '20;
Somebody's platter, somebody's urn;
Mr. and Mrs.
Isaac Stern°—   45
All gaily jumbled
So it's automatic
To believe you've stumbled
On your great-aunt's attic.
Helter-skelter   50
But large as life,
A room by Belter
And a room by Phyfe;°
A period spinet,
A period speller;   55
The rooms that soured Mr. Rockefeller;
Rooms you can stare at, rooms you can poke in,
And a tenderhearted lobby
You can even smoke in.

28. brownstone: a style of house made with reddish-brown stones, popular in
New York just before and after the turn of the century. 40. horsecars: streetcars
pulled by horses. 45. Isaac Stern: a contemporary concert violinist. 53, 54.
Belter . . . Phyfe (fif): John H. Belter and Duncan Phyfe, nineteenth-century
cabinetmakers.

It's a fine museum,   60
Not a new museum,
But a neighborly
Sort of old-shoe museum,
Not a class museum
Where the pundits° go   65
Or a mass museum
With a Sunday show,
Not vast and grand
Like the Natural History.°
How it ever got planned   70
Is a minor mystery.
But it fits my fancy
Like applesauce and pork,
The Museum of the City of New York.

65. **pundits:** scholars, very intelligent people. 69. **the Natural History:** the Museum of Natural History in New York City displays dioramic reconstructions of dinosaurs and other animals, and primitive peoples.

Meaning and Method

1. What type of collection is found in the Museum of the City of New York? Why does the speaker prefer this collection to those of other museums?
2. Is this poem really a "love letter," or is it a humorous satire? How do you know?

Composition

Write a humorous love letter in verse or prose to an institution of some sort. For example, you can write "Love Letter to a School," "Love Letter to _____ Department Store," "Love Letter to a Movie Theater," "Love Letter to the Telephone Company," and "Love Letter to the Automobile License Bureau." Try to let your reader know your attitude toward the institution you address.

W. H. Auden

Wystan Hugh Auden is both an English and an American poet. He was born in York, England, in 1907 and was educated at Oxford. At the university, he was associated with a group of young radicals including Stephen Spender and Christopher Isherwood, both of whom became well-known writers.

Auden's early poems began to appear while he was teaching at a boys' school in Malvern during the early 1930's. These early poems, influenced by the writings of Marx, were concerned with the social and economic problems revealed by the Depression. To Auden, the economic collapse of the 1930's showed that the rigid social class structure of European society and the economic system that supported it were out of date. In his poems, he satirized the hypocrisy and the lack of spirit that he thought characterized England during this period. Technically, these early poems reflect his skill in handling the language and in capturing the rhythms of popular speech. They also show his versatility in working in a wide range of verse forms—from modern free verse to the alliterative poetry of Old English. His interest in science, which he received from his father, a doctor, appears in imagery drawn from chemistry, physics, and other scientific disciplines. But many of his early poems are marred because they are quite obscure.

He left teaching in 1935 and spent several years traveling extensively before coming to the United States in 1939 to lecture at a number of universities. America's freedom and lack of a formal social-class structure appealed to him, and he remained here and became a citizen in 1946.

After Auden came to America, he began to change his themes, and he still continued to experiment with verse forms. Gradually, he abandoned his Marxist point of view and adopted a more religious perspective on life. In his Christmas oratorio, *For the Time Being*, he investigates the importance of the Birth of Christ for modern man. His later writings have stressed the need for personal responsibility as a cure for the ills of the modern world. In addition, he has presented discussions of philosophical ideas in verse; for example, *The Age of Anxiety* is a long poem in which four persons attempt to find a solution to their spiritual problems.

In 1948, he was awarded a Pulitzer prize, and in 1953 he received the Bollingen award. The following year Auden was elected to the American Academy of Arts and Letters. He has continued to teach both in America and in England. Besides teaching, he has produced an enormous quantity of writing in a variety of literary forms: poetry, plays in verse and prose, critical essays, journalistic accounts, oratorios, and opera librettos.

Auden's poetry is frequently written in complicated verse forms, many of which are the result of his having studied foreign literatures, especially Chinese and those of southern Europe. It has been said that he, "more than any other poet, originally built the contemporary style."

O Where Are You Going?

"O where are you going?" said reader to rider,
"That valley is fatal when furnaces burn,
Yonder's the midden° whose odors will madden,
That gap is the grave where the tall return."

"O do you imagine," said fearer to farer,°   5
"That dusk will delay on your path to the pass,
Your diligent looking discover the lacking
Your footsteps feel from granite to grass?"

"O what was that bird," said horror to hearer,
"Did you see that shape in the twisted trees?   10
Behind you swiftly the figure comes softly,
The spot on your skin is a shocking disease?"

"Out of this house"—said rider to reader,
"Yours never will"—said farer to fearer,
"They're looking for you"—said hearer to horror,   15
As he left them there, as he left them there.

3. **midden:** dung hill, or an accumulation of refuse. 5. **farer:** traveler.

Meaning and Method

1. "Reader" in line 1 probably symbolizes the bookish person, the one who is active in imagination only. "Rider" represents the doer, the person of action.

   What types of persons are symbolized by "fearer" and "farer"? by "horror" and "hearer"?

2. Stanza 2 has been interpreted as a warning of failure. What other threats or warnings are contained in the first and third stanzas?

3. In the last stanza, how do "rider," "farer," and "hearer" respond to the warnings? What do their reactions have in common? What has the "he" overcome when he leaves "reader," "fearer," and "horror"?

4. Do "reader," "fearer," and "horror" represent actual figures? contrasting parts of the "he" in line 16? both?

5. A great deal of the effect of this poem is the result of Auden's use of the sound effects of words. For example, he uses *slant rhymes* in each of his pairs: "reader," "rider"; "fearer," "farer"; "hearer," "horror." Whereas normal rhymes would give an impression of harmony, these slant rhymes emphasize the disharmony of the scene. Where else does he use slant rhymes? Where does alliteration increase the unpleasant or frightening effect?

Look, Stranger, on This Island Now

Look, stranger, on this island now
The leaping light for your delight discovers,°
Stand stable here
And silent be,
That through the channels of the ear   5
May wander like a river
The swaying sound of the sea.

Here at the small field's ending pause
When the chalk wall falls to the foam, and its tall ledges

2. **discovers:** *here,* reveals.

Oppose the pluck   10
And knock of the tide,
And the shingle° scrambles after the suck-
ing surf, and the gull lodges
A moment on its sheer side.

Far off like floating seeds the ships   15
Diverge on urgent voluntary errands;
And the full view
Indeed may enter
And move in memory as now these clouds do,
That pass the harbor mirror   20
And all the summer through the water saunter.

12. shingle: rounded, waterworn fragments of rock often found on beaches.

Meaning and Method

1. The speaker is probably describing the southeast coast of England ("this island") with its chalk cliffs and rough surf. What is his attitude toward the place?
2. Much of the effect of this description is achieved not by visual images but by sounds and by line breaks. For example, in the second stanza, words with a harsh /k/ sound are repeated to give an impression of the roughness of the surf. What are these words? What other sounds add to this impression of roughness? How does the arrangement of lines on the page add to the impression of the seashore?
3. Line 15 has the first and only mention of a man-made object—ships. What are the connotations of the word *voluntary* (line 16)? With what is it intended to contrast? How important a place do these man-made objects occupy in the description of nature?
4. In what way is the harbor a "mirror" (line 20)? Does the harbor water literally reflect objects? Does the harbor as a whole reflect life, and does it mirror the universe?
5. This poem appears in the Modern Library edition of Auden's *Selected Poems* under the title "Seascape." Do you think the poem is primarily a word-picture, or is the poet making a comment about nature? Is the stranger in the title meant to be a specific person, perhaps the author himself? Is he everyman? Does it matter?

The Unknown Citizen

(To JS/07/M/378 This Marble Monument Is Erected by the State)

He was found by the Bureau of Statistics to be
One against whom there was no official complaint,
And all the reports on his conduct agree
That, in the modern sense of an old-fashioned word, he
    was a saint,
For in everything he did he served the Greater Community.   5
Except for the War till the day he retired
He worked in a factory and never got fired,
But satisfied his employers, Fudge Motors Inc.
Yet he wasn't a scab° or odd in his views,
For his Union reports that he paid his dues,   10
(Our report on his Union shows it was sound)
And our Social Psychology workers found
That he was popular with his mates° and liked a drink.
The Press are convinced that he bought a paper every day
And that his reactions to advertisements were normal in
    every way.   15
Policies taken out in his name prove that he was fully insured,
And his Health-card shows he was once in hospital but left
    it cured.
Both Producers Research and High-Grade Living declare
He was fully sensible to the advantages of the Installment Plan
And had everything necessary to the Modern Man,   20
A phonograph, a radio, a car and a frigidaire.
Our researchers into Public Opinion are content
That he held the proper opinions for the time of year;
When there was peace, he was for peace; when there was war,
    he went.
He was married and added five children to the population,   25

---

9. **scab:** a worker who refuses to join a labor union or replaces a unionized worker during a strike; a strikebreaker. 13. **mates:** companions, comrades.

"The Unknown Citizen," copyright 1940 and renewed 1968 by W. H. Auden, from *Collected Shorter Poems 1927–1957* by W. H. Auden. Reprinted by permission of Random House, Inc. and Faber and Faber Ltd.

Which our Eugenist° says was the right number for a parent
   of his generation,
And our teachers report that he never interfered with
   their education.
Was he free? Was he happy? The question is absurd:
Had anything been wrong, we should certainly have heard.

26. **Eugenist:** a specialist in eugenics, the science of improving human beings mentally and physically by controlling heredity.

Meaning and Method

1. The Unknown Soldier is an unidentified soldier whose body is selected to receive national honors as a representative of all those who died in a war, especially in one of the world wars.

    How is the Unknown Citizen like and unlike the Unknown Soldier? Why is there a double irony about the word "unknown" in the title?
2. What is a "saint" in the "modern sense" (line 4)? What does the subtitle (To JS/07/M/378 . . .) show about the society? For example, what type of society would erect a monument to such a "saint"? a religious society? a conformist one? a nonconformist one? a machine-oriented society? a society where human values are given great emphasis? a society where human values are given little emphasis?
3. What is indicated by the capitalization of such words and phrases as "Bureau of Statistics," "Greater Community," "Union," "Social Psychology," "Eugenist"?
4. Why did Auden give his poem a singsong quality, and why did he use such forced or obvious rhymes as "Inc." and "think," "retired" and "fired," and "day" and "way"?
5. What aspect of modern society does this poem satirize? How do you know that the speaker does not mean to praise the Unknown Citizen or the society?

Language: Collective Nouns

In line 14, Auden writes, "The Press are convinced that . . . ." The word *Press* is a collective noun and may be used to mean the individual members of the press or the press as a group or whole. Here, it is used to mean the former.

A collective noun takes a singular verb when it refers to the group as a unit. But if the noun refers to the individual members of the group and not to the group taken as a whole, it takes a plural verb.

The following sentences illustrate the difference in usage:

(a) The committee (the group) was appointed to study the problem of air pollution.

(b) The committee (the individuals) were of different opinions as to the solutions to the problem.

Use the following collective nouns in sentences in which the word takes (a) a singular verb, (b) a plural verb.

1. band   3. jury   5. team
2. class   4. squad

Composition and Discussion

1. Examine some magazine advertisements and some television commercials. Write your analysis of what you think is advertising's concept of the average man or woman.

2. Discuss whether or not you think that Auden has presented a fair picture of modern man. If not, what has he omitted? Do you know anybody like the Unknown Citizen? If so, do you think he or she is typical of the society you live in? What are some of the things we don't know about the Unknown Citizen?

Theodore Roethke
[1908–1963]

The poet James Dickey described Theodore Roethke's face as having "an expression of constant bewilderment and betrayal, a continuing agony of doubt." Paradoxically, from this agony Roethke fashioned many of his best and strongest poems. Although Roethke suffered numerous humiliations in his life, he managed, through poetry, to transform many of these defeats into something beautiful. In his poetry, Roethke explored and revealed his inner self, his subconscious dreams and nightmares, and his various psychological states. He wrote long, discursive free-verse narratives about what he thought or felt; as one critic has pointed out "the universe of Roethke's poems is a completely subjective one." Yet in revealing his own experiences, Roethke was tracing the "spiritual history . . . of all haunted and harried men."

Roethke was born in Saginaw, Michigan, and lived in his home state until he graduated from the University of Michigan in 1929. While he was growing up, he spent many hours in his father's greenhouse, where he learned about plant life. Many of his poems are notable for the precision and sensitivity with which he describes plant and animal life. After his graduation, Roethke attended Harvard, where he was encouraged to write poetry. And, like many other poets, he eventually became a teacher—at Bennington College, Pennsylvania State University, and the University of Washington.

Among the honors he received were the Pulitzer prize for *The Waking* (1953) and the Bollingen prize for *Words for the Wind* (1958). But despite his success, he was never totally secure about his talent or his achievement.

Night Journey

Now as the train bears west,
Its rhythm rocks the earth,
And from my Pullman berth

I stare into the night
While others take their rest.   5
Bridges of iron lace,
A suddenness of trees,
A lap of mountain mist
All cross my line of sight,
Then a bleak wasted place,   10
And a lake below my knees.
Full on my neck I feel
The straining at a curve;
My muscles move with steel,
I wake in every nerve.   15
I watch a beacon swing
From dark to blazing bright;
We thunder through ravines
And gullies washed with light.
Beyond the mountain pass   20
Mist deepens on the pane;
We rush into a rain
That rattles double glass.
Wheels shake the roadbed stone,
The pistons jerk and shove,   25
I stay up half the night
To see the land I love.

Meaning and Method

1. The poet creates the impression of a train ride at night by using
   three types of images: visual, auditory, and kinesthetic, that is, felt
   with the muscles and nerves. List the images that give a sense of
   (a) the brief glimpses of the passing landscape, (b) the noise of the
   train as it moves, and (c) the bodily awareness of the train's motion
   that characterizes this night journey.
2. The image "bridges of iron lace" (line 6) not only gives a visual
   impression of the railroad bridge but also indicates the speed of the
   train. What other images or words suggest the train's speed?
3. The basic meter of this poem is iambic trimeter; that is, most of the
   lines contain three feet of iambs. Considering the setting, why is
   such a meter appropriate?
4. What is the speaker's attitude toward the scene he is watching?
5. What is the theme?

Dolor *

I have known the inexorable° sadness of pencils,
Neat in their boxes, dolor of pad and paperweight,
All the misery of manila folders and mucilage,°
Desolation in immaculate public places,
Lonely reception room, lavatory, switchboard,   5
The unalterable pathos of basin and pitcher,
Ritual of multigraph,° paper clip, comma,
Endless duplication of lives and objects.
And I have seen dust from the walls of institutions,
Finer than flour, alive, more dangerous than silica,°   10
Sift, almost invisible, through long afternoons of tedium,
Dropping a fine film on nails and delicate eyebrows,
Glazing the pale hair, the duplicate gray standard faces.

* **Dolor:** mental anguish, sorrow. **1. inexorable:** unalterable, unyielding. **3. mucilage:** glue. **7. multigraph:** an office duplicating machine. **10. silica:** an element in sand that, finely powdered, is found in the air of certain factories. Continual inhalation will result in lung disease.

Meaning and Method

1. In lines 1–7, the speaker presents a catalogue of things connected with many jobs in offices and other places of business. What are his reactions to these things? What words and phrases indicate his reactions? Line 8 sums up his basic objection to this type of life. Paraphrase this line.
2. What type of "institutions" is the poet speaking of in line 9? What is the effect of these institutions on the people who work there? Is the "dust" he mentions in line 9 literal or figurative dust? Why is this dust "more dangerous than silica" (line 10)?

Composition

One of the major problems facing business corporations is to give variety to the dull, repetitive jobs most people are assigned to perform. For example, many factory workers are forced to do the same job day after day; the same is true for office workers. Employees become bored and careless; many do as little work as possible, stay home, or quit.

Among the suggestions offered to remedy this problem are (a) hav-

"Dolor," copyright 1947 by Theodore Roethke, from *Words for the Wind* by Theodore Roethke. Reprinted by permission of Doubleday & Company, Inc.

ing the workers perform different jobs periodically, (b) letting workers participate in making decisions that will affect their jobs, (c) automating all routine jobs, (d) changing the length of the working day, and (e) decreasing the number of working days.

In a composition, discuss the benefits resulting from and/or the problems created by these suggestions. If you can, offer other ideas that you feel will add variety to routine jobs.

The Sloth *

In moving-slow he has no Peer.
You ask him something in his Ear,
He thinks about it for a Year;

And, then, before he says a Word
There, upside down (unlike a Bird),   5
He will assume that you have Heard—

A most Ex-as-per-at-ing Lug.°
But should you call his manner Smug,
He'll sigh and give his Branch a Hug;

Then off again to Sleep he goes,   10
Still swaying gently by his Toes,
And you just *know* he knows he knows.

* Sloth: a slow-moving mammal that hangs upside down from the branches of the tree in which it lives. 7. Lug: *slang*, a fellow, usually one who is clumsy or stupid.

Meaning and Method

1. What is the effect of the hyphenation of "Ex-as-per-at-ing" (line 7)?
2. Does the sloth not answer questions because he is lazy? because he does not care about other people's opinions? both?
3. What is the poet's attitude toward the sloth? Is it negative? positive? neither? angry? humorous?

Karl Shapiro

When Karl Shapiro was drafted by the Army in 1941, he asked his fiancée to be his literary agent. Like many young writers, he had had difficulty in finding a publisher for his works: his first book of verse, *Poems* (1935), was published at his own expense. His fiancée, Evalyn Katz, arranged and edited the poems, and obtained a publisher for his second collection, *Person, Place and Thing* (1942).

Unlike his first effort, which was not even reviewed by the critics, this volume received an enthusiastic response. Encouraged by the book's reception, Shapiro continued writing while he was stationed in the Pacific. He sent many new poems home to his future wife, who again prepared them for publication. The resulting book, *V-Letter and Other Poems,* won the Pulitzer prize for poetry in 1945. During his Army service in New Guinea and the Dutch East Indies, Shapiro wrote still another book, *Essay on Rime* (1945), a blank verse tour de force appraising modern poetry.

After he achieved recognition as a poet, Shapiro became increasingly interested in analyzing the relation of the poet to society. The interest in "the poet's function" was evident in his next volume of poetry, *Trial of a Poet* (1947), in which he described the "plight of the poet who comes into conflict with society." Since then Shapiro has written several prose collections of criticism, including one, *Beyond Criticism* (1953), in which he argued against those poets who exalted poetry as a "substitute religion" or used it as "social propaganda." Poetry should not be written by intellectuals for other intellectuals, a situation that he felt was common in modern poetry. Rather, poetry should be "the fullest expression of personality," and not only of the mind.

Two years after leaving the Army, Shapiro became Consultant in Poetry at the Library of Congress, and in 1948, joined the faculty of Johns Hopkins University, where he had been an undergraduate. At Johns Hopkins, he lectured on poetry and taught creative writing. For five years beginning in 1950 Shapiro was the editor of *Poetry: A Magazine of Verse.* At present, he is on the faculty of the University of Nebraska.

Auto Wreck

Its quick soft silver bell beating, beating,
And down the dark one ruby flare
Pulsing out red light like an artery,
The ambulance at top speed floating down
Past beacons and illuminated clocks   5
Wings in a heavy curve, dips down,
And brakes speed, entering the crowd.
The doors leap open, emptying light;
Stretchers are laid out, the mangled lifted
And stowed into the little hospital.   10
Then the bell, breaking the hush, tolls once,
And the ambulance with its terrible cargo
Rocking, slightly rocking, moves away,
As the doors, an afterthought, are closed.

We are deranged, walking among the cops   15
Who sweep glass and are large and composed.
One is still making notes under the light.
One with a bucket douches° ponds of blood
Into the street and gutter.
One hangs lanterns on the wrecks that cling,   20
Empty husks of locusts, to iron poles.

Our throats were tight as tourniquets,°
Our feet were bound with splints, but now,
Like convalescents intimate and gauche,
We speak through sickly smiles and warn   25
With the stubborn saw° of common sense,
The grim joke and the banal° resolution.
The traffic moves around with care,
But we remain, touching a wound
That opens to our richest horror.   30

18. douches (doo'shəz): cleanses with a stream of water. 22. tourniquets
(toor'nə·ketz): bandages, or anything to stop the flow of blood by compression.
26. saw: a saying, maxim, or proverb. 27. banal (bă'nel or bə·nal'): meaningless from overuse; hackneyed.

Already old, the question Who shall die?
Becomes unspoken Who is innocent?
For death in war is done by hands;
Suicide has cause and stillbirth, logic;
And cancer, simple as a flower, blooms.   35
But this invites the occult mind,
Cancels our physics with a sneer,
And spatters all we know of dénouement°
Across the expedient° and wicked stones.

38. dénouement (dā·n$\overline{oo}$·män′): the final outcome, particularly the final unraveling of a complex plot of a novel, play, etc. **39. expedient:** useful; concerned merely with one's own interests rather than what is right.

Meaning and Method

1. In lines 1–14, the speaker describes an ambulance arriving at the
   scene of an auto wreck. What words in these lines personify the
   ambulance? What words in lines 4–6 suggest that the ambulance is
   being compared to an airplane? Do these words also suggest a comparison with an angel, perhaps the angel of mercy?
2. Why does the ambulance bell beat in line 1 but toll in line 11?
   What are the connotations of the phrase *its terrible cargo* (line
   12)? Does it suggest the ambulance is on a personal or an impersonal mission? Does the ambulance symbolize death? mercy? both?
3. What are the attitudes of the policemen toward the accident? How
   do these differ from the attitudes of the spectators? What words or
   phrases in lines 15–30 indicate that the bystanders feel as if they
   too have been injured in the accident? Which figures in lines 22–24
   employ medical terminology to explain this feeling? Why might the
   bystanders feel that they have been injured? Why would not the
   policemen share this feeling?
4. In lines 25–28, the speaker describes how the bystanders begin to
   talk again. Possibly one says, "They shouldn't have been driving so
   fast"—an example of "the stubborn saw of common sense" (line
   26). Give an example of a "grim joke" and a "banal resolution"
   (line 27).
5. In lines 31–39, the speaker meditates on death in general. What
   examples of death seem natural or logical to the speaker in lines
   31–35? What does he mean when he says that "this" (line 36)—
   the auto accident—cancels "our physics" (line 37)? In your answer
   compare death by suicide to death in an accident.
6. What is the theme of the poem?

October 1

That season when the leaf deserts the bole°
And half-dead seesaws through the October air
Falling face-downward on the walks to print
The decalcomania of its little soul—
Hardly has the milkman's sleepy horse   5
On wooden shoes echoed across the blocks,
When with its back jaws open like a dredge°
The van comes lumbering up the curb to someone's door and
    knocks.

And four black genii muscular and shy
Holding their shy caps enter the first room   10
Where someone hurriedly surrenders up
The thickset chair, the mirror half awry,
Then to their burdens stoop without a sound.
One with his bare hands rends apart the bed,
One stuffs the china-barrel with stale print,   15
To bear the sofa toward the door with dark funereal tread.

The corner lamp, the safety eye of night,
Enveloped in the sun blinks and goes blind
And soon the early risers pick their way
Through kitchenware and pillows bolt upright.   20
The bureau on the sidewalk with bare back
And wrinkling veneer is most disgraced,
The sketch of Paris suffers in the wind,
Only the bike, its nose against the wall, does not show haste.

Two hours—the movers mop their neck and look   25
Filing through dust and echoes back and forth.
The halls are hollow and all the floors are cleared
Bare to the last board, to the most secret nook;

1. bole: the trunk of a tree. 7. dredge: a large, powerful scoop or suction apparatus that clears out or deepens channels or harbors.

But on the street a small chaos survives
That slowly now the leviathan° ingests,°   30
And schoolboys and stenographers stare at
The truck, the house, the husband in his hat who stands and
    rests.

He turns with miserable expectant face
And for the last time enters. On the wall
A picture-stain spreads from the nail-hole down.   35
Each object live and dead has left its trace.
He leaves his key; but as he quickly goes
This question comes behind: Did someone die?
Is someone rich or poor, better or worse?
What shall uproot a house and bring this care into his eye?   40

30. **leviathan** (lə·vī′ə·thən): a gigantic unidentified water beast mentioned in the Bible; any enormous creature or thing, as a whale or a large ship. **ingests:** takes in so as to digest or eat, here used humorously.

Meaning and Method

1. Why do the images in lines 1–4 make October an appropriate time of year for the events of this poem to take place?
2. What is the "stale print" (line 15) with which the moving man "stuffs the china-barrel"? Does the speaker's description of the moving men as "four black genii muscular and shy" (line 9) indicate that his attitude toward moving is humorous? that he feels that supernatural forces are at work? both? neither? something else?
3. How do the moving men change the normal atmosphere of the house (lines 14–20)? What happens to the furniture when it is put out on the street in lines 21–23? What is meant literally and figuratively by the phrase "a small chaos" (line 29)? What, literally, is the "leviathan" (line 29)? Does the speaker's use of this word show the same attitude he revealed when he called the moving men "genii"?
4. What is the husband's attitude when he returns to the empty house in lines 33–40? Do any signs remain in the house of his life there? Why do you think he asks the three questions in lines 38–40?
5. What is the tone of the poem—happy, sad, ironic, hopeful? How would you answer the questions in lines 38–40? What is the theme of the poem?

Composition

Most people have seen a friend move away from a neighborhood, or have moved themselves. Write a composition, based on personal or imagined experience, in which you mention the thoughts and emotions you had in moving from a place or in seeing a friend move away.

Muriel Rukeyser

In the 1930's when aviation was relatively new and hazardous, Muriel Rukeyser decided that she wanted to learn how to fly a plane. She therefore enrolled in an aviation school; but, although she passed the ground-course, her parents refused to sign a permit allowing their daughter, legally a minor, to fly. Her time in the school was not wasted, however, because Miss Rukeyser incorporated her knowledge of aviation in her early poems; her first collection, published in 1935 when she was twenty-two, was entitled *Theory of Flight*.

Miss Rukeyser's writing has continued to reflect her involvement in the events and scenes of her time. She was born in New York City in 1913 and attended Vassar College. Her desire to become a reporter and a writer led her to leave Vassar after two years. Shortly after leaving school, she was hired by *The Student Review* and was sent to Alabama to cover the Scottsboro trial, a case in which nine Negroes were tried for a crime of which they were widely believed to be unjustly accused and illegally convicted. Since that time, Miss Rukeyser has been involved in civil rights movements and other social causes.

Her poetry reflects her deeply felt emotional commitment to social justice. It has also documented the loss of personal direction and the alienation which she believed was widespread in the modern world. Her writing is not entirely pessimistic; in her works published since the end of the second World War, there has been a strong affirmative assertion that this alienation and loss of direction can be overcome by a belief in love.

Boy with His Hair Cut Short

Sunday shuts down on a twentieth-century evening.
The El° passes. Twilight and bulb define
the brown room, the overstuffed plum sofa,
the boy, and the girl's thin hands above his head.
A neighbor radio sings stocks, news, serenade.   5

He sits at the table, head down, the young clear neck exposed,
watching the drugstore sign from the tail of his eye;
tattoo, neon, until the eye blears, while his
solicitous tall sister, simple in blue, bending
behind him, cuts his hair with her cheap shears.   10

The arrow's electric red always reaches its mark,
successful neon! He coughs, impressed by that precision.
His child's forehead, forever protected by his cap,
is bleached against the lamplight as he turns head
and steadies to let the snippets drop.   15

Erasing the failure of weeks with level fingers,
she sleeks the fine hair, combing: "You'll look fine tomorrow!
You'll surely find something, they can't keep turning you
    down;
the finest gentleman's not so trim as you!" Smiling, he raises
the adolescent forehead wrinkling ironic now.   20

He sees his decent suit laid out, new-pressed,
his carfare on the shelf. He lets his head fall, meeting
her earnest hopeless look, seeing the sharp blades splitting.
the darkened room, the impersonal sign, her motion,
the blue vein, bright on her temple, pitifully beating.   25

2. **El:** a shortened form for "elevated train," that is, a train which runs on
tracks elevated above the city streets. The elevated structure blocks out light
from the buildings surrounding it.

Meaning and Method

1. How does the description of the setting in lines 1–8 emphasize the connotations of dreariness and confinement suggested by the opening phrase "Sunday shuts down" (line 1)?
2. Who are the "they" in line 18, and what does the boy want from them? Why does the boy admire the neon sign described in lines 11' and 12? What does the neon sign symbolize? What is ironic about the boy's admiring it?
3. What words or phrases in lines 21 and 22 indicate the effort the boy is making?
4. Do the boy and his sister have a warm, human relationship or a cold, impersonal one? How are they unlike the modern world represented by the neon sign in lines 7 and 8, 11 and 12, and 24?
5. Is the poet an objective observer, or is she emotionally involved in the situation she describes? If the latter, what emotion does she exhibit? Does this emotion make the poem seem sentimental?

Composition and Discussion

1. The poem, written during the Depression, illustrates some of the social effects of the economic collapse that began in 1929. Do some research in the library about the causes and the economic, social, and political effects of the Depression. What has been done to prevent such a widespread economic collapse from recurring? Discuss whether or not the American economy could be again subject to a depression.

2. Areas near railroad and elevated subway lines have generally been less desirable places to live because of the noise and the pollution. The same is true of highways and airports.

Orally or in writing discuss the steps that have been taken to reduce the noise and pollution caused by planes, automobiles, and trains. What additional things should be done to reduce their harmful effects?

Effort at Speech Between Two People

Speak to me.   Take my hand.   What are you now?
I will tell you all.   I will conceal nothing.
When I was three, a little child read a story about a rabbit

who died, in the story, and I crawled under a chair:
a pink rabbit: it was my birthday, and a candle   5
burnt a sore spot on my finger, and I was told to be happy.

Oh, grow to know me.   I am not happy.   I will be open:
Now I am thinking of white sails against a sky like music,
like glad horns blowing, and birds tilting, and an arm about me.
There was one I loved, who wanted to live, sailing.   10

Speak to me.   Take my hand.   What are you now?
When I was nine, I was fruitily sentimental,
fluid: and my widowed aunt played Chopin,°
and I bent my head on the painted woodwork, and wept.
I want now to be close to you.   I would   15
like the minutes of my days close, somehow, to your days.

I am not happy.   I will be open.
I have liked lamps in evening corners, and quiet poems.
There has been fear in my life.   Sometimes I speculate
On what a tragedy his life was, really.   20

Take my hand.   Fist my mind in your hand.   What are
    you now?
When I was fourteen, I had dreams of suicide,
and I stood at a steep window, at sunset, hoping toward death:
if the light had not melted clouds and plains to beauty,
if light had not transformed that day, I would have leapt.   25
I am unhappy.   I am lonely.   Speak to me.

I will be open.   I think he never loved me:
he loved the bright beaches, the little lips of foam
that ride small waves, he loved the veer of gulls:
he said with a gay mouth: I love you.   Grow to know me.   30

What are you now?   If we could touch one another,
if these our separate entities could come to grips,
clenched like a Chinese puzzle . . . yesterday

13. Chopin (shō·pan'): Frederic Chopin (1810–1849), a Polish-born pianist-composer who is famous for works that seem to reflect strong emotions.

I stood in a crowded street that was live with people,
and no one spoke a word, and the morning shone.   35
Everyone silent, moving. . . . Take my hand.   Speak to me.

Meaning and Method

1. One of the two persons in this poem speaks in each six-line stanza, and the other person speaks in each four-line stanza. What words or phrases in lines 10 and 19 and 20 indicate that the second speaker is a woman? How does line 27 confirm this impression?
2. In the first, third, and fifth stanzas, the first speaker—presumably a man—tells the woman about his childhood and adolescence. How would you characterize this speaker? Has his life been happy? If so, why? If not, why not?
3. In the second, fourth, and sixth stanzas, the woman speaks about someone she had loved, someone from whom she is now parted, either by choice or by death. Are her memories of her love happy? sad? both? What does the woman reveal about her character in line 18? Was she primarily like or unlike the man she loved, described in lines 10 and 28–30? Did she and the man communicate deeply with each other?
4. The poem begins and ends with the phrase "Speak to me." Yet throughout the poem, each of the two people has spoken alternately. In what way did they *not* speak to each other? Do they seem more concerned with the other person than with themselves?
5. Read the poem aloud, making sure to pause when you reach the spaces that ordinarily do not appear between sentences in a line of verse (see line 1, for example). Do you think that the unusual pauses give an impression of the effort of communicating? of something else? Explain.

Composition

In a composition, discuss the effects of television and film on communication. Have television news broadcasts replaced newspapers as our primary source of information about world and national events? Do people respond more favorably to films than to books? Consider in your discussion the benefits and the disadvantages of the shift from print to pictures. Does the immediacy of the visual presentation outweigh the loss of detailed analysis found in printed material? Give details and particulars; examples, real or hypothetical; or comparisons and contrasts to illustrate your arguments.

Delmore Schwartz

[1913–1966]

"Cerebral" and "intellectual" are words that have been used to describe the work of Delmore Schwartz. His works, however, are far from the coldly logical abstractions these words may call to mind. His poems are passionate, though controlled, explorations of "philosophical" questions, intense searches for meaning and value. In his poems and in his life, deep tension and drama result from what the critic Alfred Kazin called his "old-fashioned faith in reason" coming into conflict with the world as it is, and particularly with the fact of time. Time, to Schwartz, made beauty transient and life meaningless, and his thoughts about time obsessed and tortured him.

Schwartz was born in Brooklyn of Russian-Jewish parents. He majored in philosophy at New York University and did graduate work in that subject at Harvard for two years. His first book, *In Dreams Begin Responsibilities* (1938)—a collection of fiction, poetry and drama—was highly praised. From 1943 until 1955, he was associated with the *Partisan Review,* serving as an editor and frequently contributing critical essays and creative works. Schwartz also taught at various universities.

As he grew older, he became increasingly paranoic. His inability to cope with a world he thought was persecuting him led to his estrangement from his wife and his friends, and he dropped out of sight for some time. He was found dead of a heart attack at age fifty-two in a cheap New York hotel in which he had been living.

In the Naked Bed, in Plato's Cave

In the naked bed, in Plato's cave,°
Reflected headlights slowly slid the wall,
Carpenters hammered under the shaded window,
Wind troubled the window curtains all night long,
A fleet of trucks strained uphill, grinding,   5
Their freights covered, as usual.
The ceiling lightened again, the slanting diagram
Slid slowly forth.
          Hearing the milkman's chop,
His striving up the stair, the bottle's chink,
I rose from bed, lit a cigarette,   10
And walked to the window. The stony street
Displayed the stillness in which buildings stand,
The street-lamp's vigil and the horse's patience.
The winter sky's pure capital
Turned me back to bed with exhausted eyes.   15

Strangeness grew in the motionless air. The loose
Film grayed. Shaking wagons, hooves' waterfalls,
Sounded far off, increasing, louder and nearer.
A car coughed, starting. Morning, softly
Melting the air, lifted the half-covered chair   20
From underseas, kindled the looking-glass,
Distinguished the dresser and the white wall.
The bird called tentatively, whistled, called,
Bubbled and whistled, so! Perplexed, still wet
With sleep, affectionate, hungry and cold. So, so,   25

1. **Plato's cave:** In *The Republic*, the philosopher Plato used the example of a cave, with a fire at the open end, to teach man not to rely on his senses for true knowledge. According to the parable, man is chained in the cave so that he can see only the back wall. Behind him pass objects that cast shadows on the wall. Man sees (that is, experiences with his senses) these shadows which he takes to be real, but they are only appearances. Reality (true knowledge) is found in the objects that cast the shadows, and these objects are abstract ideas that can be perceived only with the mind.

"In the Naked Bed, in Plato's Cave" from *In Dreams Begin Responsibilities* by Delmore Schwartz, copyright 1938 by New Directions. Reprinted by permission of the publisher, New Directions Publishing Corporation.

O son of man, the ignorant night, the travail°
Of early morning, the mystery of beginning
Again and again,
                              while Time is unforgiven.

26. travail: anguish, distress, pain.

Meaning and Method

1. What words or phrases in lines 1–15 indicate that the speaker is describing a sleepless night? What indications are there that time is passing?
2. What images in lines 1–15 reinforce the allusion to Plato's cave in line 1? Does the speaker feel that he understands the events of day-to-day happenings? What does his identification of his own bed— "the naked bed"—with Plato's cave show about the speaker's attitude toward life? What words or phrases in lines 16–25 recall Plato's cave again? What does the speaker's statement, "The loose / Film grayed" (lines 16 and 17) show about his attitude toward daily life?
3. The specific descriptions of lines 1–25 lead up to the abstract conclusion of lines 26–28. Does the speaker think that man understands the life he leads? that he perceives reality?
4. Why is time unforgiven? Is the tone of lines 25–28 bitter? resigned? disturbed? something else?

For Rhoda

Calmly we walk through this April's day,
Metropolitan poetry here and there,
In the park sit pauper and *rentier*,°
The screaming children, the motor car   5
Fugitive about us, running away,
Between the worker and the millionaire
Number provides all distances,

3. *rentier* (räṅ·tyä′): *French,* one who owns or derives a fixed income from invested capital or lands.

It is Nineteen Thirty-Seven now,
Many great dears are taken away,
What will become of you and me   10
(This is the school in which we learn . . .)
Besides the photo and the memory?
(. . . that time is the fire in which we burn.)

(This is the school in which we learn . . .)
What is the self amid this blaze?   15
What am I now that I was then
Which I shall suffer and act again,
The theodicy° I wrote in my high school days
Restored all life from infancy,
The children shouting are bright as they run   20
(This is the school in which they learn . . .)
Ravished entirely in their passing play!
(. . . that time is the fire in which they burn.)

Avid its rush, that reeling blaze!
Where is my father and Eleanor?   25
Not where are they now, dead seven years,
But what they were then?
                              No more? No more?
From Nineteen-Fourteen to the present day,
Bert Spira and Rhoda consume, consume
Not where they are now (where are they now?)   30
But what they were then, both beautiful;
Each minute bursts in the burning room,
The great globe reels in the solar fire,
Spinning the trivial and unique away.
(How all things flash! How all things flare!)   35
What am I now that I was then?
May memory restore again and again
The smallest color of the smallest day:
Time is the school in which we learn,
Time is the fire in which we burn.   40

18. **theodicy:** an attempt to reconcile the existence of evil with the concept
of a benign God.

Meaning and Method

1. What are the connotations of line 1, *Calmly we walk through this April's day*? Are these connotations carried through in the images in lines 2–5, or do some of the images make the line appear ironic? What impression is created by the long run-on sentence of lines 1–11 punctuated only by commas?

2. What do you think is the meaning of the statement, "Between the worker and the millionaire / Number provides all distances (lines 6 and 7)? Does number also provide "all distances" in our life? Is number a meaningful form of measurement in the speaker's view?

3. Does the speaker feel his present self will leave a strong impression on the world? How does he differ from his younger self? from the children at play?

4. The speaker, who seems to be walking with someone he loves, remembers two people whom he has not seen for some time, "Bert Spira and Rhoda" (line 29). What were they like when he knew them? What has time done to them?

5. From lines 33 and 34, do you think that the speaker feels human life is important in the universal scheme of things? Does he think that memory will overcome time, or does he simply hope that it will have some effect? Can we ever bring back the persons we once were, or once knew?

6. What is meant by the refrain? What words or images in the poem carry the idea of burning?

Composition

In the poem, Schwartz asks, "What shall become of you and me?" Would people be happier if they knew what would happen to them? Would they be less happy? In your topic sentence, give your answer to the question of whether or not people would be happier if they knew the future. Then, use specific examples to support your general statement.

Robert Hayden

Although Negro history and folklore are two of Robert Hayden's main interests, he feels that the poems of black poets should not be limited to racial experiences. Nor does he feel that they should be "judged by standards different from those applied to the work of other poets." In his own books of verse, *Heart-Shape in the Dust* (1940) and *A Ballad of Remembrance* (1962), he has written about such varied subjects as seagulls, the experience of diving, and the Mexican city of Veracruz, as well as about Negro life and history. And in *Kaleidoscope*, his anthology of Negro poetry, he has also tried to bring out the variety of subject matter and approaches used by black writers.

Hayden was born in Detroit in 1913 and did his undergraduate work at Wayne State University in that city. After earning an M.A. in English literature at the University of Michigan, he taught for two years at that university. In 1946, he joined the faculty of Fisk University, where he is at present professor of English.

Hayden was awarded the prize for poetry at the first World Festival of Negro Arts, which was held in Dakar, Senegal, in 1965. He is also the poetry editor of the magazine *World Order*.

"Summertime and the Living * . . ."

> Nobody planted roses, he recalls,
> but sunflowers gangled there sometimes,
> tough-stalked and bold
> and like the vivid children there unplanned.
> There circus-poster horses curveted°   5
> in trees of heaven
> above the quarrels and shattered glass,
> and he was bareback rider of them all.

* **Summertime and the Living:** a reference to a song that begins "Summertime, and the living is easy." The song is from George Gershwin's opera *Porgy and Bess* (1935), which tells a story of life in the Negro section of Charleston, South Carolina. 5. **curveted:** pranced.

No roses there in summer—
oh, never roses except when people died—   10
and no vacations for his elders,
so harshened after each unrelenting day
that they were shouting-angry.
But summer was, they said, the poor folks' time
of year. And he remembers   15
how they would sit on broken steps amid

The fevered tossings of the dusk, the dark,
wafting hearsay with funeral-parlor fans
or making evening solemn by
their quietness. Feels their Mosaic° eyes   20
upon him, though the florist roses
that only sorrow could afford
long since have bidden them Godspeed.

Oh, summer summer summertime—

Then grim street preachers shook   25
their tambourines and Bibles in the face
of tolerant wickedness;
then Elks° parades and big splendiferous
Jack Johnson° in his diamond limousine
set the ghetto burgeoning   30
with fantasies
of Ethiopia spreading her gorgeous wings.

20. **Mosaic:** referring to the Old Testament leader Moses. **28. Elks:** a fraternal organization. **29. Jack Johnson:** the first Negro heavyweight champion of the world. He held the heavyweight title from 1908 through 1915.

Meaning and Method

1. In what ways do sunflowers contrast with roses? How do sunflowers symbolize the community the poet describes?
2. How do the childhood daydreams (see lines 5–8) contrast with the present surroundings? How did the daydreams of the community (see lines 30–32) contrast with their surroundings? What do the child's daydream and that of the community have in common?
3. What is meant by the phrase, "the florist roses / that only sorrow could afford" (lines 21 and 22)? Is the tone of this statement ironic?

Randall Jarrell
[1914–1965]

During the second World War, Randall Jarrell served in the Air Force as a control-tower operator at an airfield in Arizona where B-29 bomber crews were trained. Although he never saw combat, his involvement in the war effort intensified his sense of "the pain of human guilt." Jarrell had written about this suffering in his first collection of poems, *Blood for a Stranger*, published in 1942, the year he entered military service. But the enormous destruction resulting from the war filled him with outrage. His war poems, most of which deal with the air corps, exposed the horror, boredom, and inhumanity that armed conflict causes, and showed how the war mutilates the young both physically and psychologically.

His reputation as a poet is equaled, if not surpassed, by his reputation as a critic. Throughout his life, he contributed essays to various literary magazines: *Sewanee Review*, *The Kenyon Review*, *Poetry*, and others. *Poetry and the Age* (1953) contains some of his most profound critical opinions. The poet Robert Lowell praised Jarrell as a critic by saying he was "the only man I have ever met who would make other writers feel that their work was more important to him than his own."

Jarrell, a native of Nashville, Tennessee, studied under John Crowe Ransom at Vanderbilt University. When Ransom left Vanderbilt for Kenyon College, Jarrell, who had received his M.A. in 1938, followed and taught at Kenyon for two years. Jarrell always considered teaching a privilege; he said that if he were rich, he would pay to be able to teach. For almost twenty years, he lectured at the Women's College of the University of North Carolina, located in Greensboro. From his students and the community, he received "a personal reverence that was incomparably more substantial and poignant than the empty, numerical, long-distance blaze of national publicity." He died in Greensboro after being struck by an automobile.

The Death of the Ball Turret Gunner

In Selected Poems, *Randall Jarrell wrote, "A ball turret was a plexiglass sphere set into the belly of a B-17 or a B-24, and inhabited by two .50 caliber machine-guns and one man, a short small man. When this gunner tracked with his machine-guns a fighter attacking his bomber from below, he revolved with the turret; hunched upside-down in his little sphere, he looked like the fetus in the womb. The fighters which attacked him were armed with cannon firing explosive shells. The hose was a steam hose."* *

From my mother's sleep I fell into the State,
And I hunched in its belly till my wet fur froze.
Six miles from earth, loosed from its dream of life,
I woke to black flak and the nightmare fighters.
When I died they washed me out of the turret with a hose.   5

Meaning and Method

1. Which words or phrases in the first four lines stress the image of birth.
2. In line 1 the speaker is saying that there seemingly was but a moment between his birth and his entering military service. What are the connotations of the word *State?* What is suggested by Jarrell's equating the State with the airplane?
3. The wet fur (line 2) refers to the fur on the collar of the airman's flying suit or jacket; it is wet from perspiration. How can line 2 also be interpreted as reducing man to merely an animal?
4. What is the irony in the statement "loosed from its dream of life, / I woke to . . . the nightmare fighters" (lines 3 and 4)? Which is more real to the gunner—his prewar life or the moments before his death?
5. What is the tone of the poem? For example, is it one of bitter irony? sympathy? glorification of the dead man?

* Randall Jarrell, *Selected Poems* (New York: Knopf, 1955), page xiii.

"The Death of the Ball Turret Gunner" from *Selected Poems* by Randall Jarrell. First appeared in *Little Friend, Little Friend*. Reprinted by permission of Mary Von S. Jarrell.

Eighth Air Force

If, in an odd angle of the hutment,°
A puppy laps the water from a can
Of flowers, and the drunk sergeant shaving
Whistles O *Paradiso!*—shall I say that man
Is not as men have said: a wolf to man?   5

The other murderers troop in yawning;
Three of them play Pitch,° one sleeps, and one
Lies counting missions, lies there sweating
Till even his heart beats: One; One; One.
O *murderers!* . . . Still, this is how it's done: 10

This is war. . . . But since these play, before they die,
Like puppies with their puppy; since, a man,
I did as these have done, but did not die—
I will content the people as I can
And give up these to them: Behold the man!°   15

I have suffered, in a dream, because of him,
Many things;° for this last savior, man,
I have lied as I lie now. But what is lying?°
Men wash their hands, in blood, as best they can:
I find no fault in this just man.°   20

---

1. **hutment:** a group of huts, as in a camp. 7. **Pitch:** a card game. 15. **Behold the man!:** a translation of the Latin phrase, *ecce homo* (ek′sē hō′mō). Pilate spoke these words when he brought Jesus before those who wished to have him crucified. (See John 19:5.) 16–17. **I . . . things:** a reference to the words spoken by Pilate's wife. (See Matt. 27:19.) 18. **what is lying?:** the antithesis of Pilate's words to Jesus, "What is truth?" (See John 18:38.) 19–20. **wash . . . man:** In Matthew 27:24, Pilate "washed his hands before the multitude, saying, I am innocent of the blood of this just person . . ." before delivering Jesus to be crucified. In John 19:6, Pilate told the crowd, "I find no fault in him."

"Eighth Air Force" from *Losses* by Randall Jarrell, copyright 1948, by Harcourt Brace Jovanovich, Inc. Reprinted by permission of the publisher.

Meaning and Method

1. What are the connotations of the statement that man is *a wolf to man* (line 5)? Why would this seem particularly true in time of war? Does the speaker feel that this statement characterizes man fully? In your answer, comment on the illustrations of man's behavior in war given in lines 1–4. What characteristics of man do these incidents symbolize? Why does the speaker not answer the question in line 5?

2. In lines 6 and 10, the airmen are described unequivocally as "murderers." Does the speaker condemn them totally for their acts, or does he sympathize with them in some way?

3. In lines 12–20, the speaker may be an officer who will send these men out to die, and is perhaps lying to them about their chances of survival, or the value of their mission. How is the speaker like Pilate? What reason does the officer give for sending the airmen out to die? Does he feel guilty for what he is doing? Does he feel he is doing it for the good of mankind? Do all people share in the guilt?

4. To whom does the "him" (line 16) refer? To Christ? to mankind? to both?

5. Why is it ironic that today a man can repeat statements similar to those made when Christ was condemned to die and that the same wrongs, the same acts are repeated? Is man the "last savior" of mankind? Explain.

John Frederick Nims

Writing about his early life, John Frederick Nims commented that he had had "a quite ordinary childhood, without unusual griefs or exultations." Like other boys in Muskegon, Michigan, where he was born in 1914, he took part in sports and social activities. Unlike many other boys, however, he found in the public library of the town an atmosphere of "exciting gloom" and spent many hours there reading various sorts of adventure stories.

His hours in Muskegon's public library were eventually followed by hours in the libraries of Notre Dame University (from which he received a B.A. in 1937 and an M.A. in 1939), and the University of Chicago (from which he received a Ph.D. in 1945). He returned to Notre Dame to teach literature, and he spent several years lecturing at European universities. Since 1962, he has been a professor at the University of Illinois.

Nims has taught courses in comparative literature, which is the study of relationships between foreign literature and English and American writing. This interest in foreign literature led him to translate works by the classical Greek playwrights and the poetry of the Spanish mystic St. John of the Cross. His most important collection of poems is *The Iron Pastoral* (1947).

Love Poem

My clumsiest dear, whose hands shipwreck vases,
At whose quick touch all glasses chip and ring,
Whose palms are bulls in china, burs in linen,
And have no cunning with any soft thing

Except all ill-at-ease fidgeting people: 5
The refugee uncertain at the door
You make at home; deftly you steady
The drunk clambering on his undulant floor.

Unpredictable dear, the taxi drivers' terror,
Shrinking from far headlights pale as a dime   10
Yet leaping before red apoplectic streetcars—
Misfit in any space. And never on time.

A wrench in clocks and the solar system. Only
With words and people and love you move at ease.
In traffic of wit expertly maneuver   15
And keep us, all devotion, at your knees.

Forgetting your coffee spreading on our flannel,
Your lipstick grinning on our coat,
So gayly in love's unbreakable heaven
Our souls on glory of spilt bourbon float.   20

Be with me, darling, early and late. Smash glasses—
I will study wry music for your sake.
For should your hands drop white and empty
All the toys of the world would break.

Meaning and Method

1. In a love poem, the poet usually praises the beauty of his beloved
   and mentions how wonderful she is. How does the first stanza reverse the stereotyped format of a love poem? What is the effect of
   the first stanza on the reader?
2. Is the title of the poem ironic? Or does it accurately describe the
   poem? Explain.

Margaret Abigail Walker

"I Want to Write, I Want to Write the Songs of My People," the title of Miss Walker's first published poem, is in many respects the theme of her literary life. She was sixteen when the poem was published in *The Crisis*, the official magazine of the NAACP. Later she said, "As an adolescent, I wrote every single day I lived. It was like eating and sleeping and breathing, I guess. I wanted to express the feeling of the Negro people and my own especially."

Miss Walker, a minister's daughter, was born in Birmingham, Alabama, in 1915. She lived in the South until she enrolled in Northwestern University. After her graduation, she moved to Chicago and worked at a variety of jobs—as a social worker, reporter, secretary, and magazine editor. In 1939, Miss Walker enrolled in the creative-writing program at the University of Iowa. Since graduating with a master's degree from Iowa, she has taught at various colleges in the South.

Her only book of poems, *For My People*, was published by Yale University as part of their Younger Poets Series. Miss Walker has also written a novel, *Jubilee* (1966), which she submitted as part of her work at the University of Iowa's Writers' Workshop.

Iowa Farmer

I talked to a farmer one day in Iowa.
We looked out far over acres of wheat.
He spoke with pride and yet not boastfully;
he had no need to fumble for his words.
He knew his land and there was love for home   5
within the soft serene eyes of his son.
His ugly house was clean against the storm;
there was no hunger deep within the heart
nor burning riveted within the bone,
but here they ate a satisfying bread.   10

Yet in the Middle West where wheat was plentiful;
where grain grew golden under sunny skies
and cattle fattened through the summer heat
I could remember more familiar sights.

Meaning and Method

1. What words or phrases show that the Iowa wheat farmer was a contented man? Did his son share his attitude? What do you think caused the farmer to feel contented?
2. Did the speaker share the feelings of the farmer? Why may lines 8 and 9 be interpreted literally and figuratively? What do you think are the "more familiar sights" the speaker remembers? How does the knowledge that the poet is black help you understand these lines?
3. Is the tone of the poem one of bitter envy? of sadness? of melancholy? something else?

Childhood

When I was a child I knew red miners,
dressed raggedly and wearing carbide lamps.°
I saw them come down red hills to their camps
dyed with red dust° from old Ishkooda mines.
Night after night I met them on the roads,   5
or on the streets in town I caught their glance;
the swing of dinner buckets in their hands,
and grumbling undermining all their words.

I also lived in low cotton country
where moonlight hovered over ripe haystacks,   10
or stumps of trees, and croppers'° rotting shacks
with famine, terror, flood, and plague near by;
where sentiment and hatred still held sway
and only bitter land was washed away.

2. carbide lamps: lights worn on the miners' helmets. 4. red dust: probably from the clay soil in which many coal mines are found. 11. croppers: sharecroppers, or tenant farmers who pay part of their crop as rent for the land.

Meaning and Method

1. The "more familiar sights" the speaker remembers in "Iowa Farmer" are described in detail here. Were the miners she knew as a child as proud and content as the Iowa farmer?

2. How do the farms in "low cotton country" (line 9) contrast with that of the Iowa farmer? Is there any beauty in this land? If so, does beauty or ugliness predominate? Why is the land described as "bitter" (line 14)?

3. The Iowa farmer seemed calm and contented. The sharecroppers in this poem, however, feel stronger emotions—sentiment, hatred, and terror. How might the difference in their situations account for the difference in emotional attitude?

4. The land of the Iowa farmer is described on a sunny summer day. Both scenes in this poem, however, take place at night. What is suggested by the contrast in time between the two poems?

Peter Viereck

Peter Viereck is a historian as well as a poet. His first book, a historical study entitled *Metapolitics: From the Romantics to Hitler* (1941), has been called "the best account of the intellectual origins of Nazism available to the general public." He is also a political essayist, and he has come to be recognized as a leader of the "New Conservatism," a group that is opposed to the extremists of both the left and the right.

His initial collection of verse, *Terror and Decorum* (1948) was awarded the Pulitzer prize for poetry. As a poet, Viereck frequently writes from a detailed and almost historical perspective. Critics have objected to what they see as his desire to teach and to preach. This didacticism often deprives the readers of the pleasure of discovering the theme for themselves. But in his best work, he shows his ingenuity in structuring his poems and his skill in using popular speech.

The poet was born in New York City in 1916. After graduating with honors from Harvard, he continued studying there for his Ph.D. in history, which he received in 1942. After serving with the Army in Africa and Italy during the second World War, he returned home to begin a career in education. Since 1948, he has taught at a number of universities.

"Vale" from Carthage *
(*Spring, 1944*)

I, now at Carthage. He, shot dead at Rome.
Shipmates last May. "And what if one of us,"
I asked last May, in fun, in gentleness,
"Wears doom, like dungarees, and doesn't know?"

* **Vale** (vā′lē) : *Latin,* farewell. **Carthage:** an ancient city-state in North Africa (near Tunis in modern Tunisia) that was destroyed by the Romans in 146 B.C. During the second World War, the allied armies used Tunisia as a supply depot for the invasion of Sicily and Italy.

He laughed, *"Not see Times Square° again?"* The foam,   5
Feathering across that deck a year ago,
Swept those five words—like seeds—beyond the seas
   Into his future. There they grew like trees;
     And as he passed them there next spring, they laid
     Upon his road of fire their sudden shade.   10
Though he had always scraped his mess-kit pure
And scrubbed redeemingly his barracks floors,
Though all his buttons glowed their ritual-hymn
Like cloudless moons to intercede for him,
No furlough fluttered from the sky. He will   15
Not see Times Square—he will not see—he will
Not see Times
        change; at Carthage (while my friend,
Living those words at Rome, screamed in the end)
I saw an ancient Roman's tomb and read
"Vale" in stone. Here two wars mix their dead: 20
     Roman, my shipmate's dream walks hand in hand
     With yours tonight ("New York again" and "Rome"),
     Like widowed sisters bearing water home
     On tired heads through hot Tunisian sand
     In good cool urns, and says, "I understand."   25
Roman, you'll see your Forum Square no more;
What's left but this to say of any war?

5. **Times Square:** the movie and theater center of New York City.

Meaning and Method

1. The poem was written in 1944 at the height of the Italian campaign in the second World War. What details of character and setting are given in lines 1 and 2? How does the ellipsis—that is, the omission of one or more words—in line 1 make the two statements more emphatic?
2. Why is line 5 ironic? Why is it also poignant? What effect does the speaker achieve by italicizing the friend's words?
3. What is the speaker like? What was his friend like? How would you describe their friendship?
4. The "they" in line 8 and the "their" in line 10 refer to the friend's five words, "Not see Times Square again." What are the two possible meanings of "sudden shade" in line 10? What is ironic about the fact that the friend died in the spring?

5. The word "furlough" means a pass or a permit, official permission to be absent from duty. In view of what might be considered the friend's attempt to propitiate or please the "gods" (lines 11–14), why is line 15 so ironic and so sad?

6. What effect is achieved by the repetition and the punctuation in lines 15–17?

7. The subject of "says" (line 25) is "dream," which is personified in line 21. What is it that is understood?

8. What does the word "this" (line 27) refer to? to the poem itself? to the "I understand"? to the theme that wars have no importance in history, that all they accomplish is the killing of young men? to the idea that all dead soldiers are brothers? to all of these?

9. This poem contains a number of contrasts and comparisons. For example, "doom" is likened to "dungarees," which are usually associated with everyday living and with durability, and line 10 has "shade" over a "road of fire."

Explain the significance and/or symbolism in the comparison and contrast of (a) the dead city of Carthage with the Eternal City of Rome, (b) Forum Square with Times Square, (c) the buttons on the friend's tunic with cloudless moons, and (d) the soldiers' dreams with widowed sisters?

Composition

Write a critical evaluation of the poem analyzing its structure. Discuss the use of understatement, especially in the final couplet. Would ending the poem with a powerful denunciation of war have been as effective?

John Ciardi *

Poet, teacher, editor, critic, translator—John Ciardi has become one of the best known names in modern poetry. Although his text *How Does a Poem Mean?* (1959) caused some controversial comment when an excerpt from it first appeared in *Saturday Review*, it is accepted by many teachers of poetry as an excellent approach to the genre.

He began by saying that, "A poem is a formal structure in which many elements operate at the same time." Since it is such a structure, the study of a poem necessitates analysis, but Ciardi did not mean that the analysis, once completed, can be substituted for the poem. Rather, he says, "the only reason for taking a poem apart is that it may be put back together again more richly."

Ciardi was born in Boston in 1916. He studied at Tufts College and did graduate work at the University of Michigan. After teaching for two years, he enlisted in the Air Force and served as a gunner on a bomber. Many of the poems in his collection *Other Skies* (1947) were based on his war experiences and his readjustment to civilian life.

After the war, Ciardi resumed his teaching career, first at Harvard and then at Rutgers University. He also became the poetry editor of *Saturday Review*, a position he still holds. In 1961, he decided to give up the "planned poverty" of full-time teaching to undertake various publishing enterprises, notably writing books and poems for children. He has translated all three sections of Dante's *Divine Comedy*. Ciardi has also lectured extensively throughout the United States.

* Ciardi (Char'dē).

On Flunking a Nice Boy Out of School

I wish I could teach you how ugly
decency and humility can be when they are not
the election° of a contained mind but only
the defenses of an incompetent. Were you taught
meekness as a weapon? Or did you discover,   5
by chance maybe, that it worked on mother
and was generally a good thing—
at least when all else failed—to get you over
the worst of what was coming. Is that why you bring
these sheepfaces to Tuesday?
                                        They won't do.   10
It's three months work I want, and I'd sooner have it
from the brassiest lumpkin in pimpledom, but have it,
than all these martyred repentances from you.

3. election: *here,* conscious choice.

Meaning and Method

1. The speaker is a teacher. Why has he "flunked" the boy to whom
   he is speaking?
2. What kind of person is the boy? What attitudes of his particularly
   annoy the teacher? In your answer, explain the phrases "meekness
   as a weapon" (line 5) and "martyred repentances" (line 13).
3. According to the speaker, when is "humility" a positive quality?
   When is it negative? Does he care whether he receives the formali-
   ties of respect that many teachers demand? Does he care about
   respect in any other way?
4. Is "nice" in the title used ironically? Why or why not?
5. What is the effect produced by the brevity of "They won't do" (line
   10)?
6. What is the theme of the poem?

"On Flunking a Nice Boy Out of School" from *Person to Person* by John Ciardi, copyright 1964 by Rutgers, The State University. Reprinted by permission of the author.

Gwendolyn Brooks

In a review of Gwendolyn Brooks's novel *Maud Martha* (1953), a critic wrote that this autobiographical story of a Negro girl growing up in Chicago narrated "with sensitivity and restraint the emotional depths of a seemingly simple, uneventful life." The same characteristics—sensitivity and restraint—mark Miss Brooks's poetry. Like the novel, her poems are about seemingly uneventful lives. Many of these poems are set in Bronzeville, a fictional Negro community on Chicago's South Side. Her first collection of verse, *A Street in Bronzeville* (1945) describes the joys and sorrows of ghetto life.

Although Miss Brooks was born in Topeka, Kansas, in 1917, she has spent most of her life in the areas of Chicago she describes so accurately in her writing. She began writing poetry before she was ten, and when she was thirteen, one of her poems was published in a children's magazine. She was graduated from Wilson Junior College and worked for a short time as a typist. In 1939 she married Henry Blakely and for many years devoted most of her time to raising a family.

For her second volume of poetry, *Annie Allen* (1949), Miss Brooks became the first Negro to be awarded the Pulitzer prize. Since then, she has gathered together two other collections of poems, *The Bean Eaters* (1960) and *Selected Poems* (1963) and has written a number of short stories and book reviews. She has also taught creative writing at a number of colleges in Chicago.

Piano After War

On a snug evening I shall watch her fingers,
Cleverly ringed, declining to clever pink,
Beg glory from the willing keys. Old hungers
Will break their coffins, rise to eat and thank.
And music, warily, like the golden rose   5
That sometimes after sunset warms the west,
Will warm that room, persuasively suffuse

That room and me, rejuvenate a past.
But suddenly, across my climbing fever
Of proud delight—a multiplying cry.   10
A cry of bitter dead men who will never
Attend a gentle maker of musical joy.
Then my thawed eye will go again to ice.
And stone will shove the softness from my face.

Meaning and Method

1. Is the speaker listening to the music he is describing, or is he imagining himself as a listener? How do you know? Is the pianist someone he knows? a person in a concert hall?

2. What do you think the speaker means when he says that the music will "rejuvenate a past" (line 8)?

3. How will his experiences in war affect his pleasure in listening to music? Will he ever be able to be his past self again? Why or why not?

4. The poet creates an impression of the room, the people in it, and the contrasting moods of the people by means of connotative words. What do the connotations of *snug* (line 1) tell you about the atmosphere of the room—an atmosphere that reflects the pianist's personality? Why does the word subsequently prove to be ironic? What does the repetition of "clever" in line 2 tell you about the pianist? about the speaker's attitude toward her? How does the speaker imagine he will respond to the music (lines 5–8)?

5. Figurative language is richly woven throughout the sonnet. Why is the personification "Old hungers / Will break their coffins" (lines 3 and 4) particularly appropriate in a poem about the aftermath of war? What does it tell about the speaker's desires for beauty and comfort during the war? Is the "golden rose" (line 5) a flower or a color? Does it have connotations of both? What is meant, literally and figuratively, by "my thawed eye" (line 13)? How do the metaphors in lines 13 and 14 sum up the theme of the poem?

6. Instead of using normal end rhymes such as boy/joy, the poet used *near rhymes* in which the final consonant sounds of the accented syllables of each word are the same, but the vowel sounds are different. For example, in the first quatrain, the near rhymes are fi*ngers*/hu*ngers* and pi*nk*/tha*nk*.

What are the near rhymes in the next two quatrains? in the concluding couplet? Why do you think the poet chose to use a rhyme scheme in which the rhymes are discordant rather than harmonious?

Mentors *

For I am rightful fellow of their band.
My best allegiances are to the dead.
I swear to keep the dead upon my mind,
Disdain for all time to be overglad.
Among spring flowers, under summer trees,   5
By chilling autumn waters, in the frosts
Of supercilious winter—all my days
I'll have as mentors those reproving ghosts.
And at that cry, at that remotest whisper,
I'll stop my casual business. Leave the banquet.   10
Or leave the ball—reluctant to unclasp her
Who may be fragrant as the flower she wears,
Make gallant bows and dim excuses, then quit
Light for the midnight that is mine and theirs.

* **Mentors:** guides, trusted teachers.

Meaning and Method

1. "Mentors" is a companion sonnet to "Piano After War." The
speaker is the same man, and he expands on the idea or attitude that
was inherent in the first sonnet—that he will never forget his dead
comrades, or the anguish, ugliness, and cruelty of the war.
    According to line 1, why will he not forget them? Does he feel
that he has only escaped their fate by chance?
2. Why will the ghosts be "reproving" (line 8)? What effect will they
have on his pleasures? Will he change his actions or mood easily
when he remembers the dead, or will mourning be a difficult
duty?
3. In the last line, the speaker says that "midnight" is his time as well
as that of the ghosts. Why is life as dark for him as for the dead?
4. In this sonnet Miss Brooks uses almost the same near-rhyme scheme
that she did in "Piano After War." The difference is that there is
one full rhyme in the sestet—*wears/theirs.* How does the use of
rhyme bring the poem to a close?

Truth

And if sun comes
How shall we greet him?
Shall we not dread him,
Shall we not fear him
After so lengthy a   5
Session with shade?

Though we have wept for him,
Though we have prayed
All through the night-years—
What if we wake one shimmering morning to   10
Hear the fierce hammering
Of his firm knuckles
Hard on the door?

Shall we not shudder?—
Shall we not flee   15
Into the shelter, the dear thick shelter
Of the familiar
Propitious° haze?

Sweet is it, sweet is it
To sleep in the coolness   20
Of snug unawareness.

The dark hangs heavily
Over the eyes.

18. **Propitious** (prō·pish′əs) : indicating favorable circumstances.

Meaning and Method

1. In this poem, the speaker wonders what would happen if the truth
we say we desire—and weep for and pray for—finally appeared.
Would it be welcomed? feared? ignored? Explain the paradox: we
weep and pray for truth, but we also fear it. Why would truth be
feared? Are there times when truth should be avoided?

2. The poet presents an antithesis between light and dark; what symbolic value does each have?

3. What words or phrases in the poem personify truth? Is truth presented as something pleasant? powerful? easy to deal with? something else?

   Would the personification have had the same effect if truth had been described as "her" rather than "him"? Why or why not?

4. In *Murder in the Cathedral*, the poet and playwright T. S. Eliot wrote: "Humankind cannot bear very much reality." Do you think the speaker of the poem would agree with this statement? Why or why not? Does she seem to feel human beings are strong? weak? admirable? unadmirable? something else?

Composition

Write a composition personifying your concept of the abstraction *truth*. Or personify *falsehood, joy, grief, hatred, knowledge, time,* or *peace*. In your personification, try to let your reader see the character you are describing, as well as feel what this character is like. Develop the composition so as to present a definition of the abstraction you are personifying.

Naomi

Too foraging° to blue-print or deploy!°—
To lift her brother;
Or tell dull mother
That is not it among the dishes and brooms,
It is damper   5
Than what you will wipe out of sills and down from the
     moldings of rooms
And dump from the dirty-clothes hamper;

Or say "Do not bother
To hug your cheese and furniture"
To her small father;   10

1. **foraging:** searching about or rummaging around for something, especially for food or supplies. **deploy:** place in position, according to plan.

Or to register at all the hope of her hunt or say what
It was not.

(It was, by diligent caring,
To find out what life was for.

For certainly what it was not for was forbearing.)   15

Meaning and Method

1. What are Naomi's parents like? For example, do they have broad or narrow interests? Do they seem to care about finding out what "life was for" (line 14)? What do the connotations of *dull mother* (line 3) and *small father* (line 10) tell you about Naomi's attitudes toward her parents?
2. Do Naomi and her parents communicate with one another? Does she try to tell them her problems? Does she feel they would understand? Does she regard them as models of what to be—or what not to be?
3. What is Naomi's "hunt" (line 11)? Is her method of hunting to be involved with life? detached from life? both?
4. What is the tone of the last line? What does the word "forbearing" suggest about Naomi's character? Is Naomi being satirized? presented as a model to be imitated?

For Clarice It Is Terrible Because with This He Takes Away All the Popular Songs and the Moonlights and Still Night Hushes and the Movies with Star-eyed Girls and Simpering Males

They were going to have so much fun in the summer.
But winter has come to the edges of his regard.
Not the lace-ice, but the bleak, the bleak steep sorrow.
Not the shy snow, not the impermanent icicles but the hard
The cruel pack and snarl of the unloved cold.   5

There is nowhere for her to go.
There is no tenderness on whom she may frankly cry.

There is no way to unlatch her face
And show the gray shudder
Of this hurt hour   10
And the desert death of tomorrow.

Meaning and Method

1. In lines 1–5, the speaker explains what is meant by the "winter" (line 2) of Clarice's boyfriend's mood by contrasting two types of images about winter. What do the connotations of *lace-ice* (line 3), *shy snow* (line 4), and *impermanent icicles* (line 4) have in common? How do these connotations contrast with those of *the bleak steep sorrow* (line 3) and *the hard / The cruel pack and snarl of the unloved cold* (lines 4 and 5)?
2. What do such phrases as "gray shudder" (line 9), "hurt hour" (line 10), and "desert death" (line 11) show about Clarice's reactions to her friend's change of attitude? What characteristic of her situation described in lines 6–9 makes her feel worse than she would otherwise feel?
3. What is the attitude of the adult speaker to the end of Clarice's romance? Is the speaker's attitude as expressed in the title ironic? sardonic? amused? tolerant? Does the poem indicate that the speaker understands the unhappiness the girl is experiencing?

Robert Lowell

The early poetry of Robert Lowell is the work of a man torn by a constant conflict: how to find the morality and peace he passionately desires in a world that he sees as evil and violent. The New England in which he grew up is presented as a corrupt, decaying society, founded by Puritans who hypocritically sought freedom by fencing "their gardens with the Redman's bones," and by extension, the decay of New England represents the decline of all of American society.

The bitter tone of much of this early poetry is created by the poet's feeling that he is not immune from the disease that spread through American society, that he too is caught in the web of corruption. At times, his attitude toward the past is ambivalent, seemingly rejecting it and accepting it simultaneously, but in point of fact, he has repudiated much of his heritage.

The Lowell family heritage is rich in tradition. Their antecedents may be traced to the founding of the colonies; the poet's grandfather was a younger brother of the poet James Russell Lowell, and Amy Lowell was a distant relative. Robert was raised in the exclusive Beacon Hill section of Boston and attended St. Mark's School, where he was taught by Richard Eberhart (see page 183). He went to Harvard for two years, transferring to Kenyon College in order to study the classics with John Crowe Ransom. In 1940, he rejected his family's Protestantism for Roman Catholicism.

At the beginning of the second World War, he tried to enlist in the armed forces but was rejected. Two years later, he was arrested for failing to comply with the Selective Service Act. At his trial Lowell explained that he believed the Allied bombing of cities was morally indefensible and he therefore could not serve in the military. His plea to be regarded as a conscientious objector was rejected, and he was sentenced to a prison term of a year and a day. Actually, he spent only five months in jail.

Lowell's poetry is filled with allusions to past literature and history. Paradoxically, his rebellion against his heritage is set in poems of traditional forms—forms that he uses with enormous skill and virtuosity. His early poetry, which has been called "a poetry of deep passion and fierce tension," achieves much of its effect from having strong protest "bottled" in old, rigid metrical forms.

Eventually, Lowell abandoned traditional verse forms: "I couldn't get my experience into tight metrical forms." His later poems, *Life Studies* (1959), differ not only metrically but also thematically from those in his early collections, notably his Pulitzer prize winning *Lord Weary's Castle* (1946). Instead of commenting primarily on society, the poems in *Life Studies* are "confessional" poems in which he subjects his family and himself to both censure and sympathy. These poems are highly personal revelations about his psychological struggles, marital problems, and other difficulties. Many of these poems appear to be a form of self-therapy; that is, the poem is a method of relieving the psychological tension building up within the poet.

Lowell's confessional technique has influenced a number of younger poets, especially Sylvia Plath and W. D. Snodgrass. Because of this influence and because of the power of his verse, Lowell is considered by many as the most important American poet to appear since the second World War.

The Holy Innocents *

Listen, the hay-bells tinkle as the cart
Wavers on rubber tires along the tar
And cindered ice below the burlap mill
And ale-wife° run.° The oxen drool and start
In wonder at the fenders of a car,   5
And blunder hugely up St. Peter's hill.°
These are the undefiled by woman—their

* **The Holy Innocents:** Matthew 2:1–16 describes how the Magi told Herod, the king of Palestine, that they had come in search of the newborn king of the Jews. Herod considered Jesus his rival and sought to find out where he was living in order to have him killed. When he failed to find Jesus, he had all the children two years old or under slaughtered. These children are known as the Holy Innocents. **4. ale-wife:** a fish of the herring family widely used for food. **run:** the route by which the fish migrate to the spawning ground. **6. St. Peter's hill:** the hill in Rome on which stands St. Peter's Cathedral.

Sorrow is not the sorrow of this world:
King Herod shrieking vengeance at the curled-
Up knees of Jesus choking in the air,   10

A king of speechless clods and infants. Still
The world out-Herods Herod;° and the year,
The nineteen-hundred forty-fifth of grace,
Lumbers with losses up the clinkered° hill
Of our purgation;° and the oxen near   15
The worn foundations of their resting place,
The holy manger where their bed is corn
And holly torn for Christmas. If they die,
As Jesus, in the harness, who will mourn?
Lamb of the shepherds, Child, how still you lie.   20

12. out-Herods Herod: a reference to *Hamlet*, Act III, Scene 2, line 16. In
medieval religious plays, Herod was portrayed as a raging, screaming tyrant.
14. clinkered: A clinker is an earthy residue left by coal, etc., in burning. 15.
purgation: cleansing from guilt.

Meaning and Method

1. Which images in the first stanza are used, more than likely, to represent the relationship of the past and the present and of the man-
made world and the natural world?
2. The oxen are symbols of innocence. What is the figurative meaning
of "their / Sorrow is not the sorrow of the world" (lines 7 and 8)?
3. What does the statement "Still / The world out-Herods Herod"
(lines 11 and 12) indicate about the poet's opinion of the modern
world? How may the phrase "speechless clods and infants" (line 11)
be interpreted to mean those who are spiritually undeveloped?
4. In lines 13–15, the poet compares the movement of the year in
which he wrote the poem (1945) to the movement of the oxen
described in lines 4–6. What does the phrase "clinkered hill" (line
14) indicate about the speaker's view of the world? about man's
struggles against evil? Why is the phrase "of grace" (line 13) ironic?
5. What is the literal goal of the oxen in lines 15–18? the symbolic
goal? From lines 18 and 19, do you think Lowell feels that holy
innocence makes any impression on the modern world?
    In the last line, the poet uses the Lamb, the conventional symbol
for Christ. Does the statement that the Child lies still indicate that
God is not a vital force in the modern world? What is the tone of
the last three lines?

Salem *

In Salem seasick spindrift° drifts or skips
To the canvas flapping on the seaward panes
Until the knitting sailor stabs at ships
Nosing like sheep of Morpheus° through his brain's
Asylum. Seaman, seaman, how the draft   5
Lashes the oily slick about your head,
Beating up whitecaps! Seaman, Charon's raft°
Dumps its damned goods into the harbor-bed—
There sewage sickens the rebellious seas.
Remember, seaman, Salem fishermen   10
Once hung their nimble fleets on the Great Banks.°
Where was it that New England bred the men
Who quarted° the Leviathan's° fat flanks
And fought the British Lion° to his knees?

---

* **Salem:** a city and port north of Boston, Massachusetts. In colonial times it was famous as a whaling port. 1. **spindrift:** sea spray. 4. **Morpheus:** the god of dreams in Greek mythology; popularly known as the god of sleep. 7. **Charon's raft:** In Greek mythology, Charon was the boatman who transported souls of the dead across the River Styx to Hades, the underworld. 11. **Great Banks:** a fishing ground in the Atlantic Ocean east of Newfoundland. 13. **quarted:** divided into quarters. **Leviathan:** an unidentified water creature mentioned in the Bible; *here*, the speaker equates Leviathan with the whale. 14. **British Lion:** symbol of the British Empire.

Meaning and Method

1. In the first seven lines, the speaker seems to be describing a scene below the deck of a ship anchored in Salem harbor. The panes of the portholes are covered by canvas, left partly free to admit air, and this canvas flaps in the strong wind. A sailor sits knitting, perhaps trying to keep himself from going crazy. (Knitting, he "stabs at ships / Nosing like sheep of Morpheus through his brain's / Asylum.")

How is this picture different from what we usually imagine to be the life of a sailor? Does the poet use words that emphasize the beauty or the ugliness of the scene? the excitement or the dullness?

2. In lines 7–9, the speaker indicates that the harbor is polluted. Con-

sidering the reference to Charon's raft, what does the pollution symbolize?

3. In lines 10 and 11, the speaker reminds the seaman of the glorious days of Salem fishermen, when their fleets roamed far away to the Great Banks off Newfoundland. What were the other accomplishments of these Salem fishermen? What words make them seem like mythical heroes? Do you think the speaker regrets the change from the past glories of Salem to the present? Why or why not?

Language: Words from Mythology

Many names from Greek and Roman mythology have been used to form words in our language. The name *Morpheus*, for example, is the basis of the word *morphine*, a narcotic and a pain killer. The drug puts the user into a dreamy state of mind.

Among the other words or phrases that have been derived from mythology are the following:

1.	echo	5.	narcissistic
2.	gorgon	6.	panic
3.	halcyon	7.	terpsichorean
4.	lethargy	8.	uranium

Check in an unabridged dictionary to find the names from which these words were derived. Then, in a book of mythology, read the stories connected with these names. Explain how the modern English meaning of each of these words is related to the legend.

Water

It was a Maine lobster town—
each morning boatloads of hands
pushed off for granite
quarries on the islands,

and left dozens of bleak   5
white frame houses stuck
like oyster shells
on a hill of rock,

and below us, the sea lapped
the raw little match-stick   10
mazes of a weir,°
where the fish for bait were trapped.

Remember? We sat on a slab of rock.
From a distance in time,
it seems the color   15
of iris, rotting and turning purpler,

but it was only
the usual gray rock
turning the usual green
when drenched by the sea.   20

The sea drenched the rock
at our feet all day,
and kept tearing away
flake after flake.

One night you dreamed   25
you were a mermaid clinging to a wharf-pile,
and trying to pull
off the barnacles with your hands.

We wished our two souls
might return like gulls   30
to the rock. In the end,
the water was too cold for us.

11. **weir:** a fence of stakes, brushwood, etc., put into water to catch fish.

Meaning and Method

1. What is Lowell's impression of the scene? Point out words and images that give his feeling toward the setting.
2. Which images suggest destruction and deterioration? What is suggested by the couple's looking at a weir in which fish are trapped? Does this image imply they are married? Explain lines 31 and 32.
3. The poem tells of a failing relationship between a man and a woman. What in stanza 7 suggests the futility of the woman's attempts to save the relationship?

M. Carl Holman

When Holman was appointed Information Officer for the United States Commission on Civil Rights in the early 1960's, he left both a teaching position at Clark College in Atlanta, Georgia, and a position as editor of a weekly newspaper, the *Atlanta Inquirer*, to take the job. Holman knew from some of his personal experiences as a black man the problems with which the commission was to deal and the need for publicizing these problems.

Moses Carl Holman was born in Minter City, Mississippi, in 1919. He received degrees from Lincoln University in Missouri and the University of Chicago. Shortly after graduation from Chicago with an M.A., Holman became an English instructor at Hampton Institute in Virginia. Holman had started writing poetry while in school, and his poems have since been published in magazines and anthologies. His work has been described as revealing "good craftsmanship, arresting imagery, and a sophisticated outlook."

Notes for a Movie Script

Fade in the sound of summer music,
Picture a hand plunging through her hair,
Next his socked feet and her scuffed dance slippers
Close, as they kiss on the rug-stripped stair.

Catch now the taxi from the station,   5
Capture her shoulders' sudden sag;
Switch to him silent in the barracks
While the room roars at the corporal's gag.

Let the drums dwindle in the distance,
Pile the green sea above the land;   10
While she prepares a single breakfast,
Reading the V-mail° in her hand.

12. **V-mail:** letters written on specially prepared forms, transmitted on microfilm and enlarged on photographic paper for final delivery; used during the second World War.

"Notes for a Movie Script" by M. Carl Holman. Reprinted by permission of the author.

Ride a cold moonbeam to the pillbox°
Sidle the camera to his feet
Sprawled just outside in the gummy grasses,   15
Swollen like nightmare and not neat.

Now doorbell nudges the lazy morning:
She stills the sweeper for a while,
Twitches her dress, swings the screendoor open,
Cut—with no music—on her smile.   20

13. pillbox: a small, round, concrete emplacement for a machine gun or anti-
tank gun.

Meaning and Method

1. The poet uses several terms that are part of the jargon of movie-
   making—such as "fade in" (line 1) and "cut" (line 20). What
   other words or phrases make the poem seem to be a series of "notes
   for a movie script"?
2. What do you find out about the characters from these "notes" and
   about their relationship to each other? What is the plot of the
   movie? Why did the poet omit proper names? Are the characters
   individual personalities or types? Why do you think they have been
   portrayed this way?
3. Why is the last line ironic? Why does the poet emphasize that
   at this point there should be "no music"? How does the contrast
   between this direction and that given in line 1 indicate the change
   that has taken place from the beginning to the end of the "script"?

May Swenson

The critic and poet Mark Van Doren said that he liked May Swenson's poems because they are "brilliant and interesting," unlike many other contemporary poems, which he felt were "brilliant and dull." Part of Miss Swenson's brilliance lies in her experiments in poetic form. Like E. E. Cummings, she arranges the typography of her verse to emphasize certain ideas and in some cases shapes the lines to reflect the subject matter. Another aspect of her talent is her ability to describe an object, frequently an animal, in exact detail and simultaneously to suggest the universal implications inherent in that object. As the critic Howard Moss notes, "her surfaces are wonderfully painted and lead to surprising and mysterious depths."

Miss Swenson was born in Logan, Utah, in 1919 and attended Utah State University. She moved to New York City shortly after graduation. Her first collection of verse, *Another Animal*, appeared in 1954. Since then, she has written three other volumes: *A Cage of Spines* (1958), *To Mix with Time* (1963), and *Half Sun Half Sleep* (1967). She has also written poems for children, *Poems to Solve* (1965), and several plays.

Lion

In the bend of your mouth soft murder
   in the flints of your eyes
   the sun-stained openings of caves
Your nostrils breathe the ordained air
   of chosen loneliness   5

Magnificently maned as the lustrous pampas
   your head heavy with heraldic curls
   wears a regal frown between the brows
The wide bundle of your chest
   your loose-skinned belly frilled with fur   10
   you carry easily sinuously pacing on suede paws

Between tight thighs
   under the thick root of your tufted tail
   situated like a full-stoned fruit beneath a bough
   the quiver of your never-used malehood is slung   15

You pace in dung on cement
   the bars flick past your eyeballs
   fixed beyond the awestruck stares of children
Watching you they remember their fathers
   the frightening hairs in their fathers' ears   20

Young girls remember lovers too timid and white
   and I remember how I played lion with my brothers
   under the round yellow-grained table
   the shadow our cave in the lamplight

Your beauty burns the brain   25
   though your paws slue° on foul cement
   the fetor° of captivity you do right to ignore
   the bars too an illusion

Your heroic paranoia° plants you in the Indian jungle
   pacing by the cool water-hole as dawn streaks the sky   30
   and the foretaste of the all-day hunt
   is sweet as yearling's blood
   in the corners of your lips

26. slue: slide, skid, twist. **27. fetor:** stench. **29. paranoia:** a mental disorder characterized by delusions of persecution or of grandeur.

Meaning and Method

1. What words or phrases in stanzas 1–3 make the description of the lion realistic? What are the connotations of *ordained air, heraldic curls, regal brow,* and *suede paws?*
2. What memories does the sight of the lion recall for (a) children, (b) young girls, and (c) the speaker? How do each of these memories differ?
3. In the last stanza, the speaker says that the lion imagines itself in the Indian jungle. And in doing so, she raises the question "What is reality?"

   Which seems more real to the lion—his life in a cage or his imagined life in the jungle? Which world—the real or the imagined —appears more inviting? Is the lion symbolic of the condition of the artist in the modern world? Why or why not?

4. What is the speaker's attitude toward the lion? Fear? pity? envy? a combination of attitudes?

5. What is the effect created by the lack of punctuation? Does the lack of punctuation suggest that the scene described occurs in an instant of time? that it is the poet's immediate reaction upon seeing the lion? something else?

Richard Wilbur

The poetry of Richard Wilbur is characterized by his mastery of poetic technique. It is clear from reading his work that he has experimented with the subtle relationship that exists between the idea or theme of a poem and the poetic form appropriate for the expression of that idea. For example, a variety of stanzaic patterns and the groupings of stanzas might be used to separate the various parts of the poem while making evident the coherence of the entire work. Wilbur has also experimented with varied metrical patterns—combining, for example, iambic and trochaic measures. As one critic has commented, the magic of Wilbur's poetry may come from the fact that he "submits himself to the slow task of fitting matter to design, theme to object."

Richard Wilbur was born in New York City in 1921, but was raised in a rural section of New Jersey. He went to Amherst College with the intention of becoming a journalist; but before he could become a writer, he was inducted into military service and saw action in Italy during the second World War. When he returned home, he decided to study English literature, and, like so many other poets, went on to become a college teacher—first at Wellesley College and then at Wesleyan University.

Wilbur's first collection of poetry, published shortly after he returned from military service, contains few poems directly related to the war. The selections in *The Beautiful Changes and Other Poems* (1947) are, for the most part, "a joyous celebration of all that is wild and free and full of life." This note of celebration runs through many of his subsequent poems, particularly those in his Pulitzer prize winning *Things of This World* (1956), in which he emphasizes the marvels inherent in such "ordinary" things as laundry hanging from a clothesline. The celebration is balanced and tempered by an equally strong note of skepticism, a skepticism that causes him to question the value of many of the actions and ideas of contemporary man.

Juggler

A ball will bounce, but less and less. It's not
A lighthearted thing, resents its own resilience.
Falling is what it loves, and the earth falls
So in our hearts from brilliance,
Settles and is forgot.   5
It takes a sky-blue juggler with five red balls

To shake our gravity up. Whee, in the air
The balls roll round, wheel on his wheeling hands,
Learning the ways of lightness, alter to spheres
Grazing his finger ends,   10
Cling to their courses there,
Swinging a small heaven about his ears.

But a heaven is easier made of nothing at all
Than the earth regained, and still and sole within
The spin of worlds, with a gesture sure and noble   15
He reels that heaven in,
Landing it ball by ball,
And trades it all for a broom, a plate, a table.

Oh, on his toe the table is turning, the broom's
Balancing up on his nose, and the plate whirls   20
On the tip of the broom! Damn, what a show, we cry:
The boys stamp, and the girls
Shriek, and the drum booms
And all comes down, and he bows and says good-by.

If the juggler is tired now, if the broom stands   25
In the dust again, if the table starts to drop
Through the daily dark again, and though the plate
Lies flat on the table top,
For him we batter our hands
Who has won for once over the world's weight.   30

Meaning and Method

1. According to the speaker, why does a ball resent "its own resilience" (line 2)?
2. The word "gravity" in line 7 has a double significance or interpretation. One is the scientific meaning of "gravitational force." Considering the poet's use of "not / A lighthearted thing" and "resents its own resilience," what do you think is the second meaning of gravity?
3. In stanzas 2 and 3, the juggler creates his own world. What words or phrases are used to develop this image of a miniature universe, a heaven of five red balls? And what then is meant by "But a heaven is easier made of nothing at all / Than the earth regained"?
4. In the fourth and fifth stanzas, the juggler turns to the things of our daily life. He has "won for once over the world's weight" literally by making objects that are heavy behave as if they were light, and objects that belong down go up.

    What is the reaction of the audience to these feats? Which words or phrases in the fourth stanza convey the feelings of excitement and enthusiasm? What happens to these objects and the spectators' reactions to them when the juggler ends his act? What words and phrases in stanza 5 convey a tone opposite to that of stanza 4?
5. Like the word "gravity" in line 7, the word "weight" in the last line has two meanings. One refers to heaviness. What is the figurative meaning?
6. What is the theme of the poem?

Year's End

Now winter downs° the dying of the year,
And night is all a settlement of snow;
From the soft street the rooms of houses show
A gathered light, a shapen atmosphere,
Like frozen-over lakes whose ice is thin   5
And still allows some stirring down within.

I've known the wind by water banks to shake
The late leaves down, which frozen where they fell

1. **downs** (verb): covers with a soft, feathery, fluffy substance.

And held in ice as dancers in a spell
Fluttered all winter long into a lake;   10
Graved° on the dark in gestures of descent,
They seemed their own most perfect monument.

There was perfection in the death of ferns
Which laid their fragile cheeks against the stone°
A million years. Great mammoths° overthrown   15
Composedly have made their long sojourns,
Like palaces of patience, in the gray
And changeless lands of ice. And at Pompeii°

The little dog lay curled and did not rise
But slept the deeper as the ashes rose   20
And found the people incomplete, and froze
The random hands, the loose unready eyes
Of men expecting yet another sun
To do the shapely thing they had not done.

These sudden ends of time must give us pause.   25
We fray into the future, rarely wrought°
Save° in the tapestries of afterthought.
More time, more time. Barrages of applause
Come muffled from a buried radio.
The New-year bells are wrangling with the snow.   30

11. **graved**: engraved. 13–14. **ferns . . . stone**: *that is*, fern leaves that left
their imprints on once-molten stone. 15. **mammoths**: huge elephants that are
now extinct. Their remains have been preserved in glaciers. 18. **Pompeii**
(pom·pā'): a Roman city in Italy destroyed by the eruption of the volcano,
Mount Vesuvius, in A.D. 79. The hardening of the molten lava preserved many
things in the city, including bodies of people and animals. 26. **wrought**: *here*,
molded or shaped. 27. **Save**: except.

Meaning and Method

1. In lines 1–4, the speaker outlines a winter scene at the end of the
   year. What characteristics of the snow are emphasized in the word
   "downs" (line 1) and in the phrase "soft street" (line 3)? How do
   the characteristics of houses—human products—contrast with those
   of snow?
2. What is meant by lines 5 and 6: "Like frozen-over lakes whose ice is

thin / And still allows some stirring down within"? Is this simile an
appropriate description of the end of the year? Is the end of the year
really a stop, a finishing, or is the idea of a year—with a beginning
and an end—a human attempt to give form to man's existence?

3. In lines 7–20, the speaker gives four examples of plants and animals
who were preserved in death, and whose attitudes toward death are
in a sense preserved. What are these examples? Do the deaths seem
right or orderly—even beautiful to the speaker?

4. What is meant by lines 21–24? What were the people "unready"
for? Why were they "incomplete"? How and why do the responses
of the people to death contrast with that of the little dog in lines
19 and 20? with the animals and plants previously described?

5. What do you think is meant by the phrase "These sudden ends of
time" (line 25)? by "We fray into the future" (line 26)? Does the
speaker seem to think that human life can ever be shaped or
ordered? Why does he ask for "More time, more time" (line 28)?

6. The "New-year bells" in line 30 may be interpreted as symbols of
human time—in this case, man's insistence that the time in which
human lives are measured has many ends and many beginnings,
and that, in a sense, no end is permanent. The "snow" in line 30
may symbolize nature's time—the advance of the seasons that is
reflected in man's constant progress from youth (spring) to death
(winter). How does man seem to deal with the idea that he cannot
shape or control his life?

Piazza di Spagna,* Early Morning

I can't forget
How she stood at the top of that long marble stair
Amazed, and then with a sleepy pirouette°
Went dancing slowly down to the fountain-quieted square;

Nothing upon her face   5
But some impersonal loneliness—not then a girl,

* **Piazza di Spagna:** a square in Rome that can be reached by descending the
Spanish Steps, a long stairway characterized by a sweeping zigzag arrangement.
There is a fountain in the square. **3. pirouette** (pir′o͞o·et′): in dancing, a rapid
whirling upon the toes; *here*, a slow, but whirling motion.

"Piazza di Spagna, Early Morning" from *Things of This World*, © 1956, by Richard
Wilbur. Reprinted by permission of Harcourt Brace Jovanovich, Inc.

But as it were a reverie of the place,
  A called-for falling glide and whirl;

As when a leaf, petal, or thin chip
Is drawn to the falls of a pool and, circling a moment above it,   10
      Rides on over the lip—
  Perfectly beautiful, perfectly ignorant of it.

Meaning and Method

1. Is the speaker unable to forget the girl because she was a striking individual? because her movement reflected and enhanced the setting? something else? What are the girl's characteristics? What does line 12 tell about her?

2. What two scenes are compared in the poem? In what ways are they similar? What does the speaker admire about each scene?

3. Each four-line stanza is rhymed *abab*, and each consists of lines of varying lengths. In what ways do the rhyme scheme and the line lengths reflect the visual imagery of the poem?

Denise Levertov

Denise Levertov's early life and education were unorthodox and unusual. She was born in England in 1923, and was educated "privately," primarily by random reading in her home, which she has described as "a house full of books." The variety of her education is reflected in some of the interests she chose to pursue as a young woman. She studied ballet, worked as a civilian nurse in London during the second World War, and wrote poetry (her first book of verse, *The Double Image*, was published in England in 1946).

She married an American novelist, Michael Goodman, in 1947, moved to the United States in 1948, and became a naturalized American citizen in 1956. The change of milieu had a "very stimulating" effect on her work, according to Miss Levertov, "for it necessitated the finding of new rhythms in which to write, in accordance with new rhythms of life and speech." Instead of using the traditional forms, which had characterized her British poems, she chose free forms for her American poems. Her verse shows the influence of an avant-garde movement known as "projective verse," whose practitioners believe that lines of poetry should be shaped or determined by "the breath of the poet"—that is, by the rhythms of the poet's normal speech.

The change in Miss Levertov's verse did not occur suddenly. Her second book of verse, *Here and Now* (1957), was not published until eleven years after the appearance of her first book. Since then, she has been a relatively prolific poet, producing five volumes of verse between 1958 and 1967.

Merritt Parkway

As if it were
forever that they move, that we
keep moving—
    Under a wan sky where
    as the lights went on a star   5
      pierced the haze & now
    follows steadily
           a constant
    above our six lanes
    the dreamlike continuum° . . .   10

And the people—ourselves!
  the humans from inside the
  cars, apparent
  only at gasoline stops
             unsure,   15
    eyeing each other

        drink coffee hastily at the
      slot machines & hurry
    back to the cars
    vanish
    into them forever, to   20
    keep moving—

Houses now & then beyond the
sealed road, the trees / trees, bushes
passing by, passing   25
    the cars that
      keep moving ahead of
    us, past us, pressing behind us
          and

10. **continuum** (kən·tin′yōō·əm): something that is continuous, of which no separate parts are able to be seen.

"Merritt Parkway" from *The Jacob's Ladder* by Denise Levertov, © 1958, 1959, 1960, 1961 by Denise Levertov Goodman. Reprinted by permission of the publisher, New Directions Publishing Corporation.

> over left, those that come   30
> toward us shining too brightly
> moving relentlessly
>
> in six lanes, gliding
> north & south, speeding with
> a slurred sound—   35

Meaning and Method

1. The Merritt Parkway is a highway in western Connecticut, but it could be a superhighway in any other part of the United States. Who might be the "they" and the "we" (line 2) who move along the highway? Do you think "they" are cars? other people? What does the deliberate vagueness of these pronouns indicate about the nature of superhighways? about the speaker's attitude toward them?
2. In lines 4–10, the speaker contrasts the cars' lights with the single star that pierces the haze. How is the star different from the moving cars? What might the star symbolize?
3. Why does the speaker seem to regard the humans inside the cars as being depersonalized?
4. What are the connotations of *sealed road* (line 24)? To what literal quality of superhighways is the speaker referring in this description?
5. What words or phrases in the poem give the effect of the rushing of the cars? of their continual motion? How does the punctuation, or lack of punctuation, in the poem contribute to this effect? Why does the poem end with a dash rather than with a period? Do you think that the free verse—the particularly short line lengths and the irregular arrangement of lines on the page—is meant to contribute to this effect? If so, how?
6. What is the theme of the poem?

Composition

1. Miss Levertov wrote that William Carlos Williams "gave me instance after instance of how one's most ordinary experience could be shown in the poem as it was, invested with wonder." How does "Merritt Parkway" show the results of this "lesson" learned from Williams? In a composition, explain your answer to this question.
2. Compare the theme and style of "Merritt Parkway" and Vachel Lindsay's "The Sante-Fe Trail" (page 80).

The Jacob's Ladder *

The stairway is not
a thing of gleaming strands
a radiant evanescence°
for angels' feet that only glance in their tread, and need not
touch the stone.   5

It is of stone.
A rosy stone that takes
a glowing tone of softness
only because behind it the sky is doubtful, a doubting
night gray.   10

A stairway of sharp
angles, solidly built.
One sees that the angels must spring
down from one step to the next, giving a little
lift of the wings: 15

and a man climbing
must scrape his knees, and bring
the grip of his hands into play. The cut stone
consoles his groping feet. Wings brush past him.
The poem ascends.   20

* Jacob's Ladder: According to Genesis 28:12, the Hebrew patriarch Jacob
fell asleep and dreamed he saw a ladder set up on earth and reaching to heaven,
and he saw "the angels of God ascending and descending on it." 3. evanes-
cence (ev′ə·nes′əns): something that is passing away, or likely to pass away,
gradually or imperceptibly.

Meaning and Method

1. According to the speaker in lines 1–5, what are the characteristics
of a stairway meant only for angels, like the biblical Jacob's ladder?
For example, is it solid? delicate? What does she mean when she
says that the angels' feet "only glance in their tread" (line 4)?

"The Jacob's Ladder" from *The Jacob's Ladder* by Denise Levertov, © 1960 by
Denise Levertov Goodman. Reprinted by permission of New Directions Publishing
Corporation.

2. The angels' stairway is contrasted with one on which poets must climb. What characteristics of this stairway are described in line 6? in lines 11 and 12? Does the fact that the stairway takes on "a glowing tone of softness" (line 8) mean that it is soft? that it exists in a world full of light?

3. Is man's climb easy or difficult? What "consoles" him (line 19)? Do he and the angels—that is, inspiration—ever meet? If so, what is the result of their meeting?

4. "The Jacob's Ladder" uses an extended symbol based on the biblical Jacob's ladder to describe the poetic process. Is the poetic process a simple one of being inspired and then writing? a difficult one, in which the poet achieves all his results by hard labor? a combination of these? If so, which comes first, the labor or the inspiration?

Louis Simpson

American literature has been enriched by several poets who became expatriates from their homelands to become citizens of the United States. Not infrequently, these poets provide new insights into the meaning of American culture because they approach it as outsiders and can view it more objectively than many native Americans. Louis Simpson is such a poet.

Simpson was born on the island of Jamaica in 1923. His mother, a former actress, imparted to him her love for opera and fantasy; Simpson characterized his father, a lawyer, as a person who "had a passion for facts." The poet's memories of his parents form the basis of his poem "My Father in the Night Commanding No."

Simpson came to the United States in 1940 to enroll in Columbia University. A tour of duty as a combat infantryman during the second World War interrupted his education. He returned to Columbia after the war, completed his undergraduate courses, and remained there to work for his doctorate. He then did editorial work for a time but disliked it and instead became a teacher. At present, Simpson teaches and lectures about poetry and also goes on reading tours throughout the country.

His first collection of poems, *The Arrivistes* (1950), was characterized by his use of traditional stanzaic and metrical forms. The meaning of the poems is often found in the allusions Simpson used. The poems in this volume and in his two subsequent books—*Good News of Death* (1955) and *A Dream of Governors* (1959)—also revealed his concern with social and political problems.

With the publication of *At the End of the Open Road* (1963), which was awarded the Pulitzer prize, it was evident that his themes had changed. Simpson wrote about his reactions to contemporary America and to his personal past and present. These poems were written in free verse instead of in the more standard metrical patterns. Most critics see this change in style as an improvement: "The prosaism of his early work—which required metrics and rhyme in order to give it character as verse—now gave way to rich, fresh, haunting imagery."

A Farm in Minnesota

The corn rows walk the earth,
crowding like mankind between the fences,
feeding on sun and rain;
are broken down by hail,
or perish of incalculable drought.   5

And we who tend them
from the ground up—lieutenants
of this foot cavalry, leaning on fences
to watch our green men never move an inch—
who cares for us?   10

Our beds are sold at auction.
The Bible, and a sword—these are bequeathed
to children who prefer a modern house.
Our flesh has been consumed
only to make more lives.   15

But when our heads are planted
under the church, from those empty pods
we rise in the fields of death,
and are gathered by angels,
and shine in the hands of God.   20

Meaning and Method

1. What physical characteristics of corn in a field might have led to the metaphor in line 1? What words in line 8 extend and elaborate this metaphor?
2. In lines 11–13, Simpson uses *metonymy*, that is, the use of a closely related idea for the idea itself. How may these lines be interpreted symbolically as well as literally?
3. How may lines 14 and 15 be regarded as ironic and paradoxical?
4. The corn is compared to human beings, and the farmers are compared to plants. What words or phrases extend each of these com-

parisons? What are the connotations of the comparison of our heads
to empty pods (lines 16 and 17)? Do you think that the poet used
the corn-man and man-plant comparisons to show the connection
between all living things? to show that God's relationship to man is
similar to that of a farmer toward his plants? something else?
5. Does the speaker feel that other people care for him? value his
work? Does he value himself and his work? Does he think God
values it?

My Father in the Night Commanding No

My father in the night commanding No
Has work to do. Smoke issues from his lips;
   He reads in silence.
The frogs are croaking and the streetlamps glow.

And then my mother winds the gramophone;   5
The Bride of Lammermoor° begins to shriek—
   Or reads a story
About a prince, a castle, and a dragon.

The moon is glittering above the hill.
I stand before the gateposts of the King—   10
   So runs the story—
Of Thule,° at midnight when the mice are still.

And I have been in Thule! It has come true—
The journey and the danger of the world,
   All that there is   15
To bear and to enjoy, endure and do.

6. **Bride of Lammermoor:** Lucia di Lammermoor, the title character in an
opera by the Italian composer, Gaetano Donizetti (1797–1848). In the story,
Lucia goes mad. **12. Thule** (thoo′lē or too′lē): in ancient geography, the
northernmost limit of the habitable world; today, a settlement in northwest
Greenland, site of a U.S. military base.

Landscapes, seascapes . . . where have I been led?
The names of cities—Paris, Venice, Rome—
     Held out their arms.
A feathered god,° seductive, went ahead.   20

Here is my house. Under a red rose tree
A child is swinging; another gravely plays.
     They are not surprised
That I am here; they were expecting me.

And yet my father sits and reads in silence,   25
My mother sheds a tear, the moon is still,
     And the dark wind
Is murmuring that nothing ever happens.

Beyond his jurisdiction as I move
Do I not prove him wrong? And yet, it's true   30
     They will not change
There, on the stage of terror and of love.

The actors in that playhouse always sit
In fixed positions—father, mother, child
     With painted eyes.   35
How sad it is to be a little puppet!

Their heads are wooden. And you once pretended
To understand them! Shake them as you will,
     They cannot speak.
Do what you will, the comedy is ended.   40

Father, why did you work? Why did you weep,
Mother? Was the story so important?
     "Listen!" the wind
Said to the children, and they fell asleep.

20. **feathered god:** perhaps a reference to Quetzalcoatl (ket·säl′kō·at′l), one of
the principal gods of the Aztecs. He is also considered a culture hero of some
Central American tribes.

Meaning and Method

1. In lines 1–12, the speaker remembers a typical childhood scene. The time is evening. His father is working; his mother is either listening to a romantic opera or reading a fairy tale romance. How would you characterize the mother? the father? Does the family group seem happy? How do you know that this scene took place many years ago?

2. In lines 13–20, the speaker indicates what his life has been like since his childhood. What has he done? What is symbolically meant by the father's "No," and how has the speaker, in a sense, escaped it?

3. In lines 21–24, the speaker indicates that his situation is now reversed—he is a father with children of his own. In his mind, however, his childhood world still exists: his father still "sits and reads," and his mother responds to her fairy tale romances (lines 26–29). Although he has moved not only beyond his father's actual "jurisdiction" (line 29) but also beyond the limited world represented by his father's "No," he wonders whether any real change has occurred.

   Who are "They" (line 31), and why will they "not change"? What is implied by the fact that "They" is emphasized? Why does the speaker now see himself, his mother, and his father, as "actors" (line 33) on a stage? Why does playing the roles of "father, mother, child" (line 34) result in puppet behavior? Why are the puppets unable to speak now (see line 39)? Is the poet's use of the word "comedy" (line 40) ironic? truthful?

4. What do the questions in lines 41 and 42 reveal about the speaker's present attitude toward his parents?

Composition and Discussion

1. The use of such words as "playhouse" (line 33), "little puppet" (line 36), and "comedy" (line 40) echoes the speech beginning with "All the world's a stage" in Shakespeare's *As You Like It* (Act II, Scene 7, lines 139–66). These references have led critics to say that the theme of Simpson's poem is that people often play roles which they conceive for themselves, rather than discovering all the potentialities of their human nature and realizing these potentialities.

Do you agree or disagree with this statement of the theme? Does this theme apply to the real world—that is, do people conform to stereotyped images of themselves? Do people act according to what they believe is accepted behavior for a "teacher," a "radical student," a "parent," or a "businessman"? Does acting according to roles prevent people from becoming individuals?

2. In the poem, Simpson presents a description of a commonly found scene—a family sitting in the living room during an evening. But the poet probes beneath the commonplace and gives a picture of life that the commonplace sometimes hides.

Write a composition in which you describe an ordinary, everyday occurrence or scene, but in which you also indicate how this occurrence masks a situation that is tragic.

Oliver Pitcher

Oliver Pitcher's major literary interest is the theater. He left his native Massachusetts to come to New York City to study drama and acting. His dramatic training includes courses at Bard College and practical experience with the American Negro Theatre.

Much of Pitcher's writing is for the stage, but he has used poetry to express his feelings about the condition of the Negro. His tone is often sardonic, and his choice of subjects offbeat. Although his poems have appeared in various anthologies, only one volume of his verse, *Dust of Silence* (1958), has been published.

Salute

```
       Murderers
       of Emmet Till°
       I salute you
       and the men
       who set the                                    5
           murderers
       free I salute
       you. Twice.

       I salute
       the brothers                                   10
       of charity
       who let Bessie
       Smith° bleed to
       death. She
       had the wrong                                  15
       blood type.
       It wasn't white.
```

2. **Emmet Till**: a Negro teenager who was lynched in Mississippi in 1954.
12–13. **Bessie Smith** (1894–1937): one of the great blues singers of the twenties. She bled to death following an automobile accident because the hospital to which she was taken refused to treat a black person.

"Salute" by Oliver Pitcher. Reprinted by permission of the author.

I salute
all self-anointed°
men   20
who dole out freedoms to other
    men.

I could go on. But won't. I
salute everything, all things
that infect me with this knot   25
twisted in my subconscious; knot
of automatic distrust, unraveled.
I salute everything, all things
worthy of my confusion, my awe,
my fury, my cursing, which never   30
looks good in print . . . worthy of
my tears . . . ALL HONORABLE MEN!
I salute you.

You could go on . . . But won't.

19. **self-anointed:** *here,* for the purpose of setting themselves apart as sacred.
The word "self-anointed" is perhaps a pun on "self-appointed."

Meaning and Method

1. The tone of this poem is bitterly ironic. Why, in the context of the
   poem, is the repeated statement, "I salute you" ironic? What is
   ironic about "brothers / of charity" (lines 10 and 11) and "wrong /
   blood type" (lines 15 and 16)?
2. In line 32, the speaker alludes to Mark Antony's speech over the
   body of Caesar in *Julius Caesar* (Act III, Scene 2). Why is this
   allusion appropriate? Did Mark Antony use the phrase in the same
   ironic way?
3. In line 23, the speaker says, "I could go on. But won't." In line 34,
   he says, "You could go on . . . But won't." What is the difference
   in meaning and implication between these two statements?
4. What social attitudes or conditions does the speaker object to?
   How do the examples of Emmet Till and Bessie Smith illustrate
   these conditions? Can you think of other examples?

James Dickey

In 1966, a former college football player and fighter pilot was awarded the National Book Award in Poetry for *Buckdancer's Choice*. At that time, the judges commended James Dickey for his "clarity, subtlety, and passion. . . ."

Dickey's early poems, such as those found in *Into the Stone* (1960), are about nature and are, as one critic noted, a "poetry of enchantment, ritual, and myth." His later poems introduce a strong note of violence captured in realistic details. And Dickey's novel, *Deliverance* (1970), also continues his study of violence as well as of obsession.

James Dickey has spent most of his life in the South. He was born in Atlanta in 1923. In 1942, he registered as a student at Clemson University but left to join the Air Force. When he was discharged from the service, he entered Vanderbilt University and stayed to receive a bachelor's and a master's degree. During the Korean War, he was recalled to active duty as a pilot.

In the 1950's, Dickey taught literature and creative writing at Rice University and at the University of Florida, and then worked for several years in advertising. In 1960, he gave up his successful business career to devote his time entirely to literature.

Since then he has been a writer-in-residence at several universities, and in 1966 he was appointed the Consultant in Poetry at the Library of Congress. He has written several books of criticism, the latest being *Poets and Poetry Today: A Critical Study*.

The Lifeguard

In a stable of boats I lie still,
From all sleeping children hidden.
The leap of a fish from its shadow
Makes the whole lake instantly tremble.
With my foot on the water, I feel   5
The moon outside

Take on the utmost of its power.
I rise and go out through the boats.
I set my broad sole upon silver,
On the skin of the sky, on the moonlight,   10
Stepping outward from earth onto water
In quest of the miracle

This village of children believed
That I could perform as I dived
For one who had sunk from my sight.   15
I saw his cropped haircut go under.
I leapt, and my steep body flashed
Once, in the sun.

Dark drew all the light from my eyes.
Like a man who explores his death   20
By the pull of his slow-moving shoulders,
I hung head down in the cold,
Wild-eyed, contained, and alone
Among the weeds,

And my fingertips turned into stone   25
From clutching immovable blackness.
Time after time I leapt upward
Exploding in breath, and fell back
From the change in the children's faces
At my defeat.   30

Beneath them I swam to the boathouse
With only my life in my arms
To wait for the lake to shine back
At the risen moon with such power
That my steps on the light of the ripples   35
Might be sustained.

Beneath me is nothing but brightness
Like the ghost of a snowfield in summer.
As I move toward the center of the lake,
Which is also the center of the moon,   40

I am thinking of how I may be
The savior of one

Who has already died in my care.
The dark trees fade from around me.
The moon's dust hovers together.   45
I call softly out, and the child's
Voice answers through blinding water.
Patiently, slowly,

He rises, dilating to break
The surface of stone with his forehead.   50
He is one I do not remember
Having ever seen in his life.
The ground I stand on is trembling
Upon his smile.

I wash the black mud from my hands.   55
On a light given off by the grave
I kneel in the quick of the moon
At the heart of a distant forest
And hold in my arms a child
Of water, water, water.   60

Meaning and Method

1. What was the "miracle" (line 12) that the children believed the lifeguard could perform? Why does he attempt to perform at night the miracle he failed to perform in the daylight? Whom does he attempt to imitate? In your answer, comment on lines 9–11 and lines 33–36.

2. Lines 13–32 are a flashback to the events of the afternoon. Did the lifeguard share the children's feeling at his "defeat"?

3. In lines 37–54, the speaker imagines that the miracle has come to pass, that the child's voice "answers" his call, and that the child "rises" (line 49) and "smiles" (line 54). What words or images in these lines indicate that, despite the lifeguard's belief that the child has risen, the child is actually dead? How is this knowledge impressed upon the lifeguard in lines 59 and 60? What effect is achieved by the repetition of "water" in the last line?

4. What emotions does the lifeguard reveal in this poem? Is he responsible for the death of the boy? If not, why does he react so strongly to the drowning?
5. Throughout the poem, the poet indicates the interplay of light and darkness. What images carry this through? What do light and darkness symbolize in the poem? Do sunlight and moonlight symbolize the same things?

Composition

"The Lifeguard" relates the concern that the lifeguard had for the people under his care. In life, concern and worry for another can lead to possessiveness. Write a composition in which you discuss the distinction between love, which leads to concern and worry about someone, and possessiveness. Can parental love become possessive? Can male-female love lead to possessiveness? Suggest guidelines for people to follow in order to avoid becoming overly possessive.

Samuel Hazo

The theme of all poetry of Samuel Hazo is human dignity. His awareness of the value of the individual runs throughout the poems found in his four published volumes—*Discovery and Other Poems* (1959), *The Quiet Wars* (1962), *Listen with the Eye: Poems* (1964), and *My Sons in God* (1965).

Hazo was born in Pittsburgh in 1928. He attended the University of Notre Dame and received advanced degrees from Duquesne University and the University of Pittsburgh. Since 1955, he has been associated with Duquesne as a teacher and administrator.

Pittsburgh in Passing

Between old battles and the ones I should
be seeing, I have lost my circus eyes.
Birthdays and deathdays. I feel the glaciering
of centuries beneath the pulse of clocks
and through the blown-out candles of my blood.   5

I stand unarmed where Braddock's armies° stood.
Instead of Hurons I see acres piped
and sewered for our waste and mined with bones
of Quakers, Indians, and immigrants.
Three decades in the woods of William Penn   10

have left me kin to all the buried men
who claimed this wilderness and named this town.
Where Washington marched in buckskin, I can drive
through battlefields of signs and ironworks,
inhale unrevolutionary air   15

6. **Braddock's armies:** In 1754, the English forces under General Braddock were defeated in a battle near Pittsburgh by a combined force of French soldiers and their Huron Indian allies.

and damn the siren waking me to war-
alerts each Monday of the year. Senates
have bolstered us with bunkercaves and rockets.
A palisade° of missiles rings the town
while banking and burlesque thrive back to back   20

in the same building. Threats of surprise attack
would bench a naked tease and the most correct
of tellers flank to flank in a joint shelter.
No one objects. Shielded around the clock
by minutemen in radar shacks, we tomb   25

the Hiroshima world beside old Rome
and older Troy while mayors fatten us
with talk. No one admits we walk on skulls,
and no one prays Isaiah° back to speak
the truth without refining it to please!   30

The siren spins. The aborigines
and whites who battled here are six wars old.
Chained to a different blunderbuss,° we sleep
in cemeteries screened by warhead forts
and dream our moats are still the seven seas.   35

19. **palisade:** a barrier or fortification. 29. **Isaiah:** an eight-century B.C. Hebrew prophet who spoke out against the political policies of Judah. He foretold the destruction of the kingdom. 33. **blunderbuss:** a short gun with a large mouth used for firing at close range.

Meaning and Method

1. The poem relates the thoughts of the poet on his birthday. What words in the first stanza refer to the process of aging and dying? What is meant by the phrase "I have lost my circus eyes"? What words or phrases in the rest of the poem refer to dying?
2. According to the poet, what are the dominant characteristics of American life? How is America's present situation like its colonial past?
3. Why does Hazo feel that he is buried like the "men / who claimed this wilderness" (lines 11 and 12)?
4. Why is it ironic that the "palisade of missiles" (line 19) is found in the land claimed and settled by the Quaker William Penn?

Composition and Discussion

1. In the years following the end of the second World War, America began to spend vast sums of money to build up its military strength.

Discuss whether or not the United States should divert part of the money spent on military items to solve problems such as inadequate housing, pollution, hunger, and other domestic ills. Is defense against external attack our most pressing problem? What should be the economic priorities of the country?

2. Write a composition using a statement of the theme of the poem as your topic sentence. Then, defend or reject Hazo's evolution of the present condition of life in the United States. Is it an accurate summarization of our condition? Does it give a slanted picture—that is, has he shown only one side of the story?

Wendell Berry

Wendell Berry was born in 1934. He is a native of Henry County, Kentucky, where he still lives. He received his undergraduate and graduate degrees from the University of Kentucky. He then taught at Stanford and New York University before joining the English department of the University of Kentucky.

His published books are two novels—*Nathan Coulter* and *A Place on Earth*; three collections of poetry—*The Broken Ground*, *Findings*, and *Openings*; and a book of essays—*The Long-Legged House*. His work also includes a poetic elegy for John F. Kennedy, *November Twenty-six Nineteen Hundred and Sixty-three*.

The Guest

Washed into the doorway
by the wake of the traffic,
he wears humanity
like a third-hand shirt
—blackened with enough   5
of Manhattan's dirt to sprout
a tree, or poison one.
His empty hand has led him
where he has come to.
Our differences claim us,   10
He holds out his hand,
in need of all that's mine.

And so we're joined, as deep
as son and father. His life
is offered me to choose.   15

Shall I begin servitude
to him? Let this cup pass.°

17. Let . . . pass: a reference to Christ's words spoken as he underwent the agony in the Garden of Gethsemane on the night before he died. (Matthew 26:39.) The cup represents suffering and trials.

Who am I? But charity must
suppose, knowing no better,
that this is a man fallen   20
among thieves,° or come
to this strait by no fault
—that our difference
is not a judgment,
though I can afford to eat   25
and am made his judge.

I am, I nearly believe,
the Samaritan who fell
into the ambush of his heart
on the way to another place.   30
My stranger waits, his hand
held out like something to read,
as though its emptiness
'is an accomplishment.
I give him a smoke and the price   35
of a meal, no more

—not sufficient kindness
nor believable sham.
I paid him to remain strange
to my threshold and table,   40
to permit me to forget him—
knowing I won't. He's the guest
of my knowing, though not asked.

20–21. man . . . thieves: an allusion to Christ's parable of the Good Samaritan. In the parable, a man was attacked by thieves and left in a ditch. Only a Samaritan, the enemy of the Jews, helped the man. (See Luke 10:30–37.)

Meaning and Method

1. What does Berry mean when he says that he and the beggar are "joined, as deep / as son and father" (lines 13 and 14)? What is the bond that unites them?
2. Lines 16–18 present the speaker's thoughts as the beggar stands before him. What is his reaction? Do you think this is the usual

reaction of a person who is approached by a beggar? Would they see the beggar as an equal? Would they in some way feel superior to him? How do lines 18–26 answer the speaker's unstated idea that the beggar is responsible for his present condition and has, therefore, "got what he deserved"?

3. How does the speaker use charity as a way of paying the beggar "to remain strange / to my threshold and table" (lines 39 and 40)? as a way of preventing any human relationship from occurring? What does the speaker withhold from the beggar? Is the speaker like the Good Samaritan described in the Bible?

4. What is the theme of the poem?

5. Is the title of the poem, "The Guest," ironic? Does it accurately summarize the events that took place? Does it suggest the ideal relationship between the speaker and the beggar? Explain.

Additional Poems for Comparison, Contrast, and Study

Edward Field

[b. 1924]

Frankenstein *

The monster has escaped from the dungeon
where he was kept by the Baron,
who made him with knobs sticking out from each side of
  his neck
where the head was attached to the body
and stitching all over   5
where the parts of cadavers° were sewed together.

He is pursued by the ignorant villagers,
who think he is evil and dangerous because he is ugly
and makes ugly noises.
They wave firebrands at him and cudgels and rakes,   10
but he escapes and comes to the thatched cottage
of an old blind man playing on the violin Mendelssohn's°
  "Spring Song."

Hearing him approach, the blind man welcomes him:
"Come in, my friend," and takes him by the arm.
"You must be weary," and sits him down inside the house.   15
For the blind man has long dreamed of having a friend
to share his lonely life.

The monster has never known kindness—the Baron was cruel—
but somehow he is able to accept it now,

* **Frankenstein**: the name of the medical student who created the monster.
The name was taken from Mary Shelley's nineteenth-century novel. The novel
was made into a movie and has been followed by a number of other horror
movies, such as *The Son of Frankenstein*. The word "Frankenstein" has erro-
neously come to mean the monster itself. 6. **cadavers**: the bodies of dead persons. 12. **Mendelssohn**: Felix Mendelssohn (1809–1847), German composer.

and he really has no instincts to harm the old man,   20
for in spite of his awful looks he has a tender heart:
Who knows what cadaver that part of him came from?

The old man seats him at table, offers him bread,
and says, "Eat, my friend." The monster
rears back roaring in terror.   25
"No, my friend, it is good. Eat—gooood"
and the old man shows him how to eat,
and reassured, the monster eats
and says, "Eat—gooood,"
trying out the words and finding them good too.   30

The old man offers him a glass of wine,
"Drink, my friend. Drink—gooood."
The monster drinks, slurping horribly, and says,
"Drink—gooood," in his deep nutty voice
and smiles maybe for the first time in his life.   35

Then the blind man puts a cigar in the monster's mouth
and lights a large wooden match that flares up in his face.
The monster, remembering the torches of the villagers,
recoils, grunting in terror.
"No, my friend, smoke—gooood,"   40
and the old man demonstrates with his own cigar.
The monster takes a tentative puff
and smiles hugely, saying, "Smoke—gooood,"
and sits back like a banker, grunting and puffing.

Now the old man plays Mendelssohn's "Spring Song" on the
    violin   45
while tears come into our dear monster's eyes
as he thinks of the stones of the mob, the pleasures of
    mealtime,
the magic new words he has learned
and above all of the friend he has found.

It is just as well that he is unaware—   50
being simple enough to believe only in the present—

that the mob will find him and pursue him
for the rest of his short unnatural life,
until trapped at the whirlpool's edge
he plunges to his death.   55

Howard Moss
[b. 1922]

Horror Movie

Dr. Unlikely, we love you so,
You who made the double-headed rabbits grow
From a single hare. Mutation's friend,
Who could have prophecied the end
When the Spider Woman deftly snared the fly   5
And the monsters strangled in a monstrous kiss
And somebody hissed, "You'll hang for this!"?

Dear Dracula, sleeping on your native soil,
(Any other kind makes him spoil),
How we clapped when you broke the French door down   10
And surprised the bride in the overwrought bed.
Perfectly dressed for lunar research,
Your evening cape added much,
Though the bride, inexplicably dressed in furs,
Was a study in jaded jugulars.   15

Poor, tortured Leopard Man, you changed your spots
In the debauched village of the Pin-Head Tots;
How we wrung our hands, how we wept
When the eighteenth murder proved inept,
And, caught in the Phosphorous Cave of Sea,   20
Dangling the last of synthetic flesh,
You said, "There's something wrong with me."

The Wolf Man knew when he prowled at dawn
Beginnings spin a web where endings spawn.
The bat who lived on shaving cream,   25
A household pet of Dr. Dream,
Unfortunately, maddened by the bedlam,
Turned on the Doc, bit the hand that fed him.

And you, Dr. X, who killed by moonlight,
We loved your scream in the laboratory   30
When the panel slid and the night was starry
And you threw the inventor in the crocodile pit
(An obscure point: Did he deserve it?)
And you took the gold to Transylvania
Where no one guessed how insane you were.   35

We thank you for the moral and the mood,
Dear Dr. Cliché, Nurse Platitude.
When we meet again by the Overturned Grave,
Near the Sunken City of the Twisted Mind,
(In *The Son of the Son of Frankenstein*),   40
Make the blood flow, make the motive muddy:
There's a little death in every body.

Meaning and Method

1. In Field's poem, why do the villagers think the monster is "evil and dangerous"? Why is it that a blind man befriends the monster? How does the monster react to the blind man's kindness?
2. What specific details emphasize the humanity of the monster?
3. What is the theme of "Frankenstein"?
4. In "Horror Movie," Moss humorously talks about typical Hollywood monster movies. What serious statement does the final couplet make about human nature? about the glorification of violence in this type of movie?
5. How do lines 29–33 foreshadow the idea presented in the final couplet.
6. Edward Field in "Frankenstein" also uses a horror movie as the subject matter of his poem. How does the theme of Field's poem contrast with that of Moss's?

John Logan

[b. 1923]

The Picnic

It is the picnic with Ruth in the spring.
Ruth was third on my list of seven girls
But the first two were gone (Betty) or else
Had someone (Ellen has accepted Doug).
Indian Gully the last day of school;   5
Girls make the lunches for the boys too.
I wrote a note to Ruth in algebra class
Day before the test. She smiled, and nodded.
We left the cars and walked through the young corn
The shoots green as paint and the leaves like tongues 10
Trembling. Beyond the fence where we stood
Some wild strawberry flowered by an elm tree
And Jack-in-the-pulpit was olive ripe.
A blackbird fled as I crossed, and showed
A spot of gold or red under its quick wing.   15
I held the wire for Ruth and watched the whip
Of her long, striped skirt as she followed.
Three freckles blossomed on her thin, white back
Underneath the loop where the blouse buttoned.
We went for our lunch away from the rest,   20
Stretch in the new grass, our heads close
Over unknown things wrapped up in wax papers.
Ruth tried for the same, I forget what it was,
And our hands were together. She laughed,
And a breeze caught the edge of her little   25
Collar and the edge of her brown, loose hair
That touched my cheek. I turned my face in-
to the gentle fall. I saw how sweet it smelled.

She didn't move her head or take her hand.
I felt a soft caving in my stomach.   30
As at the top of the highest slide
When I had been a child, but was not afraid,
And did not know why my eyes moved with wet
As I brushed her cheek with my lips and brushed
Her lips with my own lips. She said to me   35
Jack, Jack, different than I had ever heard,
Because she wasn't calling me, I think,
Or telling me. She used my name to
Talk in another way I wanted to know.
She laughed again and then she took her hand;   40
I gave her what we both had touched—can't
Remember what it was, and we ate the lunch.
Afterward we walked in the small, cool creek
Our shoes off, her skirt hitched, and she smiling,
My pants rolled, and then we climbed up the high   45
Side of Indian Gully and looked
Where we had been, our hands together again.
It was then some bright thing came in my eyes,
Starting at the back of them and flowing
Suddenly through my head and down my arms   50
And stomach and my bare legs that seemed not
To stop in feet, not to feel the red earth
Of the Gully, as though we hung in a
Touch of birds. There was a word in my throat
With the feeling and I knew the first time   55
What it meant and I said, it's beautiful.
Yes, she said, and I felt the sound and word
In my hand join the sound and word in hers
As in one name said, or in one cupped hand.
We put back on our shoes and socks and we   60
Sat in the grass awhile, crosslegged, under
A blowing tree, not saying anything.
And Ruth played with shells she found in the creek,
As I watched. Her small wrist which was so sweet
To me turned by her breast and the shells dropped   65
Green, white, blue, easily into her lap,
Passing light through themselves. She gave the pale

Shells to me, and got up and touched her hips
With her light hands, and we walked down slowly
To play the school games with the others.   70

Meaning and Method

1. The poet is trying to re-create an experience he had as a teen-ager. How do lines 1–8 indicate that the teen-age boy in the poem had a carefree attitude toward girls? How does the picnic change his attitude? What was the word he understood for the "first time" (line 55)?
2. Does Ruth share the feeling—and the change—that take place in the speaker? Does she seem to react with the same intensity with which he reacts?
3. How would you describe the mood of the poem? How does the setting (described first in lines 9–15) help create the mood?
4. The poem is dramatic, that is, it unfolds until it reaches a climax. What is the climax? How does the poet build up to the climax? Is the ending of the poem (lines 67–70) anticlimactic? Why or why not?

Winfield Townley Scott

[1910–1968]

The Unfurnished Room

You stand alone in an emptied house
And stare from the sill° into a vacant room:
Wallpaper whirls around the gaping closet.
The six-over-six windows° to the east
Are reproduced at slant across the floor.   5
So this is morning, of a clear day.
Your heart, the only sound, accelerates
Because nothing yet has happened to you here
Or everything has happened and is over.

2. sill: *that is*, of the door. 4. six-over-six windows: windows that are divided, both top and bottom, into six small sections.

Mary Oliver

[b. 1935]

A Letter from Home

She sends me news of bluejays, frost,
Of stars and now the harvest moon
That rides above the stricken hills.
Lightly, she speaks of cold, of pain,

And lists what is already lost.   5
Here where my life seems hard and slow,
I read of glowing melons piled
Beside the door, and baskets filled
With fennel, rosemary and dill,°
While all she could not gather in   10
Or hide in leaves, grows black and falls.
Here where my life seems hard and strange,
I read her wild excitement when
Stars climb, frost comes, and bluejays sing.
The broken year will make no change   15
Upon her wise and whirling heart;—
She knows how people always plan
To live their lives, and never do.
She will not tell me if she cries.

I touch the crosses° by her name;   20
I fold the pages as I rise,
And tip the envelope, from which
Drift scraps of borage, woodbine, rue.°

9. fennel, rosemary, dill: Fennel is an herb of the parsley family. Rosemary is a shrub of the mint family; it symbolizes fidelity and remembrance. Dill is an herb of the parsley family. All three are used in cooking. **20. crosses:** symbols for kisses; actually they are X's. **23. borage, woodbine, rue:** Borage is a blue-flowered herb; it symbolizes courage and is thought to drive away sadness. Woodbine is another name for the Virginia creeper, a grapelike vine. Rue is a bushy herb; it symbolizes bitterness and grief, and also forgiveness.

Meaning and Method

1. What words in "The Unfurnished Room" give an impression of emptiness? What words or phrases in "A Letter from Home" emphasize the desirable qualities of the place where the speaker used to live?

2. What effect does Miss Oliver achieve by ending the poem with the word "rue"?

3. How has each poet used *setting* as a method of emphasizing the loneliness felt by the speaker?

Richard Armour

[b. 1906]

Trustworthy

The House of Representatives has voted that American Indians, no longer "hostile or uncivilized," can be trusted with guns. NEWS ITEM.

The Indian no longer
   Is hostile, as of yore.
His moral sense is stronger,
   He's gentle to the core.

He's through with bow and arrow,   5
   His knifing days are done.
No longer crude and narrow,
   He's ready for a gun,

Though somewhat slow a starter,
   What progress he has made.   10
He's set to man a mortar
   And throw a hand grenade.

This change is rather recent,
   It wasn't always thus,
But now he's very decent   15
   And civilized like us.

Back-to-Nature Writer

In books and articles he hymns the pleasures
    Of simple, golden days of long ago.
He quotes at length, and obviously treasures,
    Bucolic thoughts of Wordsworth and Thoreau.

He sometimes grieves, he sometimes shouts defiance   5
    At man too mechanized, enthralled with chrome.
Deploring deeds of industry and science,
    He writes of rustic woodlands as his home.

But do not shed for him a tear of pity
    Or hasten by his written word to judge him.   10
He lives where born, amidst a bustling city
    From which a team of horses couldn't budge him.

Meaning and Method

1. In view of the poem, what is the irony in the title "Trustworthy"?
2. What paradox becomes apparent when you compare lines 11 and 12 with lines 15 and 16 of "Trustworthy"?
3. What is the theme of "Back-to-Nature Writer"?

"Back-to-Nature Writer" from *Light Armour* by Richard Armour, copyright 1954 by Richard Armour. Reprinted by permission of McGraw-Hill Book Company.

Alan Seeger

[1888–1916]

I Have a Rendezvous * with Death

I have a rendezvous with Death
At some disputed barricade,
When Spring comes back with rustling shade
And apple-blossoms fill the air—
I have a rendezvous with Death   5
When Spring brings back blue days and fair.

It may be he shall take my hand
And lead me into his dark land
And close my eyes and quench my breath—
It may be I shall pass him still.   10
I have a rendezvous with Death
On some scarred slope of battered hill,
When Spring comes round again this year
And the first meadow-flowers appear.

God knows 'twere better to be deep   15
Pillowed in the silk and scented down,
Where Love throbs out in blissful sleep,
Pulse nigh to pulse, and breath to breath,
Where hushed awakenings are dear . . .
But I've a rendezvous with Death   20
At midnight in some flaming town,
When Spring trips north again this year,
And I to my pledged word am true,
I shall not fail that rendezvous.

* **Rendezvous** (rän′dā·vōō) : an appointment to meet.

Richard Eberhart

A biographical sketch of Richard Eberhart appears on page 183.

The Fury of Aerial Bombardment

You would think the fury of aerial bombardment
Would rouse God to relent; the infinite spaces
Are still silent. He looks on shock-pried faces.
History, even, does not know what is meant.

You would feel that after so many centuries   5
God would give man to repent; yet he can kill
As Cain could, but with multitudinous will,
No farther advanced than in his ancient furies.

Was man made stupid to see his own stupidity?
Is God by definition indifferent, beyond us all?   10
Is the eternal truth man's fighting soul
Wherein the Beast° ravens° in his own avidity?°

Of Van Wettering I speak, and Averill,
Names on a list whose faces I do not recall
But they are gone to early death, who late in school   15
Distinguished the belt-feed-lever from the belt-holding-pawl.°

12. **Beast:** perhaps a reference to the Beast mentioned in Revelations 13. The term is applied to any vicious ruler or soldier. **ravens:** devours hungrily. **avidity:** greediness. 16. **belt-feed . . . pawl:** parts of a machine gun.

"The Fury of Aerial Bombardment" from *Collected Poems 1930–1960* by Richard Eberhart, © 1960 by Richard Eberhart. Reprinted by permission of Oxford University Press, Inc., and Chatto and Windus Ltd.

Frank Horne

[b. 1899]

Kid Stuff

December, 1942

The wise guys
tell me
that Christmas
is Kid Stuff . . .
Maybe they've got   5
something there—
Two thousand years ago
three wise guys
chased a star
across a continent   10
to bring
frankincense and myrrh
to a Kid
born in a manger
with an idea in his head . . .   15

And as the bombs
crash
all over the world
today
the real wise guys   20
know
that we've all
got to go chasing stars
again
in the hope   25

that we can get back
some of that
Kid Stuff
born two thousand years ago—

Meaning and Method

1. Alan Seeger in "I Have a Rendezvous with Death" personifies both Death and Love. How are the actions of Death and Love similar? For example, how is the description of Death in the second stanza like the sleep described in the third?
2. Name the three places where Seeger thinks the rendezvous may be kept.
3. Why is it ironic that the poet expects to die in the Spring? Seeger died fighting with the French Foreign Legion during the first World War. Why does the fact that he actually died in combat add a note of poignancy to the poem?
4. How does "pledged word" (line 23)—referring to the speaker's promise to keep the rendezvous—continue the reference to love in this stanza?
5. Compare the tone of Eberhart's "The Fury of Aerial Bombardment" with that of Seeger's poem. Which poem seems to romanticize war and death? Which seems to cry out against senseless deaths?
6. What three reasons does Eberhart suggest for man's failure to end war? How has modern man used education as a way to increase man's destructive powers?
7. In line 13, why does Eberhart use names beginning with those letters?
8. "Kid Stuff" is built around a pun on the phrase "wise guys." From reading lines 1, 8, and 20, what three meanings does the phrase have?
9. What solution does Frank Horne offer in "Kid Stuff" to the problem of war? What is the idea that Christ had?

Composition

One of the criteria of good poetry is that it give man a deeper understanding of life, of his fellow human beings, and of himself. In a composition evaluate these three poems according to this criterion. Which, if any, seems to fulfill it most completely? Why or why not?

Howard Moss

[b. 1922]

Small Elegy

In the smart room where Lennie lies,
French draperies are too silk for eyes
That like their hangings plain, like their ties
Thin-striped. Lennie will no more arise

And go now where the cocktail shakers shake   5
Their crystal energies and pianists fake
Some lovelorn valentines and, on the make,
Mirrored faces join, and part, and break.

And since those wretched limbs, not custom-made
But real, and common, in a last charade°   10
Crumble into peace, who's to parade
Up Fifth and down with all his tricks of trade?

The chandelier, the chiffonier,° the waste
By-products of the golden calf, Good Taste,
Surround his body. To his Never-Faced-   15
Reality, gentlemen, a final toast!

Damn it, he had good taste! That's all he had.
He knew the nearly-good from the not-quite-bad.
Lennie wore the first vest made of plaid.
Lennie gave it up when it became a fad.   20

10. charade: a symbolic action; also a word represented in riddling verse, or by picture, tableau, or dramatic action. **13. chiffonier:** high chest of drawers.

Good-by, Lennie—fad, plaid, and madras!°
May artificial angels and high brass
Proclaim a high-fidelity Mass
When you step from, and into glass.

21. **madras:** cotton cloth that has small designs, giving it a striped, corded, or checked effect; from Madras, the city in India where the cloth was first woven.

Meaning and Method

1. Describe the type of life Lennie led. What things seemed important to him? What note does the statement that he "knew the nearly-good from the not-quite-bad" (line 18) add to his character?
2. Considering the type of life Lennie led, why is the suggested funeral service appropriate?
3. What is Moss satirizing in the poem? Lennie? "the golden calf, Good Taste" (line 14)? the artificiality of life in urban society? all of these?

Peter Viereck

A biographical sketch of Peter Viereck appears on page 234.

Kilroy *

(For John H. Finley, Jr.)

1

Also Ulysses once—that other war.°
    (Is it because we find his scrawl
    Today on every privy door
    That we forget his ancient role?)
Also was there—he did it for the wages—   5
When a Cathay-drunk Genoese° set sail.
Whenever "longen folk to goon on pilgrimages," °
Kilroy is there;
    he tells The Miller's Tale.°

2

At times he seems a paranoiac king   10
Who stamps his crest on walls and says, "My own!"
But in the end he fades like a lost tune,
Tossed here and there, whom all the breezes sing.
"Kilroy was here"; these words sound wanly gay,
    Haughty yet tired with long marching.   15

---

* **Kilroy:** During the second World War, American soldiers wrote the expression "Kilroy was here" on walls, rocks, trees, etc. **1. that other war:** the Trojan War. **6. Cathay-drunk Genoese:** Columbus, who sought a water route to Cathay (China). **7. longen . . . pilgrimages:** one of the opening lines of the General Prologue to *The Canterbury Tales* by Geoffrey Chaucer (ca. 1340–1400). In the fourteenth century, traveling long distances on a pilgrimage was regarded as quite adventurous. **9. The Miller's Tale:** the story told by the Miller in *The Canterbury Tales.* In the story, the Miller makes fun of a carpenter who is excessively fearful.

He is Orestes°—guilty of what crime?—
>   For whom the Furies still are searching;
>   When they arrive, they find their prey
(Leaving his name to mock them) went away.
Sometimes he does not flee from them in time: 20
"Kilroy was—"
>   *(with his blood a dying man*
>   *Wrote half the phrase out in Bataan.°)*

3

Kilroy, beware. "HOME" is the final trap
That lurks for you in many a wily shape: 25
In pipe-and-slippers plus a Loyal Hound
>   Or fooling around, just fooling around.
Kind to the old (their warm Penelope°)
But fierce to boys,
>   thus "home" becomes that sea,   30
Horribly disguised, where you were always drowned,—
>   (How could suburban Crete condone
The yarns you would have V-mailed from the sun?)—
And folksy fishes sip Icarian° tea.
One stab of hopeless wings imprinted your   35
>   *Exultant Kilroy-signature*
Upon sheer sky for all the world to stare:
>   *"I was there! I was there! I was there!"*

---

16. Orestes: In Greek legend, Orestes killed his mother, Clytemnestra, because she had murdered his father, Agamemnon, the king who led the Greek forces against Troy. Orestes was punished for his action by being pursued and tormented by the Furies, the goddesses who avenged unpunished crimes. **23. Bataan:** a peninsula in the Philippines where American forces, after a long siege, surrendered to the Japanese in 1942. Most of the American soldiers died in the battle or on the "death march" to the prison camp that followed their surrender. **28. Penelope:** the wife of Ulysses, who waited ten years for him to return home after the end of the Trojan War. Penelope is the symbol of loyalty and domesticity. **34. Icarian:** of Icarus, the son of Daedalus. Daedalus, a master builder, constructed artificial wings that he and his son would use to escape from Crete. Icarus, compelled by his adventurous spirit, flew too high, and the sun melted the wax that was used to fasten the wings to his back. He fell into the sea and drowned.

4

God is like Kilroy; he, too, sees it all;
That's how he knows of every sparrow's fall;   40
That's why we prayed each time the tightropes cracked
On which our loveliest clowns contrived their act.
The G.I. Faustus° who was
                         everywhere
Strolled home again. "What was it like outside?"   45
Asked Can't, with his good neighbors Ought and But
And pale Perhaps and grave-eyed Better Not;
For "Kilroy" means: the world is very wide.
               He was there, he was there, he was there!
And in the suburbs Can't sat down and cried.   50

43. **Faustus:** a legendary German philosopher who sold his soul to the devil in return for power and knowledge.

Meaning and Method

1. What do Ulysses, Columbus, Chaucer's pilgrims, Orestes, Icarus, and Faustus have in common? What does each add to the character of "Kilroy"?
2. Why should Kilroy beware of "Home"? Why will he "drown" at home?
3. Why is God like "Kilroy"?
4. What types of persons are represented by *Can't, Ought, But, Perhaps,* and *Better Not?* How does Kilroy differ from them?
5. What does "Kilroy" symbolize? What is the theme of the poem?

Composition and Discussion

1. In a composition, discuss the effectiveness of "Kilroy" as a symbol for the spirit of adventure. Originally, the phrase "Kilroy was here" was written on walls, doors, and other places as a joke. Does the trivial origin and use of this phrase weaken the symbolism?

Also consider the allusions that Viereck used to characterize "Kilroy" as the symbol of the spirit of adventure. For example, were the soldiers at Bataan searching for adventure or had they merely received an unlucky and unwanted assignment?

2. Compare the treatment of war in this poem to its treatment in Viereck's "*Vale* from Carthage," (page 234). Which poem seems to idealize war? Which re-creates the pathos of death in war?

John Updike

[b. 1932]

Ex-Basketball Player

Pearl Avenue runs past the high-school lot,
Bends with the trolley tracks, and stops, cut off
Before it has a chance to go two blocks,
At Colonel McComsky Plaza. Bert's Garage
Is on the corner facing west, and there,   5
Most days, you'll find Flick Webb, who helps Bert out.

Flick stands tall among the idiot pumps—
Five on a side, the old bubble-head style,
Their rubber elbows hanging loose and low.
One's nostrils are two S's, and his eyes   10
An E and O. And one is squat, without
A head at all—more a football type.

Once Flick played for the high-school team, the Wizards.
He was good: in fact, the best. In '46
He bucketed three hundred ninety points,   15
A county record still. The ball loved Flick.
I saw him rack up thirty-eight or forty
In one home game. His hands were like wild birds.

He never learned a trade, he just sells gas,
Checks oil, and changes flats. Once in a while,   20
As a gag, he dribbles an inner tube,
But most of us remember anyway.
His hands are fine and nervous on the lug wrench.
It makes no difference to the lug wrench, though.

Off work, he hangs around Mae's Luncheonette.   25
Grease-gray and kind of coiled, he plays pinball,

Sips lemon cokes, and smokes those thin cigars;
Flick seldom speaks to Mae, just sits and nods
Beyond her face toward bright applauding tiers
Of Necco Wafers, Nibs, and Juju Beads.   30

Meaning and Method

1. What are the connotations of the proper names in the first stanza—
   Pearl Avenue, Colonel McComsky Plaza, Bert's Garage? What is
   the effect of ending the stanza with "Flick Webb, who helps Bert
   out"? What are the connotations of the name *Flick?*
2. If one of the gasoline pumps, described in lines 7–12, is "more a
   football type," what are the others meant to suggest? Why did
   Updike use such words and phrases as "Five on a side," "idiot
   pumps," "bubble-head style," and "rubber elbows"?
3. When was Flick a happier person? What is meant by "The ball
   loved Flick" (line 16)? What contrast is offered by lines 23 and 24?
4. How do lines 28–30 indicate that Flick lives in remembrance of
   things past?
5. What is the theme of the poem?

Composition and Discussion

Have an open-class discussion or write a composition about the role
of athletics in the high school curriculum. Should the school emphasize
the major sports, such as football and basketball, which only a few
students can play, or should it develop a program of intramural sports,
for both boys and girls? In order to arrive at an answer to this question,
you should begin by defining the educational goals of the athletic program. Should sports stress competition? fair play? sound physical development? Once you have defined the goals of the program, then
suggest methods of achieving those goals.

Daniel Hoffman

[b. 1923]

The Seals in Penobscot Bay *

The seals in Penobscot Bay

hadn't heard of the atom bomb,
so I shouted a warning to them.

Our destroyer (on trial run) slid by
the rocks where they gamboled° and played;   5

they must have misunderstood,
or perhaps not one of them heard

me over the engines and tides.
As I watched them over our wake

I saw their sleek skins in the sun   10
ripple, light-flecked, on the rock,

plunge, bubbling, into the brine,
and couple & laugh in the troughs

between the waves' whitecaps and froth.
Then the males clambered clumsily up   15

and lustily crowed like sea cocks,°
sure that their prowess held thrall°

---

* **Penobscot Bay:** a bay in Maine that has a naval base. **5. gamboled:** frolicked.
17. sea cocks: valves which control the pipes that go through the vessel's hull
to the water. **17. thrall:** in bondage.

"The Seals in Penobscot Bay" from *An Armada of Thirty Whales* by Daniel Hoffman,
© 1954 Yale University Press. Reprinted by permission of the author.

all the sharks, other seals, and sea gulls.
And daintily flipped the females,

sea wenches with musical tails;   20
each looked at the Atlantic as

though it were her looking-glass.
If my warning had ever been heard

it was sound none would now ever heed.
And I, while I watched those far seals,   25

tasted honey that buzzed in my ears
and saw, out to windward, the sails

of an obsolete ship with banked oars
that swept like two combs through the spray.

And I wished for a vacuum of wax   30
to ward away all those strange sounds,

yet I envied the sweet agony
of him who was tied to the mast,°

when the boom, when the boom, when the boom
of guns punched dark holes in the sky.   35

25–33. And I . . . mast: an allusion to the *Odyssey*. In Homer's epic, Ulysses
and his crew must sail past the place where the Sirens live. The irresistible
singing of these creatures lured sailors to their destruction. To escape the
Sirens, Ulysses put wax in the ears of the members of the crew; he lashed himself to the mast so that he could hear the Sirens' song but could not steer the
ship toward them.

Meaning and Method

1. Describe the life led by the seals. Why is it ironic that the speaker
   is on board a destroyer?
2. How is the speaker like Ulysses? How are the seals like the Sirens?
3. Why does Hoffman desire "a vacuum of wax / to ward away all
   those strange sounds"? According to the Greek legend, the Sirens
   led men to their deaths. How does the situation described in the
   poem differ from the Greek myth?

Conrad Aiken
[b. 1889]

Watch Long Enough,
and You Will See the Leaf

Watch long enough, and you will see the leaf
Fall from the bough. Without a sound it falls:
And soundless meets the grass. . . . And so you have
A bare bough, and a dead leaf in dead grass.
Something has come and gone. And that is all.　　　　5

But what were all the tumults in this action?
What wars of atoms in the twig, what ruins,
Fiery and disastrous, in the leaf?
Timeless the tumult was, but gave no sign.
Only, the leaf fell, and the bough is bare.　　　　10

This is the world: there is no more than this.
The unseen and disastrous prelude, shaking
The trivial act from the terrific action.
Speak: and the ghosts of change, past and to come,
Throng the brief word. The maelstrom° has us all.　　　　15

15. maelstrom: a turbulent, terrifying, and irresistible force; a whirlpool.

Meaning and Method

1. Aiken suggests that external events are only outward signs that signify the culmination of many internal, hidden struggles. How does the fall of a leaf illustrate this?
2. What is the tone of the poem? Is it objective? angry? sad? Does the final sentence of the poem (line 15) convey an atmosphere of despair? resignation? How does Aiken use the two meanings of *mael-*

strom to connect the literal description of the falling leaf with the theme?

Composition and Discussion

Orally or in writing, discuss the implications of Aiken's theme that everything in the world will end in death and destruction. Is it overly pessimistic? Is it realistic? Does the idea that everything ends in death lead to a "live for today" philosophy? Give reasons why you agree or disagree with Aiken's view of the world.

Alan Dugan
[b. 1923]

Morning Song

Look, it's morning, and a little water gurgles in the tap.
I wake up waiting, because it's Sunday, and turn twice more
than usual in bed, before I rise to cereal and comic strips.
I have risen to the morning danger and feel proud,
and after shaving off the night's disguises, after searching   5
close to the bone for blood, and finding only a little,
I shall walk out bravely into the daily accident.

Allen Ginsberg
[b. 1926]

In Back of the Real

          In back of the real
    railroad yard in San Jose
        I wandered desolate
    in front of a tank factory
        and sat on a bench   5
near the switchman's shack.

    A flower lay on the hay on
        the asphalt highway
    —the dread hay flower

                    I thought—It had a   10
              brittle black stem and
                    corolla° of yellowish dirty
              spikes like Jesus' inchlong
                    crown, and a soiled
              dry center cotton tuft   15
                    like a used shaving brush
              that's been lying under
                    the garage for a year.

              Yellow, yellow flower, and
                    flower of industry,   20
              tough spikey ugly flower,
                    flower nonetheless,
              with the form of the great yellow
                    Rose in your brain!
              This is the flower of the World.   25

12. corolla: the petals of a flower.

Meaning and Method

1. In "Morning Song" Alan Dugan summarized his attitude toward
   modern life in the phrase "daily accident." What connotations of
   the phrase underscore the idea that he feels helpless to control his
   life? How may "searching / close to the bone for blood" be interpreted literally and figuratively?
2. In "In Back of the Real" Allen Ginsberg says he saw a yellow hay
   flower on an asphalt highway. What does the flower look like? What
   does he mean when he says it is the "flower of industry"? The flower
   symbolizes Ginsberg's attitude toward the modern world. Based on
   the description of the flower, summarize his attitude.
3. Is Ginsberg's opinion of society completely negative? For example,
   why does he point out that the "tough spikey ugly flower" is a
   "flower nonetheless"? How can man transform that dirty hay flower
   into a "great yellow / Rose"?

Sylvia Plath
[1932–1963]

Black Rook * in Rainy Weather

On the stiff twig up there
Hunches a wet black rook
Arranging and rearranging its feathers in the rain.
I do not expect miracle
Or an accident   5

To set the sight on fire
In my eye, nor seek
Any more in the desultory° weather some design,
But let spotted leaves fall as they fall,
Without ceremony, or portent.°   10

Although, I admit, I desire,
Occasionally, some backtalk
From the mute sky, I can't honestly complain:
A certain minor light may still
Leap incandescent°   15

Out of kitchen table or chair
As if a celestial burning took
Possession of the most obtuse° objects now and then—
Thus hallowing an interval
Otherwise inconsequent   20

By bestowing largess,° honor
One might say love. At any rate, I now walk

* Rook: a bird of the crow family. 8. desultory: changeable, occurring by
chance. 10. portent: warning. 15. incandescent: shining with intense brilliance.
18. obtuse: insensible, lacking acuteness of intellect or feeling. 21. largess:
liberal giving, generosity.

Wary (for it could happen
Even in this dull, ruinous landscape); skeptical,
Yet politic; ignorant   25

Of whatever angel may choose to flare
Suddenly at my elbow. I only know that a rook
Ordering its black feathers can so shine
As to seize my senses, haul
My eyelids up, and grant   30

A brief respite from fear
Of total neutrality. With luck,
Trekking stubborn through this season
Of fatigue, I shall
Patch together a content   35

Of sorts. Miracles occur,
If you care to call those spasmodic°
Tricks of radiance miracles. The wait's begun again,
The long wait for the angel,
For that rare, random descent.   40

37. spasmodic: transitory.

Meaning and Method

1. What mood is suggested by the title of the poem?
2. For Miss Plath, the sight of a rook arranging its feathers offers "A brief respite from fear / Of total neutrality." What words and phrases support the interpretation that this sight and other momentary sights assume a religious significance—that is, that they offer her a way to transcend the world?
3. Miss Plath, like Robert Lowell (see page 246), is considered a confessional poet. Do such lines as "I desire, / Occasionally, some backtalk / From the mute sky" (lines 11–13) and "The wait's begun again, / The long wait for the angel" (lines 38 and 39) mean that the poet was seeking some sign to help explain existence, to give order to the universe, to give meaning to life? Would such a sign be part of the "respite from fear / Of total neutrality"? Discuss.

Mary Oliver
[b. 1935]

The Swimming Lesson

Feeling the icy kick, the endless waves
Reaching around my life, I moved my arms
And coughed, and in the end saw land.

Somebody, I suppose,
Remembering the medieval maxim,   5
Had tossed me in,
Had wanted me to learn to swim,

Not knowing that none of us, who ever came back
From that long lonely fall and frenzied rising,
Ever learned anything at all   10
About swimming, but only
How to put off, one by one,
Dreams and pity, love and grace—
How to survive in any place.

Meaning and Method

1. What words in lines 1–3 suggest death?
2. What do lines 9–14 tell about the psychological effect on the speaker of having been thrown into the water?
3. What qualities does Miss Oliver imply are needed "to survive in any place"?

"The Swimming Lesson" from *No Voyage and Other Poems* by Mary Oliver. Reprinted by permission of the publisher, Houghton Mifflin Company.

319

Maxine Kumin

[b. 1925]

The Pawnbroker

The symbol inside this poem is my father's feet
which, after fifty years of standing behind
the counter waiting on trade,
were tender and smooth and lay on the ironed sheet,
a study of white on white, like a dandy's shirt.   5
A little too precious; custom-made.
At the end of a day and all day Sunday they hurt.
Lying down, they were on his mind.

The sight of his children barefoot gave him a pain
—part anger, part wonder—as sharp as gravel   10
inside his lisle° socks.
Polacks! he said, but meant it to mean
hod carriers,° greenhorns, peasants; not ghetto Poles
once removed. *Where are your shoes? In hock?*
I grew up under the sign of those three gold balls   15
turning clockwise on their swivel.

Every good thing in my life was secondhand.
It smelled of having been owned before me by
a redcap porter whose ticket
ran out. I saw his time slip down like sand   20
in the glass that measured our breakfast eggs. At night
he overtook me in the thicket
and held me down and beat my black heart white
to make the pawnbroker's daughter pay.

11. lisle: a type of cotton thread. 13. hod carriers: workmen who carry bricks, mortar, and other building materials in an open, long-handled, troughlike container called a hod.

On Saturday nights the lights stayed lit until ten.   25
There were cops outside on regular duty to let
the customers in and out.
I have said that my father's feet were graceful and clean.
They hurt when he turned the lock
on the cooks and chauffeurs and unlucky racetrack touts°   30
and carwash attendants and laundresses and stock-
room boys and doormen in epaulets;

they hurt when he did up accounts in his head
at the bathroom sink
of the watches, cameras, typewriters, suitcases, guitars,   35
cheap diamond rings and thoroughbred
family silver, and matched them against the list
of hot goods from Headquarters,
meanwhile nailbrushing his knuckles and wrists
clean of the pawn-ticket stains of purple ink.   40

Firsthand I had from my father a love ingrown
tight as an oyster, and returned it
as secretly. From him firsthand
the grace of work, the sweat of it, the bone-
tired unfolding down from stress.   45
I was the bearer he paid up on demand
with one small pearl of selfhood. Portionless,
I am oystering still to earn it.

Not of the House of Rothschild,° my father, my creditor
lay dead while they shaved his cheeks and blacked his mustache. 50

My lifetime appraiser, my first prince whom death unhorsed
lay soberly dressed and barefoot to be burned.
That night, my brothers and I forced
the cap of his bottle of twenty-year-old Scotch
and drank ourselves on fire beforehand   55

30. **touts:** in horse racing terminology, persons who spy on horses to gain information for betting. 49. **House of Rothschild:** a bank specializing in international finance, founded and run by the Rothschild family. Originally, the
bank was located in Germany; now it has spread throughout the world.

for the sacrament of closing down the hatch,
for the sacrament of easing down the ways
my thumb-licking peeler of cash on receipt of merchandise,
possessor of miracles left unredeemed on the shelf
after thirty days,   60
giver and lender, no longer in hock to himself,
ruled off the balanced sheet,
a man of great personal order
and small white feet.

Meaning and Method

1. What is the speaker's attitude toward her father? What did her
   father give to her? What does she mean when she says, "I was the
   bearer he paid up on demand / with one small pearl of selfhood"
   (lines 46 and 47)?
2. How do you know the pawnbroker never was rich?
3. In line 1, Miss Kumin says that "The symbol inside this poem is
   my father's feet." In what ways does the symbol of her father's feet
   capture his character? Why does she stress that they are clean? that
   they hurt all the time?

Composition

Compare and contrast the theme and tone of "The Pawnbroker"
with that of E. E. Cummings's "My Father Moved Through Dooms of
Love" (page 149).

Robert Bly
[b. 1926]

A Man Writes to a Part of Himself

What cave are you in, hiding, rained on?
Like a wife, starving, without care,
Water dripping from your head, bent
Over ground corn . . .

You raise your face into the rain   5
That drives over the valley—
Forgive me, your husband,
On the streets of a distant city, laughing,
With many appointments,
Though at night going also   10
To a bare room, a room of poverty,
To sleep among a bare pitcher and basin
In a room with no heat—

Which of us two then is the worse off?
And how did this separation come about?   15

Meaning and Method

1. Contrast the scene described in lines 1–4 with that in lines 7–9.
2. How do the days of the husband seem to differ from his nights? How is the room where he spends his nights like a cave?
3. Is the separation between a husband and wife? between the interior and the exterior character of the speaker? between two aspects of the speaker's character—one more primitive, the other more sophisticated?

"A Man Writes to a Part of Himself" from *Silence in the Snowy Fields* by Robert Bly, Wesleyan University Press, 1962, copyright © 1962 by Robert Bly. Reprinted by permission of the author.

LeRoi Jones
[b. 1934]

Preface to a Twenty Volume Suicide Note

Lately, I've been accustomed to the way
The ground opens up and envelops me
Each time I go out to walk the dog.
Or the broad edged silly music the wind
Makes when I run for a bus—   5

Things have come to that.

And now, each night I count the stars,
And each night I get the same number.
And when they will not come to be counted
I count the holes they leave.   10

Nobody sings anymore.

And then last night, I tiptoed up
To my daughter's room and heard her
Talking to someone, and when I opened
The door, there was no one there . . .   15
Only she on her knees,
Peeking into her own clasped hands.

Meaning and Method

1. Which images suggest the meaninglessness and sorrow of life? For example, what does the line *Nobody sings anymore* connote about the effect of modern life upon the individual?
2. How does the young girl's attitude toward life contrast with that of her father's?
3. Does the tone seem to change with line 12? If so, how?

Howard Nemerov
[b. 1920]

Boom!

Sees Boom in Religion, Too

Atlantic City, June 23, 1957 (AP).—President Eisenhower's pastor said tonight that Americans are living in a period of "unprecedented religious activity" caused partially by paid vacations, the eight-hour day, and modern conveniences.

"These fruits of material progress," said the Rev. Edward L. R. Elson of the National Presbyterian Church, Washington, "have provided the leisure, the energy, and the means for a level of human and spiritual values never before reached."

Here at the Vespasian-Carlton, it's just one
religious activity after another; the sky
is constantly being crossed by cruciform
airplanes, in which nobody disbelieves
for a second, and the tide, the tide   5
of spiritual progress and prosperity
miraculously keeps rising, to a level
never before attained. The churches are full,
the beaches are full, and the filling-stations
are full, God's great ocean is full   10
of paid vacationers praying an eight-hour day
to the human and spiritual values, the fruits,
the leisure, the energy, and the means, Lord,
the means for the level, the unprecedented level,
and the modern conveniences,° which also are full.   15
Never before, O Lord, have the prayers and praises
from belfry and phonebooth, from ballpark and barbecue

15. conveniences: toilets.

the sacrifices, so endlessly ascended.
It was not thus when Job° in Palestine
sat in the dust and cried, cried bitterly;   20
when Damien° kissed the lepers on their wounds
it was not thus; it was not thus
when Francis° worked a fourteen-hour day
strictly for the birds; when Dante° took
a week's vacation without pay and it rained   25
part of the time, O Lord, it was not thus.
But now the gears mesh and the tires burn
and the ice chatters in the shaker and the priest
in the pulpit, and thy name, O Lord,
is kept before the public, while the fruits   30
ripen and religion booms and the level rises
and every modern convenience runneth over,°
that it may never be with us as it hath been
with Athens and Karnak and Nagasaki,°
nor thy sun for one instant refrain from shining   35
on the rainbow Buick by the breezeway
or the Chris Craft with the uplift life raft;
that we may continue to be the just folks we are,
plain people with ordinary superliners and
disposable diaperliners, people of the stop'n'shop   40
'n'pray as you go, of hotel, motel, boatel,
the humble pilgrims of no deposit no return
and please adjust thy clothing, who will give to thee,
if thee will keep us going, our annual
Miss Universe, for thy name's sake, Amen.   45

19. Job: According to the Bible, Job was subjected to many trials and great suffering, including the loss of all his possessions. Despite his torments, he never lost faith in God. **21. Damien:** Joseph Damien (1840–1888), a Belgian missionary priest who worked with the lepers. **23. Francis:** St. Francis of Assisi (ca. 1182–1226), who, according to legend, would preach to flocks of birds. **24. Dante:** Dante Alighieri (1265–1321), the author of the *Divine Comedy*. The "week's vacation" is Dante's allegorical journey through Hell, Purgatory, and Heaven, which is described in the *Divine Comedy*. In the Inferno (Hell), Dante goes through an icy rain which falls on the souls of the gluttonous (Canto VI). **32. runneth over:** an allusion to the line from Psalm 23, "My cup runneth over." **34. Athens, Karnak, Nagasaki:** Athens, the cultural center of the ancient world, was conquered by Sparta; Karnak, an Egyptian village, had many religious temples, all of which are now in ruins; Nagasaki was a Japanese city destroyed by the atomic bomb.

Meaning and Method

1. What tone does the poet achieve by referring to "beaches," "filling-stations," and "cruciform airplanes" to amplify the idea in the opening lines that life at the hotel is "just one religious activity after another"? Why is "cruciform airplanes" especially effective?

2. Contrast the religious fervor found in Job, Damien, St. Francis, and Dante with that described in lines 1–18.

3. In lines 16 and 17, Nemerov states that prayers and praises come from belfry (church) and phonebooth (a reference to things such as "dial-a-prayer"). Lines 17 and 18 are written with inverted word order and would ordinarily read "the sacrifices from ballpark and barbecue." What are the figurative and literal meanings of the word "sacrifice"?

4. Explain the humor in lines 11, 15, 24, 25 and 26, 27–29, 32, 42. Is the humor sly? bitter? ironic? slapstick? a combination of these?

5. Why does Nemerov write the poem as if it were a prayer?

Composition

Compare the theme of "Boom!" with that of Auden's "The Unknown Citizen" (page 200). What conclusions about both poets' view of modern society can you arrive at from reading the two poems?

Anne Sexton

[b. 1928]

The Addict

Sleepmonger,
deathmonger,
with capsules in my palms each night,
eight at a time from sweet pharmaceutical bottles
I make arrangements for a pint-sized journey.   5
I'm the queen of this condition.
I'm an expert on making the trip
and now they say I'm an addict.
Now they ask why.
Why!   10

Don't they know
that I promised to die!
I'm keeping in practice
I'm merely staying in shape.
The pills are a mother, but better,   15
every color and as good as sour balls.
I'm on a diet from death.

Yes, I admit
it has gotten to be a bit of a habit—
blows eight at a time, socked in the eye,   20
hauled away by the pink, the orange,
the green and white goodnights.
I'm becoming something of a chemical
mixture.
That's it!   25

My supply
of tablets

has got to last for years and years.
I like them more than I like me.
Stubborn as hell, they won't let go.   30
It's a kind of a marriage.
It's a kind of war
where I plant bombs inside
of myself.

Yes   35
I try
to kill myself in small amounts,
an innocuous occupation.
Actually I'm hung up on it.
But remember I don't make too much noise.   40

And frankly no one has to lug me out
and I don't stand there in my winding sheet.°
I'm a little buttercup in my yellow nightie
eating my eight loaves in a row
and in a certain order as in   45
the laying on of hands°
or the black sacrament.

It's a ceremony
but like any other sport
it's full of rules.   50
It's like a musical tennis match where
my mouth keeps catching the ball.
Then I lie on my altar
elevated by the eight chemical kisses.

What a lay me down this is   55
with two pink, two orange,
two green, two white goodnights.
Fee-fi-fo-fum—
Now I'm borrowed.
Now I'm numb.   60

42. **winding sheet:** the sheet put around a corpse. 46. **laying on of hands:** a
reference to ceremonies connected with Confirmation or Holy Orders.

Meaning and Method

1. Why is her use of pills "a kind of marriage" and "a kind of war"? What effects are the pills having upon her?
2. Explain why line 40 is ironic.
3. Which images convey the religious connotations of her nightly ritual?

Composition and Discussion

The critic M. L. Rosenthal wrote, "Many, although not all, of the confessional poets feel their own very specific experiences as somehow embodiments of the national and even international predicament and crisis."

Orally or in writing, discuss the aspects of the national and international "predicament and crisis" that might lead to a person's taking drugs. Why does one's inability to solve either personal, national, or international problems lead to drugs? Are drugs an effective way of handling such problems? Present alternative methods for solving these problems, such as political and social action.

W. D. Snodgrass

[b. 1926]

The Campus on the Hill

Up the reputable walks of old established trees
They stalk, children of the *nouveaux riches;*° chimes
Of the tall Clock Tower drench their heads in blessing:
"I don't wanna play at your house;
I don't like you any more."   5
My house stands opposite, on the other hill,
Among meadows, with the orchard fences down and falling;
Deer come almost to the door.
You cannot see it, even in this clearest morning.
White birds hang in the air between   10
Over the garbage landfill and those homes thereto adjacent,
Hovering slowly, turning, settling down
Like the flakes sifting imperceptibly onto the little town
In a waterball of glass.
And yet, this morning, beyond this quiet scene,   15
The floating birds, the backyards of the poor,
Beyond the shopping plaza, the dead canal, the hillside
    lying tilted in the air,
Tomorrow has broken out today:
Riot in Algeria, in Cyprus, in Alabama;
Aged in wrong, the empires are declining,   20
And China gathers, soundlessly, like evidence.
What shall I say to the young on such a morning?—
Mind is the one salvation?—also grammar?—
No; my little ones lean not toward revolt. They
Are the Whites, the vaguely furiously driven, who resist   25
Their souls with such passivity
As would make Quakers swear. All day, dear Lord, all day

2. *nouveaux riches: French,* persons who have recently become well-to-do.

They wear their godhead lightly.
They look out from their hill and say,
To themselves, "We have nowhere to go but down;   30
The great destination is to stay."
Surely the nations will be reasonable;
They look at the world—don't they?—the world's way?
The clock just now has nothing more to say.

Meaning and Method

1. The poem was written in about 1958, at a time when college students were thought of as the "silent generation." What do lines 4 and 5 suggest about the character of the students?
2. In what ways is Snodgrass's home (lines 6–9) unlike the campus described in line 1?
3. The "waterball of glass" symbolizes a world that is self-enclosed and is, at the same time, quite fragile. What words in lines 10–17 carry unfavorable connotations about the setting? What does Snodgrass imply might shatter the tranquility of "this quiet scene"?
4. How may the mind—that is, academic pursuits—save the student from facing tomorrow? How may the students find salvation in grammar?
5. Why do not his students revolt? What do the students mean when they say, "We have nowhere to go but down; / The great destination is to stay" (lines 30 and 31)? Do they literally mean that they will stay on the campus on the hill? Or do they mean they will try to stay in their present position of wealth and power?
6. Lines 32 and 33 present the speaker's comments on what the students have said. Is the tone sarcastic? pleasant? bitter?
7. Does the "clock" (line 34) refer to the clock in the tower mentioned in line 3? Does it symbolize the passing of time? Before answering, reread lines 18–21 and 30 and 31.
8. What criticisms did Snodgrass have about the college students of that time?

A Glossary
of Literary Terms

Abstract and Concrete Terms: *Abstract terms* are words and phrases that refer to ideas, characteristics, or intangible qualities. Abstractions have little or no appeal to any of the senses. Examples of abstract terms are *infinity, mankind, idea,* and *goodness. Concrete terms* stand for particular and individual things as opposed to generalities. They usually denote physical realities and therefore appeal to the senses and make us "see" or vividly imagine specific objects or actions. Examples of concrete terms are *red, blink, stone,* and *dime.*

Allegory: a narrative in verse or prose in which concrete characters and actions represent abstract ideas or moral qualities. An allegory carries both literal and symbolic levels of meaning. (See **Symbol.**)

Alliteration: the repetition of sounds, usually consonant sounds but sometimes vowel sounds, at the beginnings of words in the same line or in successive lines of poetry.

Allusion: a brief, casual reference to a person, place, event, or artistic or scriptural work that the author expects the reader to recognize. An allusion may be drawn from literature, history, geography, scripture, or mythology. For example, the title of Delmore Schwartz's poem "In the Naked Bed, in Plato's Cave" alludes to the Greek philosopher Plato and his parable of the cave.

Analogy: a mode of reasoning that is based on the probability that if one thing resembles another in several important particulars, it will resemble that thing in another. It is a comparison of two things alike in certain respects.

Anticlimax: see **Climax and Anticlimax.**

Aphorism: a terse, pithy statement expressing a grain of wisdom or truth. Examples include:

> "Remember that time is money."—Benjamin Franklin

> "Silence is the virtue of fools."—Francis Bacon

Apostrophe: the direct address to a deceased or absent person as if he were alive and present, or to an animal or thing, or to an abstract idea or quality as if it could understand the speaker. Apostrophe is often used with *personification.* (See **Personification.**)

Assonance: the repetition of vowel sounds with different consonants. These sounds may appear in the same line or in successive lines of poetry. For example:

> . . . the cliffs of England stand,
> Glimmering and vast, out in the tranquil bay.
> —Matthew Arnold, "'Dover Beach"

Atmosphere: the prevailing mental and emotional climate of a poem; something the reader senses or feels. **Setting** and **Mood** help to create and heighten atmosphere.

Ballad: a relatively short poem that tells a story. There are two types of ballads, *folk songs* and *literary ballads*. Folk ballads are meant to be sung; literary ballads are meant to be printed and read.

Ballad Stanza: the most common stanza—or grouping of lines—used in ballads. It is a *quatrain*, or four-line stanza, with the second and fourth lines rhyming (see **Rhyme**). Generally each quatrain has four stressed syllables in the first and third lines, and three stressed syllables in the second and fourth lines. W. H. Auden's "O Where Are You Going" (page 197) is an example of a modern poem that has a ballad stanza.

Blank Verse: unrhymed poetry, in which each line usually has ten syllables. Five of the syllables are stressed—generally the second, fourth, sixth, eighth, and tenth syllables. Such an arrangement of stressed and unstressed syllables in a ten-syllable line is called *iambic pentameter*. (See **Meter**.)

Character: a person in a play, story, novel, or poem.

Character Foil: a character who serves by contrast to set off the qualities of another character. For example, the appearance of a particularly dull, slow-witted, and unimaginative character will strengthen the reader's impression of an amusing, witty, and expressive character.

Characterization: the technique(s) an author uses to develop the personality of his characters so that they are believable persons who act consistently and speak naturally. These basic methods of characterization are the following:

(a) direct analysis by the author of the person's actions, motives, and feelings;

(b) physical description by the author of the person's appearance, actions, and surroundings, such as the room in which he or she lives or works;

(c) presentation of the person's thoughts through a stream of consciousness—that is, as thoughts and their associations are formed and run through the person's mind;

(d) presentation of the person's reactions to situations, events, and other people;

(e) presentation of the reactions of other people to the person's actions or words;

(f) presentation of the person's speech and conversations;

(g) presentation of the remarks, comments, and conversations of others about the person; and

(h) a combination of two or more of these methods.

Cliché: any trite or commonplace expression that is no longer fresh or effective because it has been used too often. The following are examples of clichés: *the time of our lives, sick as a dog, last but not least, fresh as a daisy, in the prime of life.*

Climax and Anticlimax: *Climax* is the point of greatest intensity of action or suspense in a story. Climax normally follows a buildup through successive narrative incidents. It usually occurs at the narrative's turning point but is sometimes coincidental with the dénouement (French for "unknotting") or final unraveling of the plot.

Anticlimax can be either dramatic or rhetorical. *Dramatic anticlimax* occurs in a narrative in which the climax is unexpected or is not a logical one in terms of the rising action and suspense, or in which the climax is far less than what the reader expected. *Rhetorical anticlimax*, sometimes purposeful (as in the following example), occurs in sentences or passages whose elements are arranged in an order of decreasing importance or impact. For example:

> If once a man indulges himself in murder, very soon he comes to think little of robbing; and from robbing he comes next to drinking and sabbath-breaking, and from that to incivility and procrastination.
>   —Thomas De Quincey (1785–1859)

Colloquial Speech: a manner of speaking that is characteristic of informal conversation.

Comparison and Contrast: *Comparison* is a method of clarifying and illustrating by showing the similarities between things. *Contrast* works by showing the differences.

Concrete Terms: see **Abstract and Concrete Terms.**

Conflict: a struggle between two opposing forces or characters, either man against man, man against society, man against nature, or man against himself. Concern with the outcome of the conflict is the basic element in suspense.

Connotation: an association or suggestion that a word calls to mind in addition to its literal meaning (see **Denotation**). For example, the word "king" is denotatively "the sovereign male ruler of a kingdom." The word, however, may also suggest dignity, magnificent or stately display, a specific king, the signs of kingship—throne, crown, scepter, etc.

Consonance: repetition of consonant sounds either before or after different vowel sounds; for example, *flip—flop*.

Context: for a word, the other words surrounding it and having an effect on its meaning or use. The same words may have different meanings in different contexts. For example, notice the difference in the meaning of the word "rained" in the sentence, "It rained all night," and in the following line by Stephen Crane: "The trees in the garden rained flowers."

Contrast: see **Comparison and Contrast.**

Couplet: two successive lines, usually rhymed, which form a single unit of verse.

Denotation: the literal or dictionary meaning or meanings of a word. (See **Connotation.**)

Description: The purpose of description is to make the reader share as intensely as possible in the sense experiences of the writer; that is, the writer wants his audience to see, hear, smell, taste, or touch, in imagination, those things that the writer describes.

In writing, an image or mental picture of a person, place, object, or action can be achieved through an enumeration of physical details, particulars, and sensory impressions.

Dialect: the speech that is characteristic of a particular group or of the inhabitants of a certain geographical region. In literature, dialect can be used as part of a characterization.

Dialogue: the conversation carried on by two or more characters. A monologue is a speech of one person, such as that of someone thinking aloud.

Diction: in literary work, the choice of the right word or words to convey an idea or impression clearly and effectively.

Dramatic Monologue: a type of poem in which a speaker addresses a listener or listeners who do not answer. The speaker reveals his character by commenting on a crucial problem or conflict in his life.

Dramatic Poetry: poetry in which one or more characters speak to other characters who may or may not answer. The dramatic monologue is one type of dramatic poetry.

Elegy: a poem mourning the death of an individual. It is often also a melancholy meditation on the trials and griefs of life in general. It is one type of lyric poetry. (See **Lryic**.)

End Rhyme: see **Rhyme**.

Epic: a long story-poem that relates the deeds of a heroic character, usually a national hero.

Figurative Language: language that is not meant to be interpreted on a strict, literal level because it would make no sense or little sense if it were. The "meaning" of a figurative phrase is communicated by its connotation. For example, William Wordsworth's line, "The waves beside them danced," brings to mind a picture of small waves moving rhythmically and seeming to leap as a dancer might.

Figure of Speech: a word or phrase that describes something in a way that is not literally true but may be meaningful in a deeper sense. The effect of a figure of speech on the reader is generally stronger than that produced by everyday language. (See **Irony, Metaphor, Personification, Simile,** and **Symbol**.)

Foot: a unit in measuring or *scanning* lines of poetry to determine meter. Each foot usually contains at least one stressed syllable. In addition, it usually has one or two unstressed syllables. (See **Meter**.)

Foreshadowing: a technique whereby the author hints at events to come.

Free Verse: lines that do not follow any conventional pattern of stressed and unstressed syllables. The lines do not have a regular line length. Instead, free verse relies on the rhythmic effects found in the sound of natural speech.

Haiku (Hokku): a Japanese lyric form containing seventeen syllables, divided into three lines of five, seven, and five syllables.

Hyperbole: a deliberate overstatement, often for effect; exaggeration.

Iamb: a type of poetic *foot* consisting of an unstressed syllable followed by a stressed syllable, as in the word "re·form'." The iamb is the most common type of foot found in poetry written in English. (See **Blank Verse, Foot, Meter,** and **Rhythm**.)

Iambic Pentameter: see **Blank Verse.**

Imagery: a word picture, or image, used descriptively to represent things, actions, sensations, or ideas. Although most imagery is visual, it can also include the senses of hearing, touch, smell, and taste.

Imagism: a theory of poetry formulated by Ezra Pound and further explained by Amy Lowell. Imagism stressed clarity, exactness in detail, concrete imagery, and the creation of new poetic rhythms. The movement, which lasted approximately from 1909 to 1918, included such poets as H. D., Carl Sandburg, and William Carlos Williams.

Internal Rhyme: see **Rhyme.**

Inversion (Poetic Inversion): words arranged in such a way that they reverse in some manner the normal word order of a sentence. Often inversion is used for the sake of rhyme.

Irony: in its simplest form, a figure of speech in which the writer says something in such a way that its opposite meaning is implied. For example, in Stephen Crane's poem "War Is Kind," the poet addresses a baby whose father has just been killed in a war, and tells the baby not to weep, for "war is kind." However, the example he has given—a young man who has been killed, leaving a crying, fatherless baby—shows war's cruelty and horror, and makes the reader realize that war is *not* kind.

Irony, which is usually based on contrast—often incongruous—may be present in a situation as well as in words. For example, in Shakespeare's *Romeo and Juliet*, Juliet, in order to avoid marrying Paris, takes a potion that makes her appear to be dead. She expects to awake and be reunited with Romeo. Romeo, however, seeing her, believes she is really dead and kills himself. His reaction is ironic within the context of the situation.

Light Verse: verse that is primarily humorous or entertaining.

Lyric: a poem whose sole purpose is the expression of an individual's emotions or attitudes. It is usually short and musical. (See **Elegy** and **Sonnet.**)

Metaphor: a comparison or likeness expressed in figurative language without using the words *like* or *as*. One thing is said to be another.

Meter: the pattern of stressed and unstressed syllables in verse. In the most frequent and traditional forms of verse written in English, the number of syllables and the number of stressed syllables are regular. However, most poems will contain variations in the meter.

The most common types of metric feet are: *iambic* (unstressed syllable followed by stressed syllable), *trochaic* (stressed syllable followed by unstressed syllable), *anapestic* (two unstressed syllables followed by one stressed syllable), *dactylic* (one stressed syllable followed by two unstressed syllables), and *spondaic* (two stressed syllables). (See **Blank Verse** and **Rhythm.**)

Metonymy: the use of a closely related idea for the idea itself. Calling a football "the pigskin" is an example of metonymy. (See **Synecdoche.**)

Mood: the overall emotional atmosphere or feeling created in a literary work by its tone or tones. (See **Atmosphere, Setting,** and **Tone.**)

Myth: a tale or story usually focusing on the deeds of gods or superhuman heroes. Myths are the imaginative part of legends; they played an important role in ancient cultures by helping to explain or justify the mysteries of nature and the universe, such as the origin of fire.

Narrative Poem: a poem that tells a story.

Narrator: one who narrates, or relates, a true or fictional story.

Near Rhyme: rhyme in which the final consonant sounds of the accented syllable(s) of each word are the same, but the preceding vowel or consonant sounds are different. *Port* and *chart* are near rhymes.

Onomatopoeia (on′ə·mat′ə·pē′ə): the use of words whose sounds imitate natural sounds. For example: *bang, buzz, sizzle.*

Oxymoron: a figure of rhetoric combining contradictory, paradoxical, or incongruous words. For example: *eloquent silence, wise fool.*

Parable: a short tale making a moral or religious point.

Paradox: a seeming contradiction; a statement that seems to include a contradiction and yet is true.

Parody: the conscious, exaggerated imitation of a literary style or individual work with the intention of achieving humor through distortion.

Personification: a figure of speech in which the writer attributes human qualities to animals, inanimate objects, or ideas. Personification is often used with apostrophe. (See **Apostrophe.**)

Point of View: the standpoint from which a literary work is written. The point of view usually influences the way the writer presents a subject. For example, if he is writing from the "I," or personal, point of view, he may present only details that personally affect the "I." If he is writing from the "he," or third-person, point of view, he may present details of which the participants in an action may not themselves be aware. The point of view of the speaker may or may not be that of the poet. (See **Speaker.**)

Quatrain: a four-line stanza. (See **Stanza.**)

Refrain: a group of words, a line, or a group of lines repeated throughout a poem, usually at the end of each stanza.

Repetition: the use of the same sound, word, phrase, sentence, or idea (or some slight variation of it) to achieve emphasis.

Rhetorical Question: a question asked only for oratorical or literary effect. It does not require an answer because the answer is implied in the question.

Rhyme: the repetition of two or more words reasonably close to each other in which the last vowel sound and the last consonant sound are the same. Examples: *tune—soon; he—me; leap—deep.* If the rhyme occurs at the end of the line, it is called an *end rhyme.* For example:

> The lucious clusters of the vine
> Upon my mouth do crush their wine . . .
> —Andrew Marvell, "The Garden"

If a rhyme occurs within a line, it is called an *internal rhyme.* For example:

> Much I marveled this ungainly fowl to hear discourse so plainly.
> —Edgar Allan Poe, "The Raven"

Rhyme Scheme: the pattern in which end rhyme occurs throughout a stanza or an entire poem. Rhyme schemes are usually denoted by italicized letters of the alphabet. For example, if the first and third lines of a four-line stanza rhyme, we say that the rhyme scheme is *abac* (*a* represents the rhyming lines, while *b* and *c* represent the lines that do not rhyme). If the two pairs of alternate lines in a four-line stanza rhyme, the rhyme scheme is *abab*, and if all four lines rhyme, it is *aaaa.*

Rhythm: in poetry, the recurrence or repetition of stressed and unstressed syllables in a regular pattern or manner. When rhythm in poetry is so strictly patterned that it can be measured in feet (see **Foot**), it is called meter.

Satire: the use of ridicule, sarcasm, wit, or irony in order to expose, set right, or destroy a vice or folly.

Setting: the physical background of a work; the time and place in which a story occurs.

Simile: a figure of speech in which the comparison between two unlike things is expressed directly, usually by means of *like* or *as*.

Slant Rhyme: see **Near Rhyme.**

Sonnet: a lyric poem of fourteen lines usually written in rhymed iambic pentameter. Sonnets usually follow one of two types of rhyme schemes—the Shakespearean or English (*ababcdcdefefgg*), or the Italian (*abbaabbacdecde*). However, many variations of these rhyme schemes are possible.

Speaker: the person whose voice we "hear" in the poem. (Note that the use of *I* does not necessarily mean that the speaker is the poet.)

Stanza: a group of lines that constitute a division in a poem. There is space before the first line and after the last line of each such group. In many poems, each stanza contains the same number of lines.

Style: a writer's distinctive or characteristic form of expression; the means he uses to express his thoughts effectively. Style is determined by the choice and arrangement of words, sentence structure, the use of figurative language, meter, rhythm, tone, and verse forms.

Syllabic Verse: verse in which the number of syllables per line is important and not the pattern of stressed-unstressed syllables.

Symbol: a person, place, event, or object that exists and has meaning in itself and also suggests something further, such as an attitude or a value. For example, donkeys and elephants are donkeys and elephants, but they are also symbols of opposing major political parties in the United States.

Synecdoche: the use of the part for the whole or the whole for the part. Using *redskin* for *Indian* and *law* for *policeman* are examples of synecdoche. (See **Metonymy.**)

Theme: the main idea of a literary work; the total comment about life that the author wishes to make.

Tone: the attitude of the writer toward his subject, his characters, and his readers.

Type: a character who embodies the characteristics of a group or class rather than a strong individual personality.

Understatement: the representation, through unemphatic or restrained wording, of something as less than it actually is, usually in order to achieve a subtle effect.

The
Language Arts
Program

Throughout the text, language arts principles and activities have been integrated with the presentation of literature. Most of the language arts activities appear in the *Meaning, Method, Language,* and *Composition and Discussion* questions and exercises that follow each selection. Other aspects of the language arts—particularly those concerning the origins of words—are covered in footnotes to the selections.

General Skills

Author (recognizing attitude of), 11, 12, 15, 29, 39, 44, 45, 46, 51, 55, 64, 67, 70, 74, 78, 79, 85–86, 89, 90, 92, 96, 101, 102, 103, 104, 109, 119, 124, 130, 142, 146, 179, 195, 198, 204, 205, 206, 211, 215, 220, 243, 245, 248, 251, 256, 265, 272, 281, 285, 316, 322

Characterization (inferring character of author and subject), 8, 9, 11, 12, 15, 18, 18–19, 25, 29, 34–35, 37, 41, 44, 51, 52, 55, 63, 64, 77, 90, 94, 96, 109, 116, 152, 162, 167, 179, 181, 217, 222, 226, 232, 235, 238, 244, 253, 259, 262, 272, 279, 295, 305, 308, 332; (recognizing techniques of), 11, 15, 54, 63, 77, 179

Chronology (recognizing departures from straightforward), 28, 35

Comparing and contrasting poems, techniques, characters, etc., 8, 15, 18, 22, 34, 37, 52, 54, 55, 64, 67, 71, 157, 198, 233, 324

Dictionary (using the) 37, 77–78, 89–90, 123, 167, 250

Drawing conclusions from the text, 29, 40, 45, 48, 51, 52, 54, 57, 64, 72, 79, 91, 102, 103, 107, 111–12, 113, 122, 125–26, 138, 139, 142, 145, 152, 154, 157, 158, 163, 175, 176, 181, 185, 186, 187, 188, 201, 215, 222, 261, 272, 275, 295, 305, 316, 317, 322, 323, 324, 332

Extending discussion beyond the immediate text, 48, 56, 57, 176, 275

Foreshadowing, 102, 292

Humor (recognizing techniques of), 54, 85, 86, 125, 192, 195, 206, 211, 327

Library research, 215

Meaning (recognizing from context), 47, 235, 314

Paraphrasing, 54, 113, 115, 205

Literary Types and Terms

Vocabulary Development

Speaking and Listening

Composition

Describe a room in a particular season of the year, 45

Describe impressions of a home-town or a city, 68

Describe impressions of a town seen only indirectly, 68

Personify a specific object, 69

Describe an ideal place, 101–02

By combining description and explanation, mention favor-able and unfavorable places in a town, 116

Write a character sketch, 119

Describe a place that gives the impression of being free or of being confined, 139

Personify "truth," 243

Describe an ordinary scene that has tragic overtones, 273

Exposition:

Explain whether or not Eben Flood is a symbol, 8

Discuss the role that money should play in one's life, 11

Compare the type of person you would expect to hold a certain job and the actual person who holds that position, 12

Explain why Lucinda Matlock's view of life is not satisfactory, 19

Explain why "In a Station of the Metro" is like a haiku, 29

Explain what Frost's reading "Mending Wall" suggested about his attitude toward the Berlin Wall, 54

Present your attitude toward patriotism and criticism of government, 57

Compare Frost's idea of com-mitment with that of Presi-dent Kennedy's, 57

Explain what Frost meant by "character," 57–58

Compare and contrast character of Silas and Finzer, 64

Explain who the winners in life are, 70

State some advice given to you and explain why you agree or disagree with it, 74

Explain several aphorisms, 74

Mention specific changes that indicate broader changes, 79

Summarize the central idea of "The Leaden-eyed," 79

Present personal opinion in-directly about some aspect of progress in America, 86

Explain the meaning of "The ordinary is always what one makes it," 94

Give reasons for opinions about the function of movies, 97

Using suggested sentence as a topic sentence, defend Miss Moore's definition of the function of the poet, 113

Draw conclusions about Mari-anne Moore's poetic tech-niques and themes, 120

From his poetry, illustrate Ran-som's treatment of death, 126

Present opinions agreeing or dis-agreeing with the theory that the greatest threat to America is internal, not external, 130

Analyze Miss Millay's images and choice of words, 142

Discuss whether or not modern man is defenseless against de-humanizing forces, 149

An Index
of Authors and Titles